To Penny,
Melissa, Kimberley,
James and Adam

Recreation and Leisure: City and Guilds Course 481, Parts 1 and 2

Jonathan Wright
BEd Cert Ed DipRM(MILAM)

Croner Publications Ltd
Croner House
London Road
Kingston upon Thames
Surrey KT2 6SR
Tel: 081-547 3333

Copyright © 1989 J. Wright
First published 1989
Reprinted 1990
Second edition 1991

Published by
Croner Publications Ltd,
Croner House,
London Road,
Kingston upon Thames,
Surrey KT2 6SR
Telephone: 081-547 3333

All rights reserved.
No part of this publication may be reproduced,
stored in a retrieval system, or transmitted in any form or by
any means, electronic, mechanical, photocopying, recording,
or otherwise,
without the prior permission of
Croner Publications Ltd.

The right of Jonathan Wright
to be identified as author of this work
has been asserted by him in accordance
with the Copyright, Designs and Patents Act 1988.

While every care has been taken
in the writing and editing of this book,
readers should be aware that only Acts of Parliament
and Statutory Instruments have the force of law,
and that only the courts can authoritatively
interpret the law.

British Library Cataloguing in Publication Data
Wright, Jonathan
Recreation and leisure: City and guilds course 481.
Pts. 1&2
1. Great Britain. Leisure facilities & recreation facilities. Management
I. Title
790'.06'9

ISBN 1 85524 098 X

Set in Linotype Univers
by Kudos Graphics,
Horsham, West Sussex.
Printed by Whitstable Litho Printers Ltd,
Whitstable, Kent.

Contents

List of Figures vi

Preface to the First Edition ix

Preface to the Second Edition x

Acknowledgements xi

Chapter 1 Marketing 1
What is marketing? — What business are we in? — Factors affecting marketing — Philosophy of use: programming; needs of specific groups — Publicity activities — Exercises — Past examination questions — Bibliography

Chapter 2 Provision and Control 33
National organisations — Local authorities — Commercial organisations — Community groups — The interrelationship of the providing agencies — Exercises — Past examination questions — Bibliography

Chapter 3 Resource Management 87
Personal presentation — Data storage and retrieval — Shift work — Hygiene — Health and safety — Chemicals commonly used in recreation environments — Support areas — Maintenance — Standardised Approach to Sports Halls — Swimming pools — Soft landscaping — Playing surfaces — Play areas for children — Exercises — Past examination questions — Bibliography

Chapter 4 Product Knowledge 179
Food and diet — Exercise: fitness, training — The major body systems that affect exercise — Injuries associated with recreational activities — Exercises — Past examination questions — Bibliography.

Index 240

List of Figures

1 The marketing process 1
2 Targeting promotion 4
3 The marketing mix 5
4 The interrelationship of leisure, play, recreation and sport 6
5 Programming 14
6 Programming mix 17
7 Programming to increase off-peak usage — flow chart 18
8 Programming to increase off-peak usage — timetable 19
9 Recent national campaigns 24
10 Examples of some of the graphics and logos used in recent Sports Council campaigns 25
11 Central Government departments and quasi-governmental organisations concerned with leisure and recreation provision 34
12 Locations of the National Sports Centres 39
13 Sports Council regions 42
14 National Parks — England and Wales 50
15 Long distance footpaths — England and Wales 52
16 Colne Valley Park 54
17 Arts Council 1988 — overall structure 57
18 English regional tourist boards 63
19 National Rivers Authority Regions — boundaries and regional office towns 65
20 The interrelationship of the different agencies in providing opportunities for participation in recreational activities 76
21 The advantages and disadvantages of manual and computer based data storage and retrieval systems 93
22 An example of a two-shift system 94
23 An example of a three-shift system 95
24 Emergency services 103
25 The storage of swimming pool chemicals 107
26 Daily/weekly maintenance sheet 114
27 A SASH design sports hall 115
28 SASH design sports hall — technical details 116
29 A traditional rectangular tank pool 118

30	A simple leisure pool	119
31	Windsor Leisure Pool — a large and complex leisure pool	120
32	Ways in which a competition pool or "tank" might be incorporated into a leisure pool complex	121
33	Swimming pool plant functions	122
34	The distribution of pollution in pool water	123
35	Simple filtration of solids	125
36	Slow rate sand and gravel media filter	125
37	Surface level details of upflow/overflow circulation	126
38	A typical swimming pool and plant installation	127
39	Scale for assessing total chlorine levels in swimming pool water	129
40	Hard and soft landscapes	138
41	Examples of natural and artificial sports surfaces	147
42	Uses of heavy and medium duty surfaces	148
43	Rebound resiliance — (i) ball/surface	149
44	Rebound resiliance — (ii) person/surface	150
45	Substrata — outdoor synthetic surface	150
46	Synthetic cricket wicket	152
47	Point and area elasticity	153
48	Surfaces appropriate to different recreational activities	154
49	Advantages and disadvantages of different methods of marking indoor courts	156
50	Advantages and disadvantages of different methods of marking outdoor pitches	157
51	Line marking machine for laying floor tape	158
52	Line marker for spraying lines on to hard surfaces (eg asphalt tennis courts)	158
53	Line marker for laying wet lime on grass pitches	158
54	An example of a small well-designed play area	163
55	Vitamins — sources and uses	181
56	Minerals — sources and uses	182
57	Essential food groups — summary	183
58	Short-term effects of strenuous exercise on the body	189
59	Long-term effects of strenuous exercise on the body	189
60	The human skeleton	191
61	The fused joints between the frontal, parietal and sphenoid bones of the skull — an example of immovable joints	192
62	The cartilaginous joints between the sternum and the ribs — an example of slightly movable joints	192
63	Freely movable or synovial joint (shoulder)	193

64	The hip joint — an example of a ball and socket joint	194
65	The elbow joint — an example of hinge joint	194
66	The pivot joint between the atlas and axis bones in the neck	194
67	The gliding joint between the articular processes of adjacent vertebrae	194
68	The joint between the bones of the forearm and the wrist — an example of a condyloid joint	194
69	The joint between the metacarpal joint of the thumb and the wrist — an example of a saddle joint	194
70	The way in which the attachments of the muscles influence the action of the muscle upon the joint	196
71	The principal muscles of the human body	197–8
72	The heart (simplified)	202
73	The circulatory system (simplified)	203
74	The respiratory system	205
75	The human nervous system	207
76	Rocker board and wobble board	208
77	The causal chain in injury	209
78	Classification of sports injuries — examples	211
79	Sports injuries associated with aerobics and dance	217
80	Sports injuries associated with Association football	217
81	Sports injuries associated with basketball	218
82	Sports injuries associated with batting in cricket	219
83	Sports injuries associated with bowling in cricket	220
84	Sports injuries associated with cross-country, distance, hill and road running	221
85	Sports injuries associated with judo	221
86	Sports injuries associated with Rugby football	222
87	Artificial ventilation	224
88	Chest compression	224
89	The recovery position	225
90	Sports injuries associated with ice skating	231

Preface to the First Edition

This book has been written specifically for students taking City and Guilds 481 (Parts 1 and 2) and is designed to meet the information requirements of the written examinations within a single text. It is based closely on the author's lecture notes, prepared for C&G 481 students, over a period of several years. The book is divided into four main sections, corresponding with the four main sections of the syllabus:

>Marketing; Provision and Control; Resource Management; Product Knowledge.

The exercises which are included at the end of each section are designed to provide the basis for additional practical work and research beyond the confines of the text.

Examples of previous examination questions are also included at the end of each section. The information needed in order to answer these questions will be found within the section of the text to which they relate.

This publication combines basic, factual information and graphics, with useful exercises and past examination questions all in the one volume.

It should be noted that the format of the Part 2 second written paper will be changed with effect from December 1989 to include questions similar in structure to those used on the first written paper.

Full details are contained in the pamphlet *481 Recreation and Leisure Industries,* City and Guilds, (stock number SP-00-0481, £4.00 including postage. The pamphlet is available from: The Sales Section, City and Guilds Institute, 76 Portland Place, London W1N 4AA (telephone: 071-580 3050).

Preface to the Second Edition

The original intention when preparing the Second Edition was to avoid large scale reorganisation of unchanged material, primarily for the benefit of lecturers using both editions simultaneously with their classes. The advent of the changed format of the Part 2 examinations from December 1989 meant that the sections relating to past examination questions have had to be completely restructured. Since it had already been decided to increase the number of exercises provided at the end of each main section, the opportunity has also been taken to reorganise the original exercises into a more logical sequence.

The section and exercise relating to Coaching and Officiating Qualifications has also been transferred from Provision and Control to Product Knowledge, and the section relating to Recording Accident Details from Product Knowledge to Resource Management since these are the respective sections where they are now examined.

The vast majority of the other revisions are concerned with updating the current situation with regard to national agencies, and complementing the original text with additional sections where there has been a shift in emphasis in the examinations to correspond with new developments in, what continues to be, a growing and changing industry.

Acknowledgements

I would like to thank my friends and colleagues for their help, encouragement and additional material:

Lesley Boyden, Andy Brown, Gordon Clark, David Jones, Val London, John McKenna, Andrea Moore, Carla Robinson, Chris Rutherford, Mark Shirley, Gary Smith, Karen Summerfield, Kim Tanser, John Thedham, Sheila Vincent and Russell Ward.

The author and publishers also wish to thank the following who have kindly given permission for the use of copyright material.

Arts Council structure 1988, objectives and activities reproduced from the Arts Council 43rd Annual Report and Accounts 87–88, London, 1988.

British Tourist Authority responsibilities and the use of its logo, reproduced from the British Tourist Board Annual Report 1988.

Colne Valley Park strategic plan, map and park logo reproduced from the Colne Valley Park Standing Conference Proposals for the Regional Park, October 1988. Buckinghamshire County Council.

City and Guilds of London Institute Subject 481 Recreation and Leisure Industries: syllabuses and past years' question papers for subjects 778/481.

Countryside Commission logo, information, National Parks logos and map, waymark sign and long distance footpath map reproduced from "At Work in the Countryside, 1988/89", Countryside Commission, 1988.

English Tourist Board objectives, logo and map of the Regional Tourist Boards, reproduced from the English Tourist Board Annual Report, 1987/1988.

Forestry Commission logo reproduced with kind permission of the Forestry Commission.

Historic Buildings and Monuments Commission structure, function and logo of English Heritage reproduced with kind permission of the Historic Buildings and Monuments Commission for England.

National Coaching Foundation structure and logo reproduced from "All About the NCF", National Coaching Foundation, 1988.

National Rivers Authority information reproduced from "The National Rivers Authority — A Brief Introduction"

National Trust information and logo reproduced from "National Trust Membership: See what you're saving", National Trust, 1984.

Nature Conservancy Council for England — functions and logo.

Countryside Council for Wales — logo and information reproduced from: "Landscape Wildlife People Enjoyment Understanding", CCW, 1991, "The Countryside under the Dragon's Wing", CCW, 1991.

Sports Council aims, action programme and logo reproduced from "What is the Sports Council?" fact sheet, the Sports Council, London. Information relating to the National Sports Centres and the logos of the individual National Sports Centres reproduced from "The National Sports Centres" fact sheet, the Sports Council, London. Sections of material relating to "50+", "What's Your Sport?", "Ever Thought of Sport" and "Action Sport" reproduced with kind permission of the Sports Council. SASH Technical Details reproduced from SASH "Design Guide 1: Indoor Sports Building", the Sports Council, London. Definitions relating to sports surfaces reproduced from "Specifications for Artificial Sports", Sports Council, London, 1978.

Water Authorities Association and Severn-Trent Water for additional information relating to the water authorities and the map of the boundaries and headquarters towns of the present water authorities reproduced by kind permission of the Water Authorities Association.

Wolfe Publishing Ltd, for figure 77 "The Causal Chain in Injury" from Williams, JGP "A Colour Atlas of Injury in Sports", Wolfe Medical, 1980.

1 Marketing

WHAT IS MARKETING?

Marketing is a *process* which puts the *customer* at the centre of things. It concerns *everyone* who works within an organisation but it is especially relevant in the leisure and recreation industry. This is because it is essentially a *service* industry where almost all employees come face to face with the customer. Marketing is certainly more than just selling; it is about finding out what people want and responding to it. The following flow chart shows how this might be done:

FIRST IDENTIFY

WHO ARE OUR CUSTOMERS (AND POTENTIAL CUSTOMERS)?	WHAT ARE THE ORGANISATION'S RESOURCES?
	Physical | Financial | Human

THEN IDENTIFY

THESE CUSTOMERS NEEDS AND WANTS	WHAT CAN BE PROVIDED? HOW CAN IT BE PROVIDED?

FINALLY

MATCH

THE NEEDS AND WANTS OF THE CUSTOMERS	⟷	THAT WHICH CAN BE PROVIDED

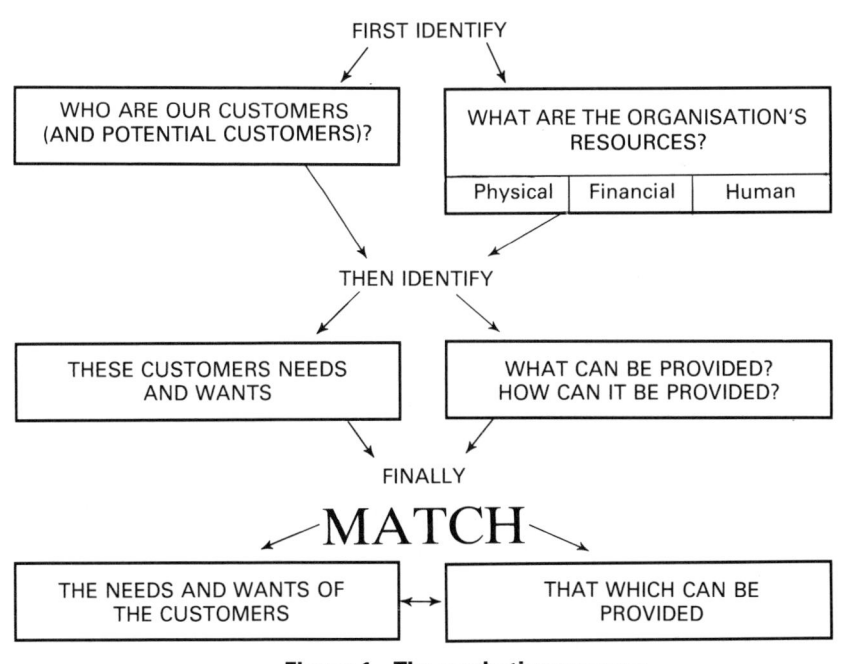

Figure 1 The marketing process

1

Who are our customers?

The answer depends on the aims of the organisation concerned, but, potentially, it includes everyone who might make use of that organisation's products, its facilities and services. A large local authority owned leisure facility with the aim of providing the best possible service to the local community might adopt a "cradle to grave" philosophy, where the market will be the whole community.

Voluntary groups and members' clubs may provide a service but could have a rather narrower view of where their market is and therefore who their customers might be; for example, this could be restricted to those who may wish to participate in, or watch, a particular sport or activity.

Commercial organisations will primarily be concerned with providing facilities and services for those who are able to pay for them.

Therefore the identification of specific groups, who may be interested in a particular set of facilities or services, is an important aspect of marketing. Such groups are often referred to as *market segments*.

What are the needs and desires of our customers?

Establishing just what the needs and desires of customers are can be difficult, particularly in the leisure and recreation industry. Even though people may be participating in the same activity, their reasons for doing so may be very different.

Reasons why individuals may participate in a particular recreational activity might include:

(a) enjoyment of that particular activity for its own sake;
(b) as a means of getting fit or keeping healthy and reducing stress;
(c) for social reasons (to be in the company of family or friends);
(d) because they wish to be associated with that activity or the people who participate in it as a means of gaining social status.

It can be seen that for many people the attraction of the actual activity itself may be of little importance, as participation is a means to a different end. Thus one activity may be as good as another and demand substitution may frequently occur, so that if a new activity were made available many customers may change to doing that instead.

The personality and skill of the person leading the sessions and the influence of fashion are other factors which may alter the demand for a particular activity.

All these factors therefore make it very difficult to establish exactly what the needs and desires of our customers are. However, one of the best ways of finding out is by talking to existing and potential customers and asking what they like or dislike about the provision and how the services and facilities might be improved. The most important aspect of this exercise is listening to their replies and suggestions.

This is referred to as "field" or "primary" research. The alternative, to use data and information published elsewhere — is known as "desk" or "secondary" research. Both methods can be of considerable value and it is important that they are used as much as is possible because some groups have greater difficulty in articulating or communicating their needs than others.

What are the resources of the organisation?

The resources of the organisation will consist of:

(a) physical resources (facilities, equipment);
(b) financial resources (the money that is available to provide any extra equipment, staffing or publicity that may be required);
(c) human resources (existing staff with special skills, abilities and interests).

What can be provided?

In leisure and recreation environments provision may consist of:

(a) products,
(b) services;
(c) benefits.

Products may include:

(a) sports clothing and equipment;
(b) food and drink;
(c) gifts and souvenirs;
(d) activities.

Services may include:

(a) the use of facilities (car parking, sports hall, weights room, showers, bar);
(b) the use of equipment;
(c) information (through reception, notices, leaflets and brochures);
(d) coaching, instruction and supervision.

Benefits may include:

(a) relaxation and enjoyment;
(b) improved health and fitness;
(c) social benefits (friendship, sense of achievement, recognition and status).

The final decision on what is to be provided will depend on the resources of the organisation being matched to the needs and desires of its customers.

One of the biggest problems in leisure is that very often the "product" is an intangible expectation or promise that must be purchased before it can be assessed whether it is value for money.

Pricing the product or service

Once it has been decided what is to be provided and where it is to be provided, it is then necessary to decide what the price of the product or service to the customer is to be.

This will not necessarily depend only on the actual cost of providing the product or service. It will also depend on whether the aim of the organisation is to provide a service or make a profit.

Promotion

The final component of marketing is promotion. Having developed a product it is then necessary to make sure that potential customers know about it, what is on offer, where, when and how much. This may be done through a number of means including advertising and promotional events.

However, the nature of the promotion will depend on who it is aimed at. The different target groups may be identified as shown in Figure 2 below:

EXISTING SERVICES TO EXISTING CUSTOMERS	EXISTING SERVICES TO NEW CUSTOMERS
NEW SERVICES TO EXISTING CUSTOMERS	NEW SERVICES TO NEW CUSTOMERS

Figure 2 Targeting promotion

The marketing mix

The marketing mix is the term used to cover four important elements that affect marketing decisions. These are known as the four "P"s:

PRODUCT, PLACE, PRICE, PROMOTION.

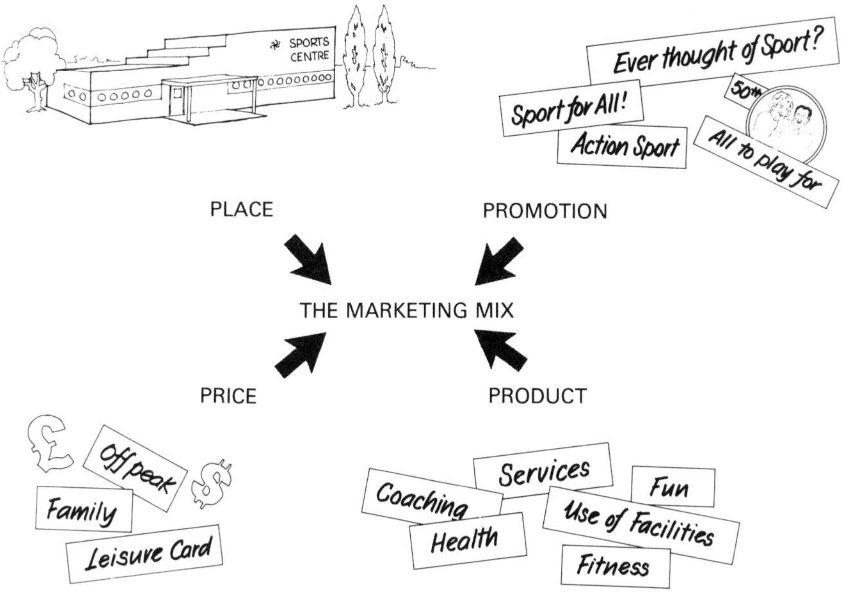

Figure 3   The marketing mix

WHAT BUSINESS ARE WE IN?

Some simple definitions to begin with

Ask any group of people what they understand by the terms "leisure", "recreation", "sport" and "play" and the number of different meanings and interpretations that are received will illustrate very clearly why some form of agreed definition has to be used by groups of people working or studying in this area. The above terms are central to the marketing of leisure and recreation services and consequently there are important professional reasons for defining these.

The following definitions have been selected as being appropriate to the needs of students studying for the City and Guilds Part 1 examinations. They are not necessarily suitable for use at higher levels of study.

Leisure is the time which allows the individual the opportunity to participate in any self-determined activity outside the recognised "working time". It may be play, recreation or sport; it may be active or passive.

Play can be a spontaneous response or activity undertaken for enjoyment, not necessarily controlled by predetermined guidelines, though it can be ordered by immediately agreed conventions.

Recreation is any activity or pastime undertaken by the individual for enjoyment and can encompass any activity participated in by the individual outside that part of the day recognised as "working time".

Sport is any activity normally with an element of competitiveness undertaken within agreed rules, regulations or conventions, where success may well depend on physical ability.

The way in which leisure, play, recreation and sport (as defined above) may be regarded as relating to each other for the purposes of the City and Guilds 481-1 examinations is illustrated in Figure 4 below:

```
              LEISURE
           ↗         ↖
         ↙             ↘
    PLAY ←——→ RECREATION ←——→ SPORT
```

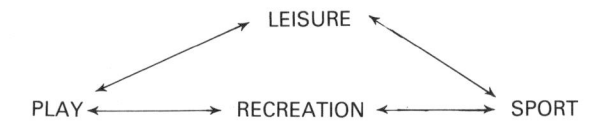

Figure 4 The interrelationship of leisure, play, recreation and sport

There are a number of approaches to obtaining a definition but it is important that the one eventually selected is appropriate to the needs of the group of people actually using it. Merely taking a definition from a dictionary is likely to result in a definition being selected that is too vague or ambiguous. It is much better that a definition should be specially constructed, based upon the best compilation of ideas available, and that this definition should stipulate as little as possible.

Active and passive leisure activities

For the purposes of the examination a distinction is made between "active" and "passive" leisure activities. Active leisure activities clearly include sports, hobbies and other interests which require active, often intense, responses from the participants.

Passive leisure activities are those which require virtually no response or effort from the individual participating in that activity. Examples of passive leisure activities might include:

(a) sleeping,
(b) sun bathing,
(c) watching television,
(d) listening to the radio,
(e) reading.

It must be noted that such a distinction can only really be made within the terms of the definitions set out above. Definitions of leisure used at higher levels of study, which relate to the freedom of choice and the quality of the experience for the individual, have no place for such a distinction.

Leisure activities which are not sports

Many leisure activities are, or course, sports but many hobbies and interests, which are not sports, *are* leisure activities. Examples include:

(a) sightseeing and visiting places of interest;
(b) eating out;
(c) shopping;
(d) participating in art and craft related activities;
(e) studying areas of personal interest (eg nature study, antiques, historic aircraft);
(f) gardening and "do it yourself" activities.

Leisure activities which are disapproved of by society as being anti-social, destructive or illegal

This group of activities frequently attracts a good deal of attention and, indeed, many opportunities for alternative leisure activities have been provided in the hope that this may reduce the number of people engaged in "unacceptable" leisure pursuits. Examples of unacceptable activities include:

(a) vandalism;
(b) drug misuse, including solvent "sniffing", alcoholism and drunkenness;

(c) brawling and football hooliganism;
(d) criminal activities engaged in for excitement, including breaking and entering, shoplifting and "taking and driving away".

General characteristics of a sport

Much lively discussion may be had in considering the merits of claims of particular activities to be called sports. Whilst there is considerable agreement in the case of activities such as football, cricket and tennis, even when these games are played professionally, the claims of snooker, chess, darts, rock climbing or even "twitching" (a competitive form of bird watching) are much more debatable. Before entering into any such discussion it is important to agree first upon precisely what the main characteristics of a sport are. Most would agree that these are:

(a) it is competitive;
(b) it has agreed rules or conventions;
(c) it has defined and measurable goals, targets or standards that may be evaluated and scored;
(d) it has an element of physical activity.

Differences and similarities between sport and recreation

Where participation in a sport is voluntary and is engaged in for fun, personal fulfilment or for personal reasons, then it is clearly also a recreational activity. However, recreational activities also include many hobbies, pastimes and crafts which are not sports. It is also difficult to find obvious similarities between sports such as professional football and Formula 1 Grand Prix motor racing and recreations such as embroidery or reading romantic novels. Generally speaking, however, both sports and recreations are:

(a) active;
(b) may be enjoyable;
(c) usually involve a degree of specialised skill or knowledge.

This quality and nature of the experience may be very different when the sport is played either professionally or as a result of some form of compulsion.

FACTORS AFFECTING MARKETING

The factors affecting marketing have been variously listed but may be said to include:

(a) location (including environmental factors);
(b) social factors;
(c) cultural influences;
(d) fashion;
(e) political factors;
(f) economic factors.

Location

The location of a leisure facility can be vital to its success. Although the physical position of facilities is important, especially if they are prominently located in such a way that they are brought to the attention of passers by, it is the *accessibility* of the facility to potential customers that is the most important single factor.

This accessibility has three important aspects:

(a) the distance between the facility and the residences or places of work of its customers;
(b) the quality of road and rail links and the availability of public transport links to the facility, together with car parking at the site;
(c) the time taken to get there (facilities placed between customers' places of work and their homes have a very obvious advantage in this respect).

Ideally facilities should be placed as close as possible to where potential customers live or work, or to those places where their customers tend to gather in their leisure time (eg city centres, seaside resorts, the countryside). This is not always possible: land may not be available or may be too expensive. In isolated rural communities, where it is not possible to site facilities within easy walking distance of the homes of the majority of customers, it is important that adequate car parking is provided. In inner city areas, however, where facilities have been specifically provided to meet the needs of a local community it may be desirable not to include a car park in the design in order to reduce the use of the facilities by customers from outside the immediate locality.

Commercial facilities may be more successful if they are situated in town and city centres where there are many more people and public transport provision is likely to be much better. This is particularly the case with facilities such as theatres, cinemas, restaurants, bars and night clubs, where customers may combine visits to more than one facility during an evening. Leisure and theme parks, and other facilities where customers may be prepared to spend several hours, need good accessability particularly by road. The increasingly high attendances at Thorpe Park and Chessington World of Adventures, which are both situated just off the M25 near London, indicate the value of good transport links and locations.

Another way in which location can be used to good effect is by placing facilities along the main road links between major towns and cities and places that are already attracting large numbers of visitors. For example, many people living in cities and towns set off on a day out without any really firm idea of exactly where they will eventually end up. Local authorities, by placing picnic sites and country parks along roads between cities and National Parks and Areas of Outstanding Natural Beauty have successfully "intercepted" large numbers of visitors and helped reduce pressure on sensitive areas and relieve congestion on the roads leading to and from them. Such parks include the Goyt Valley between Manchester and the Peak District National Park and the Colne Valley Park between West London and the Chilterns.

The location of a leisure facility, together with the transport links to and around it, will determine its *catchment area* (ie the area from which most of its customers will be drawn).

Social factors

There are many social factors affecting the marketing of leisure and recreational services. Although these may vary in extent from time to time and from place to place, such factors currently exerting an influence include:

(a) changes in birth rates and marriage patterns which have led to a decrease in the number of young people entering the workforce and an increase in the number of women re-entering the workforce;

(b) increasing amounts of leisure time available for those in work, with decreased working hours and longer holidays, and the increased use of part-time and flexible working arrangements;
(c) changes in life expectancy which, coupled with earlier retirement, have led to an increased number of active older people who have significant amounts of leisure time available to them;
(d) a significant number of disadvantaged groups, including—
  (i) people who are unemployed,
  (ii) people who are disabled,
  (iii) mothers with young children,
  (iv) ethnic and minority groups.

Over the past 20 years there has been a rapid growth in the size of the leisure market and current predictions are that this trend will continue.

Cultural influences

Culture relates to the character, traditions and history of a community, together with the interests and values of its members.

Although regional variations exist (eg the growing of leeks, whippet and pigeon racing) and have a strong tradition in some areas whilst such activites are virtually ignored in others, certain sports, especially football and cricket, are very much regarded as "national sports". Success in these activities is more likely to receive wider recognition than comparable, or even greater, success in less traditional sports such as judo, trampolining, handball or volleyball. The different levels of publicity received by medal winners at the Olympic Games reflects this.

The increase in immigration to the United Kingdom since the end of the Second World War has led to the introduction of a variety of fresh ethnic groups and cultures into British society. Although this is a process which, to a greater or lesser extent, has gone on for centuries its impact in recent years has been quite marked. Different groups may be interested in different sports, activities and entertainments and be subjected to different religious and moral influences and values.

These differences may need to be taken into account when considering the needs of customers and the way in which provision is made and programmed.

Fashion

"Fashion" is a term that may be used to describe short-term rises in the popularity of particular activities and products. Since these rises in popularity will considerably affect demand it is important to keep in touch with current trends and opinions and assess the effect that these may have on an organisation.

Short-term trends may require a rapid response but a cautious approach to heavy capital investment. Long-term trends may need a much more carefully planned and structured response. Sometimes a surge of interest may be the result of the success or appeal of an individual (eg the huge increase in gymnastics that followed the success of Olga Korbut at the 1972 Munich Olympic Games) or team (eg the success of the England football team in the 1966 World Cup brought with it a marked increase in attendances at Football League games the following season).

However, although the success of individuals or teams may spark the imagination, very often it is only through the medium of television that these successes are first brought to people's attention. Television, itself, can have a big influence in bringing about an increase in the popularity of particular sports. The BBC 2 television programme "Pot Black", making use of the technological advances that had led to the availability of colour television, brought with it a tremendous revival of interest in snooker and recent Channel 4 coverage of American football, volleyball and basketball has also created an increase in interest in these activities.

Other leisure activities that have recently been very "fashionable" and enjoyed considerable popularity have included:

(a) squash;
(b) aerobics, "pop mobility";
(c) "fun running", marathons and half-marathons.

Although possibly less popular than they were, all these activities have continued to retain a large measure of support but others, such as skate boarding, roller discos and BMX cycling, are certainly not the commercial propositions that they were.

What all these activities have had in common is that they have all been ways of improving health and fitness that were both novel and fun to participate in. It is likely that activities that will enjoy surges in popularity in the future will have similar characteristics.

Political factors

Political factors can affect leisure and recreation provision at both national and local level.

Government policies determine the extent to which the national economy is regulated. Taxation, public expenditure policy and monetary controls will all have a major influence on the ability of local authorities to provide services and the public's ability to pay for them.

Party politics will also have a considerable influence upon local authorities' priorities in providing services and the ways in which their facilities are managed and resourced.

Economic factors

Economic factors will influence the level of consumption and the standard of living of customers. They will affect the ability to pay for services and goods and influence the amount of leisure time that customers have available.

The principal economic factors affecting the marketing of leisure and recreation services include:

(a) changes in levels of income;
(b) changes in levels of employment;
(c) inflation, interest rates and foreign exchange rates;
(d) economic uncertainties.

PHILOSOPHY OF USE

The "philosophy of use" of an organisation is the underlying system of beliefs and values held by the providers or managers of a facility which determines the type of use to which it will be put.

A philosophy of use may be determined by social, political or commercial considerations.

Once determined, the philosophy of use will be reflected in the aims and objectives of the facility and the programme that it offers.

PROGRAMMING

"Leisure" is a highly "perishable" commodity. An empty badminton or squash court, an empty cinema or theatre seat or an unfilled place on a ride or aeroplane is available for only a moment in time. Once gone, it cannot ever be sold. It is therefore extremely important that the use of such facilities should be carefully planned and scheduled or timetabled in order to ensure that the maximum possible use is made of them.

Programming should also take into account the availability of staff, as well as facilities, the times at which particular groups of customers are able to attend and the range of different activities and services that will be offered in a manner that is totally integrated. The programme also needs to take into account the possibility of huge fluctuations in demand, both during the day and over the year.

In short, programming can be said to consist of those components illustrated in Figure 5 below.

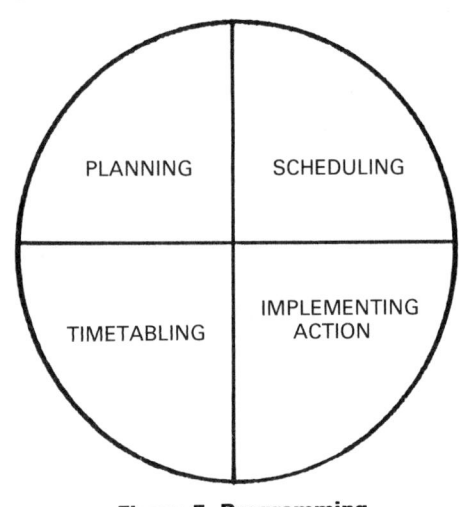

Figure 5 Programming

(circle divided into quadrants: PLANNING, SCHEDULING, TIMETABLING, IMPLEMENTING ACTION)

Approaches to programming

A number of different approaches to programming have been identified. These may be divided into two main strategies and other approaches which combine elements from each of the main strategies to a greater or lesser extent.

The two main strategies are:

(a) planned programmes directed professionally by officers of the providing organisation, often referred to as "social planning";

(b) programmes which arise from the community itself, often referred to as "community development".

Torkildsen (1983) identified a number of different approaches to programming which included the following:

(a) *the traditional approach* where programmes are based on previously used formats that have proved successful in the past;
(b) *the current trends approach* which relies upon identifying recent trends or fashions and programming activities around them;
(c) *the expressed desires approach* which is based upon asking people what they want and programming accordingly;
(d) *the authoritarian approach* which is based upon professional officers deciding what the needs are and what the community wants and programming accordingly;
(e) *the political/social approach* where pressure from groups is used as the basis for a community programme.

Each programme will have to meet different community needs. As a result different approaches to programming may be appropriate in different circumstances. Combinations or variations of these may, in the end, give the best results by being able to take a wide range of different factors into account.

Planning a programme

When planning a recreational programme, especially where the facility is managed for a local authority with the aim of providing a service for all the members of a particular community, it is important to take into account the different recreational and leisure needs of the various sections of that community and those who might be associated with specific groups within it.

These different groups and sections of the community may include:

(a) toddlers and pre-school age childen;
(b) young school age children;
(c) young teenagers;
(d) young adults aged 16–20;
(e) adults aged 21–40;
(f) middle-aged adults aged 40–55;
(g) late middle-aged and retired adults aged 55 and over;
(h) unemployed adults;

(i) manual workers;
(j) clerical workers;
(k) parents (especially mothers) with young children;
(l) ethnic minorities;
(m) physically and mentally handicapped people;
(n) members of clubs, teams and groups that may require specialist training or match facilities.

Clearly many individuals will belong to two or more of these groups and sections. Furthermore, the needs of individuals within the same group may be different but identifying the different groups that make up a community and considering their needs and how they may be catered for is an important part of the process of planning a programme.

In addition the programme should take into account:

(a) activities which are already popular and an analysis of the activities that are already offered;
(b) groups which are currently under-provided for;
(c) current trends and the need to offer some variety and novelty;
(d) the requirements of external groups (although total exclusive use of a facility should be avoided unless it is to the advantage of the organisation).

Programming mix

The programming mix is concerned with the balance of activities offered and the range and type of individuals and groups catered for. These will include those groups identified in Figure 6.

Generally, the more "community" based the programme is the more likely it is that it will require subsidy.

Crèches, disadvantaged groups and the training and coaching of high level performers may all require considerable subsidy, as indeed community work does in the majority of cases.

The inclusion of activities which are popular and economic can help offset these financial costs.

A commercially operated facility will concentrate almost exclusively on activities which are economically viable.

The objectives of the organisation must be clear and the programme based on a sound philosophy of use.

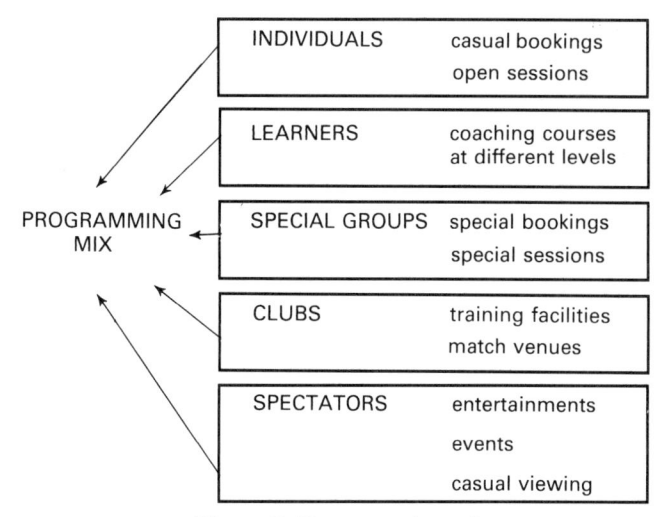

```
                    ┌─────────────────────────────────────────┐
                    │ INDIVIDUALS      casual bookings        │
                    │                  open sessions          │
                    └─────────────────────────────────────────┘
                    ┌─────────────────────────────────────────┐
                    │ LEARNERS         coaching courses       │
                    │                  at different levels    │
                    └─────────────────────────────────────────┘
PROGRAMMING         ┌─────────────────────────────────────────┐
   MIX              │ SPECIAL GROUPS   special bookings       │
                    │                  special sessions       │
                    └─────────────────────────────────────────┘
                    ┌─────────────────────────────────────────┐
                    │ CLUBS            training facilities    │
                    │                  match venues           │
                    └─────────────────────────────────────────┘
                    ┌─────────────────────────────────────────┐
                    │ SPECTATORS       entertainments         │
                    │                  events                 │
                    │                  casual viewing         │
                    └─────────────────────────────────────────┘
```

Figure 6 Programming mix

Programming to improve off-peak usage

Good programming can be very effective in improving off-peak usage of leisure facilities. Firstly, these off-peak periods will have to be identified. Generally they are likely, outside school holidays, to include early mornings and the period of the normal working day but this will vary considerably from facility to facility. Those situated in areas where there is a considerable amount of shift-work offered by employers may have very different patterns of use.

Once off-peak periods have been identified it is then necessary to consider which user groups or market segments might be free to use the facility at that time.

Activities and services that may satisfy the needs and wants of the members of those groups can then be programmed and promoted. Very often it will be found that the groups who are available to use facilities at off-peak times are those who are generally under-provided for.

This process may be summarised in the following flow chart:

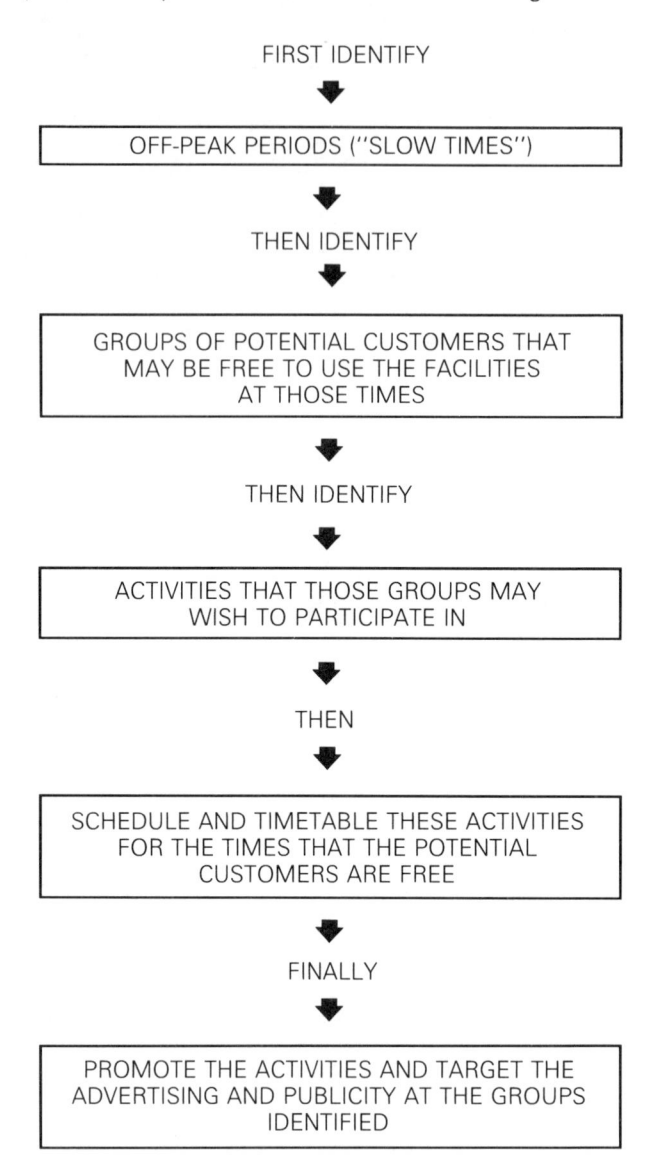

FIRST IDENTIFY
⬇
| OFF-PEAK PERIODS ("SLOW TIMES") |
⬇
THEN IDENTIFY
⬇
| GROUPS OF POTENTIAL CUSTOMERS THAT MAY BE FREE TO USE THE FACILITIES AT THOSE TIMES |
⬇
THEN IDENTIFY
⬇
| ACTIVITIES THAT THOSE GROUPS MAY WISH TO PARTICIPATE IN |
⬇
THEN
⬇
| SCHEDULE AND TIMETABLE THESE ACTIVITIES FOR THE TIMES THAT THE POTENTIAL CUSTOMERS ARE FREE |
⬇
FINALLY
⬇
| PROMOTE THE ACTIVITIES AND TARGET THE ADVERTISING AND PUBLICITY AT THE GROUPS IDENTIFIED |

Figure 7   Programming to improve off-peak usage

Examples of activites that may be programmed to increase off-peak usage are shown in Figure 8 below.

TIME	ACTIVITY/PROVISION	TARGET GROUP
07.00–08.30	Early morning swim sessions	Serious, club and keep-fit swimmers who work during normal working hours and those who have just completed a night shift
09.30–11.30	Mothers and toddlers keep-fit and recreation sessions Pre-school gymnastics sessions and play groups Crèche	Mothers with young and school age children
12.00–14.00	Lunchtime keep-fit sessions "open" recreation sessions	People who work during the normal working day but who may wish to keep fit during their lunch times
14.00–16.30	Reduced rate sessions	Primarily those who are unemployed, although it is better if the sessions are open with the same rate applying to all users
16.30–18.00	Junior sport sessions Coaching sessions	School age children

Figure 8   **Programming to increase off-peak usage — timetable**

Clubs will often be willing to fill other off-peak periods and times when facilities are under-used, eg Sunday mornings. It is often desirable, when the aim is to offer a service to all the members of a local community, to defer the allocation of a large number of club bookings until the rest of the programme has taken shape.

Some groups may have particular difficulty in fulfilling their leisure needs. Some of these groups are discussed in more detail below.

NEEDS OF SPECIFIC GROUPS THAT MAY HAVE DIFFICULTY IN FULFILLING THEIR LEISURE NEEDS

These may include:

(a) disabled people;
(b) mothers with young children;

(c) ethnic minority groups;
(d) unemployed adults.

Disabled people

The most immediate need of disabled people is to be able to gain access to the facilities:

(a) car parking bays need to be close to the building entrance;
(b) car parking bays for wheelchair users need to be at least one metre wider than standard ones;
(c) pathways need to be firm, reasonably smooth and to give good purchase;
(d) pathways should have ramps at kerb crossing points and be wide enough for two wheelchairs or prams to pass each other;
(e) ideally there should be no steps into or within the building (a design feature of the Sports Council/Bovis SASH sports halls) but where this is unavoidable ramps should be provided and, if not situated by the main entrance, be clearly signposted;
(f) within the building corridors and doors should be wide enough to give access to all areas, including:
   (i) activity areas,
   (ii) toilets and changing rooms,
   (iii) social areas, and
   (iv) spectator areas.

Attention should also be given to egress in case of a fire, since lifts should not be used in such circumstances. It is no use getting people into a building if they cannot be got out again in an emergency.

In terms of activities, experience suggests that, if they can gain access to the facilities, disabled people prefer to participate with able bodied athletes wherever possible.

Many activities can be participated in by people with varying degrees of physical disability, as demonstrated by the achievements of those who have competed in the Paralympic Games.

There is a more pressing need for specially organised sessions for those who suffer from mental handicaps. Although there are few activities which are not suitable at all, sessions may need to be carefully structured and led by experienced coaches and leaders. Exclusive use of facilities for such sessions is much more common than for those with physical or sensory difficulties.

Mothers with young children

Mothers with young children face a number of difficulties which can prevent them from participating in leisure activities (many of which are shared by women who do not have young children). The principal difficulties often include:

(a) always being on call to service the needs of their children;
(b) lack of access to cars;
(c) lack of suitable sessions and facilities at times when they may otherwise be able to participate.

Other difficulties may include financial constraints and a lack of confidence which may result from having had a break of several years from sports activities.

Ways in which mothers with young children may be helped to participate in leisure activities include:

(a) making children welcome by providing facilities for feeding, changing, "parking" prams and pushchairs and by offering crèche facilities or toddler classes at the same time as sessions for the mothers;
(b) scheduling thoughtfully and perhaps offering "women only" sessions;
(c) making payment easier, either through extending concessionary rates or by making payment more flexible (ie pay as you go, rather than for twelve-week courses);
(d) catering for families by programming activities that can be participated in by all the family together or by offering activities that permit parallel participation and by providing family changing facilities (as is now done in a number of leisure pools).

Ethnic minority groups

Before considering what is meant by an ethnic minority group it should be emphasised that "ethnic", "minority" and "racial" groups are *not* the same thing.

Ethnic relates to a group having traits and characteristics in common which may be religious, linguistic or cultural. The Jews, the gypsies and even the Irish may all be regarded as ethnic groups.

Racial relates to those who are descended from the same ancestor, especially where they inherit a common set of characteristics. Caucasians, Afro-Caribbeans and Asians are all commonly regarded as racial groups.

A minority group is one that is different from a larger group of which it is part. The differences that distinguish a minority group as being one apart may be political, cultural or racial.

An ethnic minority group will be one that is ethnic and a minority. It may also be identifiable as a racial group as well. Examples of ethnic minority groups within the United Kingdom include Vietnamese and Ugandan Asians.

Minority groups may experience problems regarding participation in leisure activities for a number of reasons, these include:

(a) religious beliefs;
(b) language differences which may make communication difficult;
(c) different cultural traditions, interests and values.

Unemployed adults

Although unemployed adults have comparatively large amounts of free time, the degree to which they take part in sports and organised recreational activities may be very limited. Often they tend to adopt an increasingly "home-centred" leisure life style: watching television, listening to the radio and doing jobs about the home. The principal reasons for many not taking part in sports activities include:

(a) lack of money to spend on sport;
(b) lack of adequate sports equipment;
(c) lack of transport;
(d) lack of motivation to take part in sport and to commit themselves to regular participation;
(e) lack of organised daytime activities;
(f) lack of knowledge of existing recreational facilities and activities;
(g) lack of expertise or confidence in the playing of sport.

Ways in which the unemployed may be encouraged to take part in sport and recreational activities include:

(a) "off-peak" pricing and low cost (or free) activities;
(b) supply and loan of appropriate equipment;
(c) provision of transport, particularly in rural areas (although mini-

buses have also been used with notable success in inner city schemes);
(d) provision of activities (where possible, actually within the community);
(e) use of a wide range of different methods of publicity;
(f) advertising activities in places where the unemployed will be (unemployment benefit offices, job centres and drop-in centres, as well as libraries and sports centres);
(g) keeping sessions "open" to those in employment;
(h) employing sports organisers or motivators to set up activities, to encourage people to "have a go" and to welcome and support those who do attend sessions.

Communicating needs

Differences in educational or social background, lack of organisation, confidence or the knowledge of who to contact can all make communication difficult.

Community groups may use a number of ways to communicate their needs. These ways may include:

(a) direct contact with managers and local politicians;
(b) letters to the press;
(c) the formation of pressure groups;
(d) publicity campaigns, events and demonstrations.

Publicity Activities

Publicity activities are very important in the promotion of leisure and recreation and for encouraging people to participate in new activities.

Although a considerable amount of publicity is generated by locally initiated events, national campaigns, sponsored and organised by national agencies, can have a tremendous impact at both national and local level. One of the most prominent, if not *the* most prominent, agencies in this respect has been the Sports Council.

The Sports Council, in addition to its on-going campaign "Sport for All" (aimed at increasing participation in sport generally) has also identified "special" low or non-participation groups. Its first campaign aimed at a

CAMPAIGN	AIM	NATIONAL AGENCY
Sport for All	To stimulate participation in sport by those who do not participate at present	Sports Council
50+ All to Play For	To stimulate participation by the 45 to 59 year old age group	Sports Council
Ever thought of Sport?	To stimulate participation by the 13 to 24 year old age group	Sports Council with Weetabix Limited
Action Sport	To encourage the unemployed to participate in sport and its organisation	Sport Council with paid staff funded through the MSC's Community Programme
What's Your Sport?	To stimulate participation in sport by women	Sports Council with the Milk Marketing Board
Look After Yourself!	To encourage individuals to achieve better health	Health Education Council
Look After Your Heart!	To reduce the incidence of heart disease by encouraging individuals to lead a healthier lifestyle	Health Education Authority with the DHSS
Watch Over the National Parks	To increase public awareness of the national parks and increase public support for them	Countryside Commission in association with the Council for National Parks

Figure 9   Recent national campaigns

special group was directed at increasing opportunities for the disabled. Since then they have organised a number of other campaigns, often in association with joint sponsors, laying down the style, content and direction for local authorities and voluntary groups to pick up and implement at local level.

Other national agencies have also initiated national campaigns and some examples of these, together with some of the recent Sports Council campaigns, are given in Figure 9.

These campaigns have all produced high quality leaflets and promotional materials that have made good use of graphic design and logos, many of which are immediately recognisable and which add considerably to the strength of the campaigns. Some examples of Sports Council graphics and logos are given in Figure 10 overleaf.

Figure 10 Examples of some of the graphics and logos used in recent Sports Council campaigns

481–1 MARKETING

Exercise 1

(a) Visit a local leisure facility and make a survey of the services offered by it.
(b) Make a note of any products available.
(c) What *benefits* would customers hope to gain by using the facility?
(d) Attempt to identify market factors which have influenced the services on offer.

Exercise 2

Produce a comparative study of three different leisure or recreational facilities, identifying their various "philosophies of use" and their principal client groups.

The different facilities should include one each from:

(a) the public sector,
(b) the commercial sector,
(c) the voluntary sector.

Exercise 3

Make a survey of the programme of activities offered by a local leisure facility.

(a) Identify the different client groups that are catered for and explain why certain activities have been scheduled for the particular times that they have.
(b) Explain how scheduling may help meet the needs of specific minority groups.

Exercise 4

Survey a number of local leisure and recreation facilities and list the ways in which they encourage participation in leisure activities by people who may have difficulty in fulfilling their leisure needs. Your answer should include reference to ONE of the following groups in detail:

(a) disabled people,
(b) mothers with young children,
(c) ethnic minority groups,
(d) unemployed adults.

Exercise 5

(a) Make a brief survey of local advertisements related to leisure and recreation services offered locally. Make a particular note of any which relate to national or local campaigns. Note: your survey should include reference to all, or some, of the following:

   (i) television,
   (ii) national and local newspapers,
   (iii) leaflets,
   (iv) notices and posters.

(b) Identify at least one promotional event that has created some publicity for a sports or leisure facility locally.

481-1 MARKETING

PAST EXAMINATION QUESTIONS RELATED TO MARKETING

Part I Written paper

1. (a) Draw a diagram to show the relationship between leisure, play, recreation and sport. (2 marks)
   (b) An activity may be regarded as both recreation and sport. State THREE other similarities between recreation and sport.
   (3 marks)
   (December 1985)
2. (a) List the words required to complete the following definition of "recreation".
   "Recreation is any _____ or _____ undertaken by the _____ for _____ and can encompass any activity participated by in the _____ outside that period of the day recognised as _____ _____." (3 marks)
   (b) List TWO characteristics of "play". (2 marks)
   (June 1990)
3. (a) Sport is an activity which has certain characteristics. List THREE of these. (3 marks)
   (b) Some people choose to take part in leisure activities which are disapproved of by society as being destructive or illegal. List TWO such activities. (1 mark)
   (c) List TWO examples of sporting activities usually provided by commercial companies. (1 mark)
   (Composite — various papers)
4. (a) List FOUR indoor recreational activities which are not sports.
   (2 marks)
   (b) List FOUR outdoor team sports requiring pitches. (2 marks)
   (c) List TWO outdoor sports played on courts. (1 mark)
   (December 1990)
5. (a) List FOUR sports involving natural inland water. (2 marks)
   (b) List FOUR passive leisure pursuits. (2 marks)
   (c) List TWO active leisure pursuits which are not sports.
   (1 mark)
   (June 1990)

6. (a) List FOUR market factors to be considered when providing for leisure needs. (4 marks)
   (b) What name is used to describe the system which allows a school to use a leisure centre during school hours, and the public to use the centre at other times? (1 mark)
   (April 1990)
7. (a) The disabled have particular leisure needs. List THREE requirements to assist their access to leisure facilities. (3 marks)
   (b) List TWO groups other than the disabled which have particular leisure needs (2 marks)
   (April 1991)
8. (a) List THREE characteristics of an ethnic minority group. (3 marks)
   (b) Give TWO examples of ethnic minority groups. (1 mark)
   (c) Give an example of a problem experienced by ethnic minorities wishing to take part in sport or recreation. (1 mark)
   (June 1987)
9. (a) Explain briefly why the unemployed sometimes have difficulty in communicating their leisure needs. (2 marks)
   (b) Name a scheme designed to encourage the unemployed to take part in sport, and list its main elements. (3 marks)
   (December 1987)
10. (a) List THREE ways in which a community group can make its recreational needs known. (3 marks)
    (b) State TWO ways in which a leisure centre manager can assess the needs of the local community. (2 marks)
    (Composite — December 1986–1987)
11. A group of people in a local community wish to promote the playing of short tennis by children. List FIVE ways in which they could persuade others to support them. (5 marks)
    (June 1991)
12. (a) Name the Sports Council campaign to increase participation in sport in inner city areas. (1 mark)
    (b) Name the Sports Council campaign to increase participation in sport by the elderly. (1 mark)
    (c) Name a local scheme which encourages the unemployed to take part in sport. (1 mark)
    (d) Name TWO groups other than the unemployed which have difficulty fulfilling their leisure needs. (2 marks)
    (December 1990)

481-2 MARKETING

PAST EXAMINATION QUESTIONS RELATED TO MARKETING

Part II Paper 2 The organisation of recreation and leisure

1. (a) Describe how a leisure complex may improve off-peak usage.
   (5 marks)
   (b) Explain briefly the term "philosophy of use". (5 marks)
   (June 1987)
2. (a) Explain what is meant by a "recreation programme". (5 marks)
   (b) List FIVE factors which affect the marketing of recreation and leisure services. (5 marks)
   (December 1987)
3. (a) State the THREE basic elements which combine to make a successful recreation programme. (6 marks)
   (b) Identify FOUR different approaches to recreation programming. (4 marks)
   (Spring 1990)
4. (a) Outline the philosophy of use associated with each of the following sectors of recreation and leisure provision:

   (i) public, (3 marks)
   (ii) private, (4 marks)
   (iii) voluntary. (3 marks)
   (June 1990)
5. Explain TWO main differences between the "philosophy of use" of a "publicly" run sports centre and a "privately" run country club.
   (10 marks)
   (April 1991)

REFERENCES AND BIBLIOGRAPHY

Arnott, A Leisure opportunities for young women. Leisure Management Vol. 6 No. 9, pp 17–20, 1986
Donkin, D The Derwentside experience. Sports Council 1986
Glyptis, S, Kay, T and Donkin, D Sports and the unemployed. Sports Council, 1986
Parker, SR The future of work and leisure. Paladin, 1972
Parker, S. The sociology of leisure. 2nd edition. Allen and Unwin 1976
A practical approach to the administration of leisure and recreation services. Croner, 3rd edition 1990
Roberts, K Contemporary society and the growth of leisure. Longman, 1978
Robinson, G Making sense of marketing. Macmillan Educational, 1986
Sport for All. Sports Council, 1986
Torkildsen, G Leisure and recreation management. E&FN Spon, 2nd edition, 1986
Wills, G *et al* Introducing marketing. Pan, 1984

2 Provision and Control

AGENCIES INVOLVED IN PROVIDING FOR LEISURE AND RECREATION

Very many different agencies are involved in the provision of opportunities for leisure and recreation in the United Kingdom. These agencies vary considerably in their aims and methods of operation, and include organisations such as theme parks, leisure centres, restaurants, sports clubs, health clubs, youth groups, play groups, community associations, charities and organisations funded by the Government. In considering their influence in providing opportunities for participation in recreational activities it is useful to categorise these agencies as:

(a) national organisations;
(b) local authorities;
(c) commercial organisations;
(d) community groups.

NATIONAL ORGANISATIONS

These are taken to include those quasi-governmental organisations that are largely dependant upon grant aid from central Government, many of which also have a regional network of services, and charities and trusts. Those to be looked at in detail are:

(a) central Government;
(b) Sports Council;
(c) Central Council of Physical Recreation;
(d) Countryside Commission;
(e) Arts Council;
(f) Forestry Commission;
(g) National Nature Conservancy Councils;
(h) tourist boards;
(i) National Rivers Authority;

(j) governing bodies of sport;
(k) National Coaching Foundation;
(l) National Playing Fields Association;
(m) National Trust;
(n) English Heritage.

Central Government

Central Government consists of many different departments, each with its own particular sphere of influence and interests, policies and ministers.

These departments provide varying levels of financial support to the different quasi-governmental organisations that share those interests. Since the members of many of these organisations are also appointed by the appropriate Minister or Secretary of State (rather than being elected representatives) their activities are not immune from political direction or influence. However, since it may be argued that their funds derive almost entirely from tax revenue it may also be argued that some

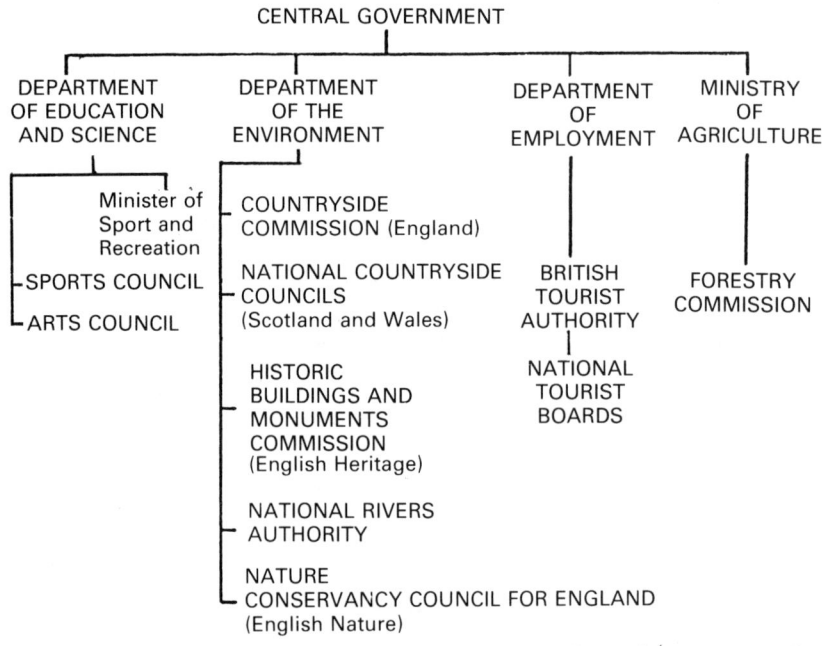

```
                        CENTRAL GOVERNMENT
    ┌──────────────┬──────────────────┬──────────────┬─────────────┐
DEPARTMENT     DEPARTMENT         DEPARTMENT      MINISTRY
OF EDUCATION   OF THE             OF              OF
AND SCIENCE    ENVIRONMENT        EMPLOYMENT      AGRICULTURE
    │              │                   │               │
    Minister of    COUNTRYSIDE
    Sport and      COMMISSION (England)
    Recreation
  SPORTS COUNCIL   NATIONAL COUNTRYSIDE   BRITISH        FORESTRY
  ARTS COUNCIL     COUNCILS               TOURIST        COMMISSION
                   (Scotland and Wales)   AUTHORITY
                                              │
                   HISTORIC                NATIONAL
                   BUILDINGS AND           TOURIST
                   MONUMENTS               BOARDS
                   COMMISSION
                   (English Heritage)

                   NATIONAL RIVERS
                   AUTHORITY

                   NATURE
                   CONSERVANCY COUNCIL FOR ENGLAND
                   (English Nature)
```

Figure 11 Central Government departments and quasi-governmental organisations concerned with leisure and recreation provision

form of political acountability is necessary. Those Government departments whose interests include areas and organisations which are of particular importance in the provision of facilities and opportunities for participation in leisure and recreational activities are shown in Figure 11.

Sports Council

Head Office:
16 Upper Woburn Place,
London WC1H 0QP
Tel: 071-388 1277

The Sports Council is an independent body which was established by Royal Charter in 1972. At that time it took over the staff and assets of the Central Council of Physical Recreation and gained responsibility for the Technical Unit for Sport. It replaced the advisory Sports Council which had been formed in 1965. It has overall responsibility for British sport and receives an annual grant from central Government. There are separate Councils for Scotland, Wales and Northern Ireland. The Sports Council structure currently consists of a chairman, two vice chairmen and members, who are all appointed by the Minister of Sport and Recreation with the authority of the appropriate Secretary of State, together with a number of employee members and observers. The Sports Council is also advised by consultative groups made up of experts and people involved in particular areas concerned with sport and recreation. These consultative groups replaced the six standing committees during the reorganisation of the Sports Council in 1988.

The Sports Council has four main aims:

(a) to increase participation in sport and physical recreation;
(b) to increase the quality and quantity of sports facilities;
(c) to raise standards of performance;
(d) to provide information for and about sport.

It attempts to achieve these aims through a comprehensive programme of action which includes:

(a) providing grants and financial aid to —
  (i) local organisations attempting to get more ordinary people into sport (in the form of regional participation grants);
  (ii) governing bodies of sport and other national organisations, to

improve administration, increase participation and raise standards of performance;
(iii) the National Coaching Foundation;
(iv) those developing new or improved sports facilities;
(b) running campaigns and programmes to promote sport and persuade people who do not at present participate to take up a sport;
(c) researching and preparing efficient and economical standard design solutions for sports buildings and systems, designing and testing innovatory facilities and systems (including artificial playing surfaces, heating/ventilation techniques and computerised administration) and funding research and feasibility studies;
(d) financing and running the campaign against drug misuse in sport;
(e) running the five National Sports Centres with their *centres of excellence*.

(This list and the following information are both taken from "What is the Sports Council? Fact Sheet" and "The National Sports Centres Fact Sheet", see Bibliography.)

The National Sports Centres

The National Sports Centres are centres for sporting excellence, run by the Sports Council. They provide some of the finest specialist sports facilities available in the United Kingdom for sportsmen and women.

The centres give priority, wherever possible, to the governing bodies of sport and other national organisations for national team preparation, training of coaches and officials and other teams and individuals striving for high standards of sports performance. When the facilities are not taken up by these priority bookings, the use of the facilities by beginners being introduced to new sports and by members of the local community is actively encouraged. Originally the National Sports Centres were established and run by the CCPR but they were transferred, together with the other assets, property and staff, to the Sports Council in 1971. Currently there are five National Sports Centres run by the Sports Council, these are:

(a) Bisham Abbey,
(b) Crystal Palace,
(c) Lilleshall,

(d) Holme Pierrepont and
(e) Plas y Brenin.

Until October 1987, there was also a National Sailing Centre at Cowes on the Isle of Wight.

All the centres have residential, training and conference facilities but, in addition, each centre is associated with providing specialist facilities for particular activities.

Bisham Abbey NSC

Bisham Abbey NSC,
Nr. Marlow,
Buckinghamshire
SL7 1RT
Tel: 062-84 76911

Situated on the banks of the River Thames, this is essentially a coaching and training facility. It has an excellent indoor training hall and various high quality artificial surfaces. The centre also has grass hockey, rugby and football pitches. The main sports catered for are tennis, hockey, Association football and weight training. The centre is also the base for the LTA's tennis school of excellence.

Crystal Palace NSC

Crystal Palace NSC,
Norwood,
London SE19 2BB
Tel: 081-778 0131

The centre, six miles south of Central London, is a multi-purpose sports facility. The sports hall, together with its swimming and diving pools and indoor arena, and the athletics stadium, with its eight-lane synthetic track, provide spectator, competition and championship facilities of international standard. In addition, the centre has a comprehensive range of other facilities including sports halls, ten squash courts, weight training facilities and a range of artificial courts and pitches.

The main sports catered for are swimming, diving and athletics, as well as those others wishing to stage national or international events.

Lilleshall NSC

Lilleshall Hall
National Sports Centre

Lilleshall NSC,
Nr. Newport,
Shropshire
TF10 9AT
Tel: 0952 603003

This centre is also essentially a coaching and training centre. Its main indoor facilities include excellent, world-class gymnastics training facilities and high standard cricket nets. Outdoor facilities include 30 acres of playing fields. Other facilities include a new sports hall, squash courts, all weather tennis courts and a synthetic pitch for football and hockey.

The Football Association is using Lilleshall as its base for major coaching activities. The FA's National School of Excellence and the FA's National Rehabilitation and Sports Injury Centre are also established there.

The main sports catered for are Association football, cricket and gymnastics.

Holme Pierrepont National Water SC

Holme Pierrepont
National Water Sports Centre

Holme Pierrepont NWSC,
Adbolton Lane,
Holme Pierrepont,
Nottingham NG12 2LU
Tel: 0602 821212

Holme Pierrepont is one of the most comprehensive water sports centres in the world. Its most outstanding facilities include an artificial white water canoe slalom course, a 2000 m regatta lake with good spectator facilities and separate water-ski lagoon with ski tow ropes. Other facilities include a comprehensive gymnasium.

The main sports catered for are canoeing, rowing, water skiing and other water sports.

Figure 12 Locations of the National Sports Centres

Plas y Brenin National Centre for Mountain Activities

Plas y Brenin
National Centre for Mountain Activities

Capel Curig,
Gwynedd,
North Wales
LL24 0ET
Tel: 06-904 214

This centre is situated within the Snowdonia National Park, which makes it an ideal base for outdoor activities, particularly those associated with mountaineering. On-site facilities include an artificial ski slope with button tow, a heated training pool and indoor climbing wall.

The main sports catered for are mountaineering, rock climbing, hill walking, canoeing, orienteering and dry slope skiing.

The centre also employs a large number of full-time specialist instructors as the majority of its work is concerned with residential courses.

Other national sports centres

The Sports Councils for Wales, Scotland and Northern Ireland also have their own national sports centres.

Regional sports councils

The Sports Council has ten regions which operate through nine regional offices. These regions are responsible for the implementation of Sports Council policies in respect of their own particular regions.

Northern Region   (Northumberland, Cumbria, Durham, Cleveland and Tyne and Wear)
Aykley Heads,
Durham DH1 5UU
Tel: 091-384 9595

North West Region   (Lancashire, Cheshire, Greater Manchester and Merseyside)
Astley House,
Quay Street,
Manchester M3 4AE
Tel: 061-834 0338

Yorkshire and Humberside (West Yorkshire, South Yorkshire, North Yorkshire and Humberside)
Coronet House,
Queen Street,
Leeds LS1 4PW
Tel: 0532 436443

East Midland Region (Derbyshire, Nottinghamshire, Lincolnshire, Leicestershire and Northamptonshire)
Grove House,
Bridgeford Road,
West Bridgeford,
Nottingham NG2 6AP
Tel: 0602 821887 and 822586

West Midlands Region (West Midlands, Hereford and Worcester, Shropshire, Staffordshire and Warwickshire)
Metropolitan House,
1 Hagley Road,
Five Ways, Edgbaston,
Birmingham B16 8TT
Tel: 021-454 3808

Eastern Region (Norfolk, Cambridgeshire, Suffolk, Bedfordshire, Hertfordshire and Essex)
26–28 Bromham Road,
Bedford MK40 2QP
Tel: 0234 45222

Greater London and South East Region (Greater London, Surrey, Kent, East and West Sussex)
PO Box 480,
Crystal Palace National Sports Centre,
Ledrington Road,
London SE19 2BQ
Tel: 081-778 8600

Southern Region (Berkshire, Buckinghamshire, Hampshire, Isle of Wight, Oxfordshire)
51a Church Street,
Caversham,
Reading,
RG4 8AX
Tel: 0734 483311

Figure 13 Sports Council regions

(From "Sport in the Community – the Next Ten Years", Sports Council.)

South Western Region (Avon, Cornwall, Devon, Dorset, Somerset, Wiltshire and Gloucestershire)
Ashlands House,
Ashlands,
Crewkerne,
Somerset TA18 7LQ
Tel: 0460 73491

The Central Council of Physical Recreation (CCPR)

Francis House,
Francis Street,
London SW1P 1DE
Tel: 071-828 3163

The CCPR is an independent voluntary body consisting of representatives of over 240 governing and representative bodies of sport and physical and recreational activities. It was founded in 1935. Its main objects are:

"1. To constitute a standing forum where all national governing and representative bodies of sport and physical recreation may be represented and may, collectively or through special groups, where appropriate, formulate and promote measures to improve and develop sport and physical recreation.
2. To support the work of other specialist sports bodies and to bring them together with other interested organisations.
3. To act as a consultative body to the Sports Council and other representative or public bodies concerned with sport and physical recreation."

(This and the following are taken from "The Central Council of Physical Recreation, A Guide: What it is and what it does", see Bibliography.)

The CCPR is organised into six divisions in order to enable it to achieve its aims and objectives effectively. They are:

Games and Sports Division
Outdoor Pursuits Division
Major Spectator Sports Division

Movement and Dance Division
Water Recreation Division
Division of Interested Organisations

These divisions directly elect the CCPR's Executive Committee so that its policies and attitudes reflect those of its membership.

The CCPR is primarily financed by annual grants from the Sports Council, although it also receives donations from its members. In addition to providing a forum for the discussion of a wide range of issues affecting sport and recreation the CCPR also provides a number of services for its members. These include:

(a) a press service;
(b) help with sponsorship;
(c) liaison with Government and local authorities;
(d) legal advice;
(e) assistance with fund raising;
(f) other information and advice services.

The CCPR also administers the Community Sports Leaders Award (CSLA) and the Basic Expedition Training Award. Both schemes are designed for people over the age of 16 who wish to gain experience and ability in organising, assisting and leading groups participating in sports and physical recreations.

The Countryside Commission

Countryside Commission,
John Dower House,
Crescent Place,
Cheltenham,
Gloucestershire GL50 3RA
Tel: 0242 521381

The Countryside Commission was established under the Countryside Act 1968 for the purpose of keeping under review "matters relating to the conservation and enhancement of landscape beauty in England and Wales and to the provision and improvement of facilities of the countryside for enjoyment, including the need to secure access for open-air recreation". The Environmental Protection Act 1990 transferred the Countryside Commission's duties with respect to Wales to a new statutory body, the Countryside Council for Wales, with effect from 1.4.91 (see page 60). The Countryside Commission is now solely concerned with countryside matters relating to England. Its members are appointed by the Secretary of State for the Environment. The

Commission is essentially an advisory and promotional body, receiving its funds directly from the Government. It owns no land or facilities itself but has the following powers in respect of countryside projects:

(a) The designation of National Parks, Areas of Outstanding Natural Beauty and long distance footpaths and bridleways and the definition of heritage coasts.
(b) To provide grants for picnic sites, country parks, information and interpretive facilities, recreational footpaths and tree and hedge planting.
(c) To undertake research into all aspects of countryside management and usage and produce educational and informative literature about the countryside in general and specific areas such as the National Parks and the long-distance footpaths.

The Commission also has an important role to play in attempting to resolve the conflicts that can arise between farming, recreational, business and conservation interests in the countryside in general, and the National Parks in particular.

The National Parks

The designation of an area as a National Park requires special legislation. The John Dower Report, 1945, defined a National Park, in application to Great Britain, as:

"... an extensive area of beautiful and relatively wild country in which, for the nation's benefit and by appropriate national decision and action,

(a) the characteristic landscape is strictly preserved;
(b) access and facilities for public open-air enjoyment are amply provided;
(c) wildlife and buildings and places of architectural and historic interest are suitably protected; while
(d) established farming use is effectively maintained."

The first ten National Parks were created between 1951 and 1957 following the National Parks and Access to the Countryside Act 1949. This gave the National Parks Commission (the forerunner of the Countryside Commission) the necessary powers for their establishment.

The most recently established National Park, the Broads Authority, was established with effect from 1.4.89, and required separate legislation. This has, in many ways, improved the overall distribution of the National Parks which are otherwise concentrated on upland and coastal areas in the north and west.

The National Parks are each controlled by a National Park Authority or joint planning board. These are made up of members appointed by the county councils and local authorities within whose areas the park is situated, together with members appointed by the appropriate Secretary of State who have special knowledge of some aspect of National Park work.

Services provided in National Parks by the National Park Authorities include:

(a) information and interpretation services (information centres, leaflets, books and other publications);
(b) a ranger or warden service;
(c) land management advice services;
(d) facilities for improving access for visitors (footpaths, stiles, waymarking);
(e) the provision of car parks and picnic sites;
(f) assistance to voluntary conservation and wildlife groups;
(g) grant aid for specific projects.

The role of the Countryside Commission is to lend support and advice on major issues to the authorities which manage the parks and to advise the Government on funding and other matters affecting their efficient running.

The Countryside Commission also organises publicity campaigns related to National Parks in conjunction with the park authorities and the Council for National Parks. An example of such a campaign was the "Watch over the National Parks" campaign, concluded in 1988, which aimed to increase public awareness of the National Parks, the ideas and principles which led to their establishment, and what they have to offer visitors. A promotional video, booklet and leaflets were all produced in 1985 as part of this campaign. Particular emphasis was placed upon the educational and information services available to party leaders planning visits to the parks.

The National Parks of England and Wales are listed overleaf:

England

Broads Authority

Broads Authority,
Thomas Harvey House,
18 Colegate,
Norwich,
Norfolk NR3 1BQ
Tel: 0603 610734

Dartmoor

Dartmoor National Park,
Parke,
Haytor Road,
Bovey Tracey,
Newton Abbot,
Devon TQ13 9JQ
Tel: 0626 832093

Exmoor

Exmoor National Park,
Exmoor House,
Dulverton,
Somerset TA22 9HL
Tel: 0398 23665

Lake District

Lake District Special Planning Board,
Busher Walk,
Kendal LA9 4RH
Tel: 0539 24555

Northumberland

Northumberland National Park and
Countryside Planning Board,
Eastburn,
South Park,
Hexham,
Northumberland
NE46 1BS
Tel: 0434 605555

North York Moors

North York Moors National Park,
North Yorkshire County Council,
The Old Vicarage,
Bondgate,
Helmsley, York YO6 5BP
Tel: 0439 70657

Peak District

Peak Park Joint Planning Board,
Aldern House,
Baslow Road,
Bakewell,
Derbyshire DE4 1AE
Tel: 062 981 4321

Yorkshire Dales

Yorkshire Dales National Park,
Yorebridge House,
Bainbridge,
Leyburn,
North Yorkshire DL8 3BP
Tel: 0969 50456

Wales

Brecon Beacons

Brecon Beacons National Park,
7 Glamorgan Street,
Brecon,
Powys LD3 7DP
Tel: 0874 4437

Pembrokeshire Coast

Pembrokeshire Coast National Park,
Dyfed County Council,
County Offices,
St Thomas' Green,
Haverfordwest,
Dyfed SA61 1QZ
Tel: 0437 764591

Snowdonia

Snowdonia National Park,
National Park Office,
Penrhyndeudraeth,
Gwynedd LL48 6LS
Tel: 0766 770274

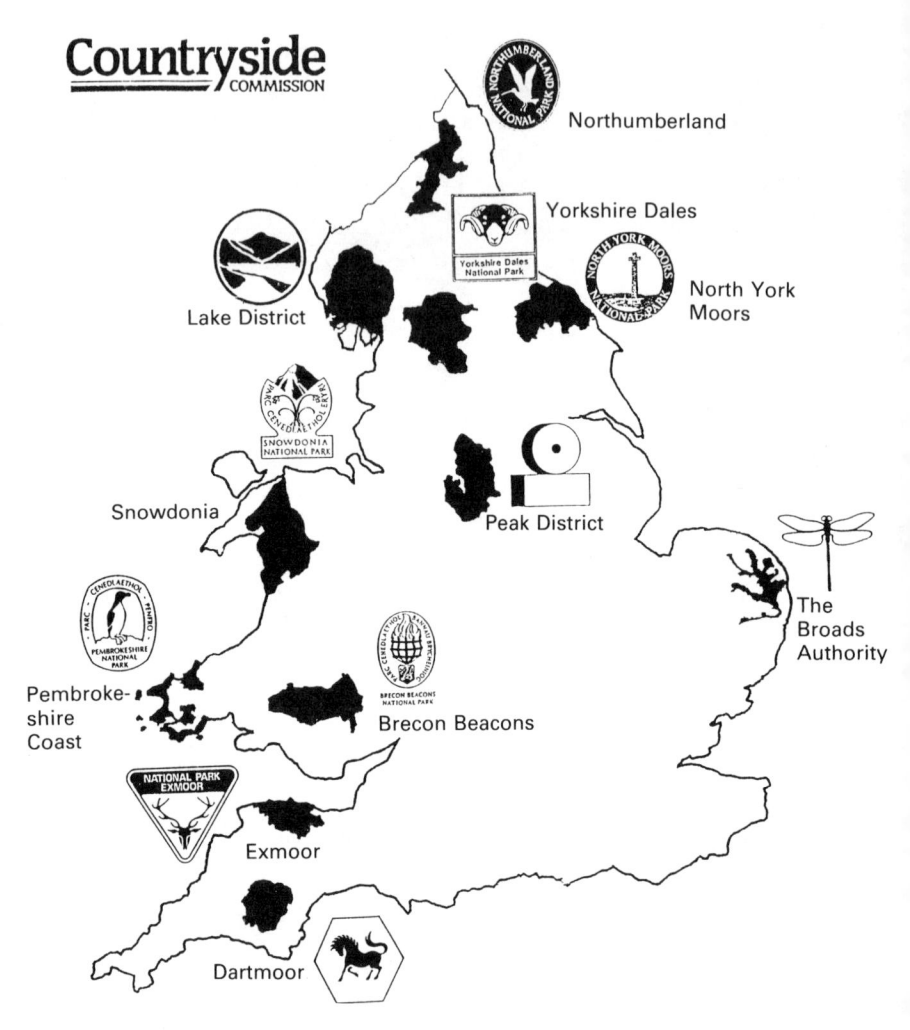

Figure 14 National Parks — England and Wales

50

The Council for National Parks

Council for National Parks,
45 Shelton Street,
London WC2H 9HJ
Tel: 071-240 3603/4

This is an independent national voluntary organisation whose objects are to promote the purposes for which the National Parks were designated: "the conservation and enhancement of natural beauty, and the promotion of the enjoyment of the areas designated as National Parks by the public".
It is composed of over 30 national and local amenity, recreation and wildlife bodies.
(Much of this information is taken from "Watch over the National Parks" and "Educational Services in the National Parks" published by the Countryside Commission, see Bibliography.)

Areas of Outstanding Natural Beauty (AONBs)

These are scenically attractive landscapes which have been identified and designated as AONBs by the Countryside Commission in order to help protect them for public enjoyment.
By August 1988 AONBs in England and Wales totalled 6675 square miles of land. Examples of AONBs include:

(a) the Norfolk coast;
(b) the Northumberland coast;
(c) the Chilterns;
(d) the Cotswolds;
(e) the Malvern Hills;
(f) the Shropshire Hills;
(g) Cannock Chase;
(h) the Wye Valley;
(i) the Gower Peninsular;
(j) the Sussex Downs.

Long distance footpaths

The Countryside Commission has also designated 13 long distance routes which have now been approved by the Government. In addition

Countryside COMMISSION

The acorn waymark sign is used in plaque or stencil form by the Countryside Commission on long distance routes

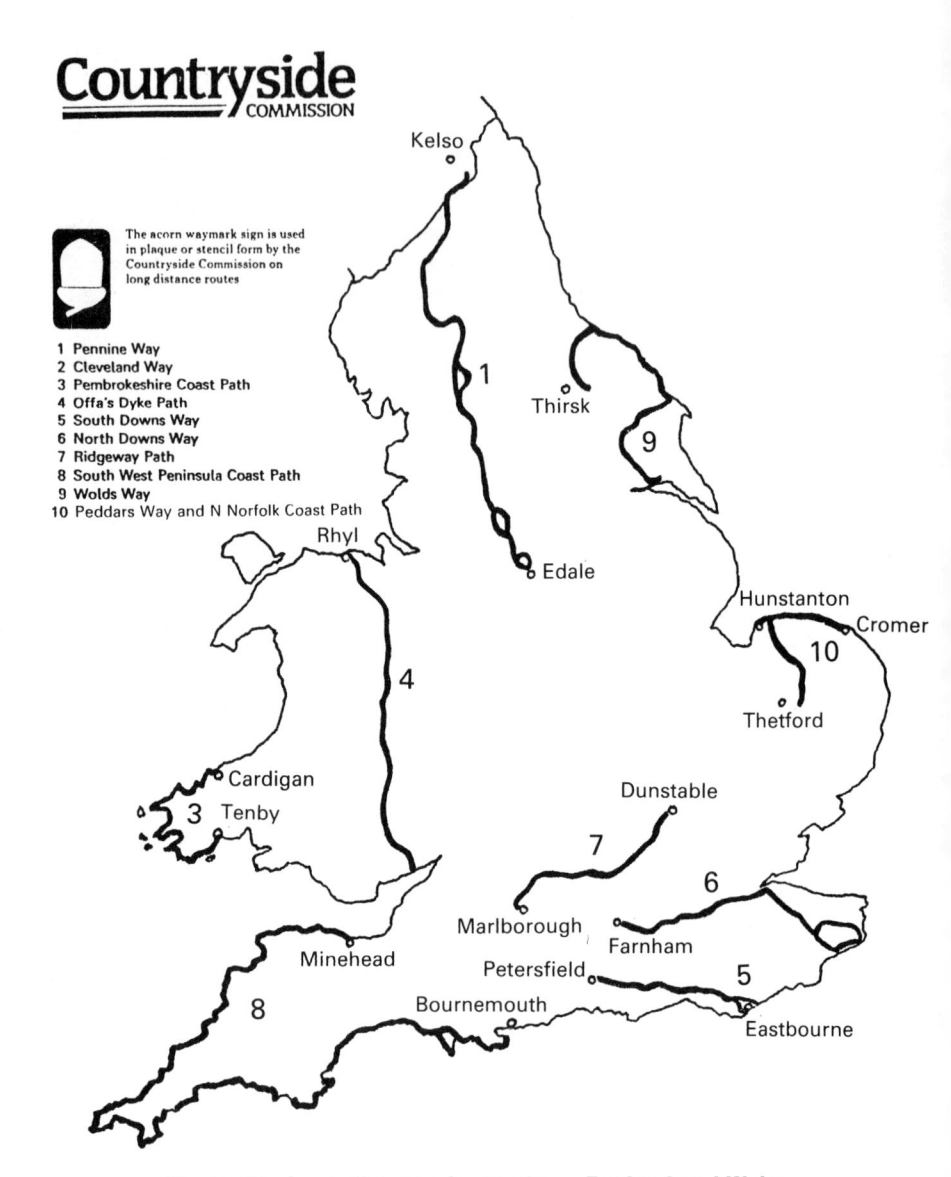

1 Pennine Way
2 Cleveland Way
3 Pembrokeshire Coast Path
4 Offa's Dyke Path
5 South Downs Way
6 North Downs Way
7 Ridgeway Path
8 South West Peninsula Coast Path
9 Wolds Way
10 Peddars Way and N Norfolk Coast Path

Kelso
Thirsk
Edale
Rhyl
Hunstanton
Cromer
Thetford
Cardigan
Tenby
Dunstable
Marlborough
Minehead
Farnham
Petersfield
Bournemouth
Eastbourne

Figure 15 Long distance footpaths — England and Wales

52

to proposing these routes, the Commission also pays for most of their upkeep and waymarking. In some instances the cost of this upkeep is considerable, particularly on eroded parts of the Pennine Way (the first LDFP to be completed, in 1965). Where possible, the routes have used existing rights of way and the remaining sections have been established largely through negotiation. The most recently opened route is the Peddars Way and Norfolk Coast Path which was completed in 1986. Work is currently in progress on the Thames Path and five further routes, including the Pennine Bridleway and the Hadrian's Wall Path, which are planned for the future.

Country parks

Country parks provide opportunities for people to enjoy the countryside. They usually provide some car parking, toilets, picnic facilities and pathways. Very often they will also provide refreshment facilities, information centres and intepretive signs and opportunities for some sporting and other recreational activities, including nature study.

Most are administered by local authorities, but frequently receive grants from the Countryside Commission in respect of particular projects. The Forestry Commission may also be an additional source of finance, particularly where the site lends itself to some measure of commercial forestry.

Regional parks

The first regional park was the Lee Valley Regional Park situated on the eastern side of London. It was established by a special Act of Parliament in 1967 and is administered by an independent statutory authority. It was the first attempt at a "green wedge" as opposed to a "green belt" policy, and so successful has it been that a number of other regional parks have subsequently been established, including the Colne Valley Park on the western side of London.

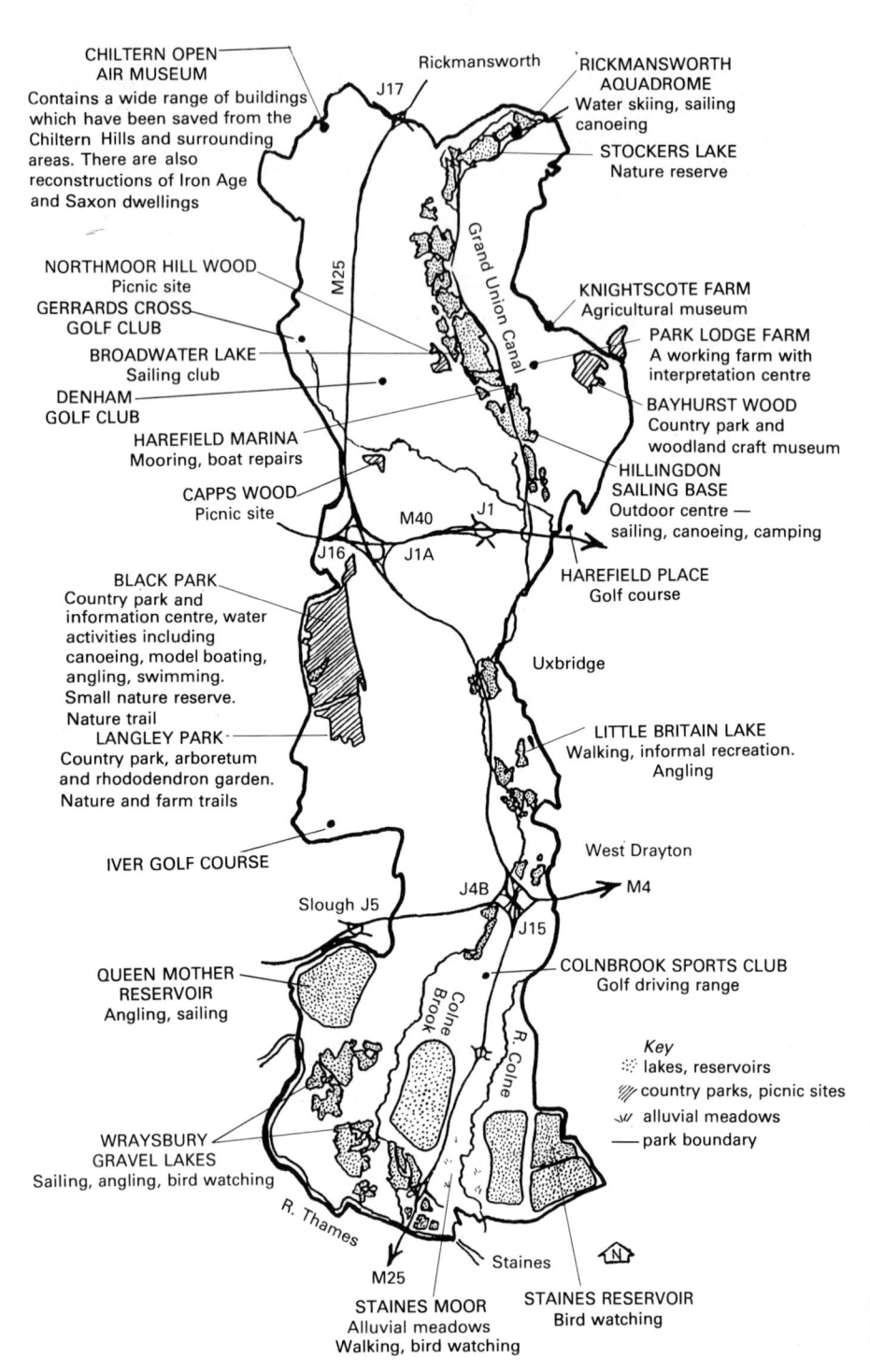

Figure 16 Colne Valley Park

The Colne Valley Park

The Chairman of the Working Party, Colne Valley Park Planning Department, County Hall, Aylesbury, Buckinghamshire, HP20 1UX
Tel: 0296 395000

The Park covers more than 40 square miles of Greater London, Buckinghamshire, Hertfordshire, Berkshire and Surrey, stretching from Rickmansworth to the Thames. It provides a first real taste of countryside on London's western doorstep.

The Colne Valley Park was conceived as a regional park in the 1960s. Local authorities agreed a strategic plan, adopted and published in 1972, which sought to protect the valley's attractive areas; to improve those marred by gravel and other works; and to help meet the leisure and recreational needs of those living within convenient travelling distance. Careful landscaping, including the planting of thousands of trees, is helping to reduce the intrusion of motorways and the urban and industrial developments within the Park.

The Park provides facilities for recreation, sport and leisure pursuits which include country parks and picnic sites (see Figure 16).

The current strategic plan, published in 1988, proposes a considerable number of major schemes to extend and develop the existing facilities and provision. These schemes include a Park Centre at Denham, the establishment of a country park centred on Little Britain Lake, the Colneside Nature and Wildfowl Centre (a nature park) at Broadwater and Harefield Lakes, nature reserves, picnic sites, landscaping, tree planting and footpath, bridleway and towpath improvements.

A Groundwork Trust has been established for the Colne Valley Park, to lead a co-ordinated programme of environmental improvement projects involving the public, private and voluntary sectors. The trust is a company limited by guarantee and has charitable status.

There are several leaflets available on the Colne Valley Park. These contain detailed information on the various activities within the Park, together with names and addresses of contacts for those wishing to pursue these interests. They are available from the Colne Valley Groundwork Trust, Denham Court, Village Road, Denham, Bucks UB9 5RG, tel: 0895 832662.

The Arts Council (The Arts Council of Great Britain)

ARTS COUNCIL

Arts Council,
105 Piccadilly,
London W1V 0AU
Tel: 071-629 9495

The Arts Council was formed in 1946. It currently operates under a revised Royal Charter granted in 1967 in which its objects are stated as:

"(a) to develop and improve the knowledge, understanding and practice of the arts
(b) to increase the accessibility of the arts to the public throughout Great Britain
(c) to advise and co-operate with departments of Government, local authorities and other bodies."

Since 1964 responsibility for the Arts Council has been vested in the Department of Education and Science.

The Council is appointed by the Minister for the Arts after consultation with the Secretaries of State for Scotland and Wales. In 1987–8 it had a chairman and 17 other members, including the chairmen and vice-chairmen of the Scottish and Welsh Arts Councils. The Council is also advised by panels and committees.

It receives grant-in-aid from the Government and acts as the principal channel for Government aid to the arts. In 1987 Government funding of the Council was announced on a three year basis, thus allowing the Council to plan further ahead and produce a three-year plan for the years 1988/89–1990/1. In this plan the Council has agreed a series of practical objectives for the artforms with which it is concerned. These artforms are listed as consisting of:

(a) dance;
(b) drama;
(c) film, video and broadcasting;
(d) literature;
(e) music;
(f) visual arts (including performance art and photography).

Activities to be funded or supported by the Council include:

(a) the continued support of the four national companies—
  (i) The Royal Opera House,
  (ii) English National Opera,

(iii) The National Theatre,
(iv) The Royal Shakespeare Company;
(b) the continued support of existing, and the establishment of, arts organisations including —
   (i) dance companies,
   (ii) opera companies,
   (iii) regional theatre companies,
   (vi) theatre buildings,
   (vii) art and photographic galleries;
(c) increased support for Afro-Caribbean and Asian arts;
(d) investment in research;
(e) touring of ballet, theatre productions, opera, orchestras, musicians and exhibitions;
(f) international arts exchange;

ARTS COUNCIL 1988
Overall Structure

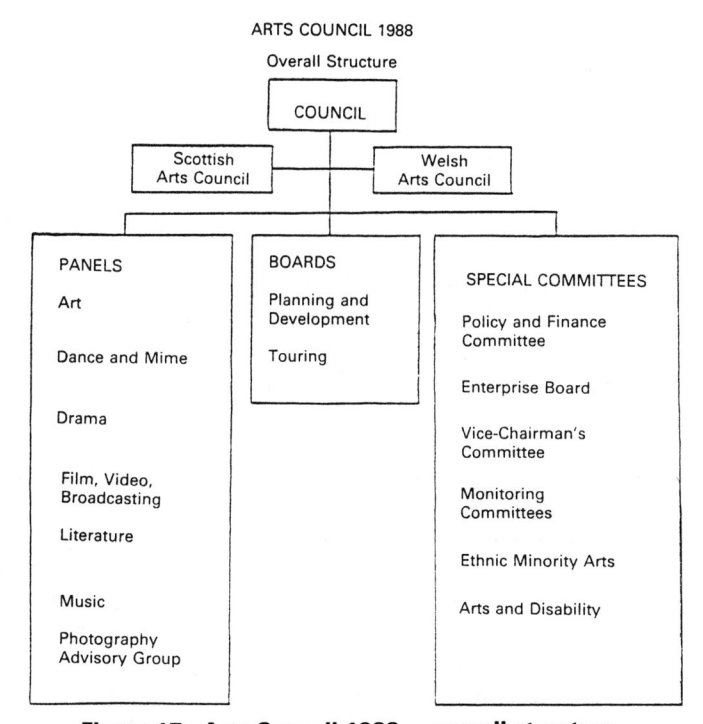

```
                          COUNCIL
        Scottish            |            Welsh
      Arts Council ─────────┼──────── Arts Council
                            |
   ┌────────────────────────┼────────────────────────┐
   PANELS                BOARDS              SPECIAL COMMITTEES
   Art                   Planning and
                         Development         Policy and Finance
   Dance and Mime                            Committee
                         Touring
                                             Enterprise Board
   Drama
                                             Vice-Chairman's
                                             Committee
   Film, Video,
   Broadcasting                              Monitoring
                                             Committees
   Literature
                                             Ethnic Minority Arts
   Music
                                             Arts and Disability
   Photography
   Advisory Group
```

Figure 17   Arts Council 1988 — overall structure

Note: The Arts Council is currently (in 1991) undergoing a complete restructuring, details of which had not been disclosed at the time of going to print.

(g) training and education;
(h) publishing information related to the arts.

There are fifteen Regional Arts Associations which are independent bodies with devolved responsibilities for developing the arts locally. There are twelve in England and three in Wales.

(Much of this information is taken from "Arts Council 43rd annual report and accounts 87–88" and "The Arts Council of Great Britain Three-Year Plan 1988/89–1990/91", see Bibliography.)

The Forestry Commission

Forestry Commission Headquarters,
231 Corstorphine Road,
Edinburgh EH12 7AT
Tel: 031-334 0303

The Forestry Commission was established by the Forestry Act 1919. Its primary role is that of timber production. The Commission is responsible to the Ministry of Agriculture, Fisheries and Food, and to the Secretaries of State for Scotland and Wales. It has a total staff of approximately 8000.

The Forestry Commission is currently the largest landowner in Britain, with three million acres. Part of the Commission's responsibility is to develop the unique recreational features and potential of its 250 forests. In order to meet the public's need for greater opportunities for access to its forests for recreational purposes the Commission has established seven forest parks. The first was opened in Argyll in 1935 and others in Snowdonia in 1937, and the Forest of Dean. In 1970, following the Forestry Act 1967 which charged the Commission also to consider conservation needs, the Commission set up a conservation and recreation branch at its headquarters and established eleven recreation planning officers to work in its conservation regions.

The Commission provides a number of facilities for leisure use. These include car parks, forest and nature trails, viewpoints, educational and interpretive facilities, visitor centres, picnic sites and, in some areas, holiday cabins, camping and caravanning facilities.

Each year there are literally millions of day visits made to Commission-owned woodlands, mainly for picnicking and walking. Although this, and increasing public concern with environmental and conservation issues, can cause a conflict of interests between the needs of commercial forestry and recreational use of the forests, the Commission has attempted to deal with any such problems with sensitivity.

Changes in legislation, knowledge and public opinion are reflected in management practices and policies. Selective clear felling and replanting with native deciduous trees in selected areas (such as along the sides of streams and the edges of plantations) and the careful contouring of new or replanted areas, especially within the National Parks, provide clear examples of such policies.

Other recreational activities, in addition to the principal ones already stated, are accommodated within the Commission's forests, where these are compatible with the forest environment, and permits are issued for activities such as orienteering, horse riding and pony trekking, fishing, sailing and, under special circumstances, some motor sports (eg car and motor cycle rallies by agreement with the Royal Automobile Club and under strict control). Charges are made where it is appropriate and considered reasonable to do so.

The Forestry Commission also produces a number of publications, information leaflets and policy statements (from which much of this information is taken, see Bibliography).

National Nature Conservancy Councils

English Nature (Nature Conservancy Council for England)

ENGLISH NATURE

Northminster House,
Peterborough PE1 1UA
Tel: 0733 340345

The Council, established under the Environmental Protection Act 1990, began work on 1.4.91. It advises the Government generally on policies relating to and affecting nature conservation in England and is responsible for the conservation of flora, fauna and geological and physiographical features, for scheduling Sites of Special Scientific Interest and for establishing and managing National Nature Reserves and Marine Nature Reserves. It also has powers to commision research and to make grants available.

This agency is one of three new country agencies, for England, Wales and Scotland, that replaced the Nature Conservancy Council, which ceased to exist on 31.3.91. In addition, the Joint Nature Conservation

Committee was established to provide a national and international overview.

Cyngor Cefn Gwlad Cymru
Countryside Council for Wales

Cyngor Cefn Gwlad Cymru,
Countryside Council for Wales,
Plas Penrhos, Ffordd Penrhos,
Bangor, Gwynedd, LL57 2LQ
Tel: 0248 370444

From 1.4.91 the Council took over the duties of the Nature Conservancy Council and the Countryside Commission in respect of Welsh countryside matters.

The Council can have up to 12 members. It meets at regular intervals in different parts of the Principality.

The Council delivers its service from a number of regional offices, as well as its central establishment at Bangor.

The Council is accountable to the Secretary of State for Wales and is responsible for providing advice on nature conservation and all other countryside matters to ministers and Government departments.

The Council also encourages and enables local authorities, voluntary organisations and other interested individuals to pursue countryside management.

The Council will also manage Wales' National Nature Reserves and encourage and control access to them. It can also create new National Nature Reserves.

The Council will influence the work of the three National Parks in Wales and work closely wtih them.

The Council will establish and maintain Sites of Special Scientific Interest, support local authorities in the protection of nationally recognised Areas of Outstanding Natural Beauty, Heritage Coasts and National Trails and support the creation and development of Country Parks and Local Nature Reserves. It will also support the work of voluntary organisations involved in the care of the countryside.

In addition to the above, the Council provides grant aid for land purchase and the provision of recreational facilities and paths, carries out research, supports environmental education and publishes information on all aspects of its work.

There are currently some 230 NNRs in Britain covering nearly 161,000 hectares (398,000 acres). Visitors are welcome on most NNRs if their activities do not conflict with conservation or research, or with the interests of owners and tenants.

Tourist Boards

British Tourist Authority

British Tourist Authority

British Tourist Authority,
Thames Tower,
Black's Road,
Hammersmith
London W6 9EL
Tel: 081-846 9000

The British Tourist Authority was established under the Development of Tourism Act 1969, along with three national tourist boards.

It is an independent statutory body and is financed mainly by grant-in-aid from the Government.

The members are appointed by the Secretary of State for Employment. The Board currently consists of eight members, including its chairman.

The responsibilities of the BTA are to:

(a) promote tourism to Britain from overseas;
(b) advise Government on tourism matters affecting Britain as a whole;
(c) encourage the provision and improvement of tourist amenities and facilities in Britain.

In order to help it meet its responsibilities, the BTA is advised by its four main committees:

(a) marketing,
(b) accommodation,
(c) British heritage,
(d) development.

As part of its activities the BTA organises promotional campaigns. In 1986/7 the BTA campaign was "Britain for All Seasons" and was designed to help fill periods of low occupancy.

The BTA also produces a considerable number of information and promotional publications.

Overseas the BTA operates a network of offices and carries out extensive marketing campaigns in different countries.

(Much of this information is taken from the BTA publications "The Who's Who of British Tourist Boards" and the "BTA Annual Report for the year ended 31.3.88", see Bibliography.)

English Tourist Board

English Tourist Board,
Thames Tower,
Black's Road,
Hammersmith,
London W6 9EL
Tel: 081-846 9000

The English Tourist Board (ETB), together with the Scottish Tourist Board and the Wales Tourist Board, was also established under the Development of Tourism Act 1969. There is a separate Northern Ireland Tourist Board.

The ETB is an independent statutory body and is financed mainly by grant-in-aid from the Government.

The members are appointed by the Secretary of State for Employment. The Board currently consists of seven members, including a chairman, who also sits on the BTA.

The objectives of the ETB are:

(a) to stimulate the development of English Tourism by encouraging the British to take holidays in England, and by the provision and improvement of facilities for tourists in England;

(b) to develop and market tourism in close co-operation with regional and national tourist boards, the BTA, local authorities and public sector organisations and the private sector;

(c) to advise Government and public bodies on all matters concerning tourism in England;

(d) to maximise tourism's contribution to the economy through the creation of wealth and jobs;

(e) to encourage and stimulate the successful development of tourism products of a high standard, which offer good value for money;

Figure 18   English regional tourist boards

(Most of this information is taken from the English Tourist Board's "Annual Report 1987/1988", see Bibliography.)

(f) to bring greater recognition to tourism as an industry for investment, employment and economic development, by providing information, and when appropriate, advice and financial support;
(g) to produce and disseminate information on tourism to the trade and the consumer;
(h) to research trends in tourism and consumer requirements to show marketing and development needs and opportunities and evaluate past performance, future prospects and the impact of tourism;
(i) to improve the industry's status and performance by encouraging and stimulating the adoption of up-to-date business methods and appropriate technology and the provision of education and training programmes;
(j) to ensure that England's unique character and heritage is recognised and protected through the sensitive management of tourism.

In order to help the ETB meet its objectives there are 12 regional tourist boards. These regional boards now administer Crown classification and holiday park grading accommodation schemes, the new holiday homes approval at a regional level. They are also responsible for co-ordinating the Tourist Information Centre network.

National Rivers Authority

Eastbury House,
30-34 Albert Embankment,
London SE1 7TL
Tel: 071-820 0101

Until 1989 there were ten regional Water Authorities for England and Wales. Their main function was to ensure that there were adequate supplies of water of a suitable quality to meet the needs of their many consumers. This included conserving, supplying and distributing water, preventing pollution and the treatment and disposal of sewage. The authorities were also responsible for land drainage and sea defences protecting low-lying land.

The Water Act 1989 divided these functions; water supply and

Figure 19 National Rivers Authority Regions — boundaries and regional office towns

sewage disposal were transferred to the water plcs and the National Rivers Authority (NRA) took over the regulatory and environmental responsibilities. The NRA came into full force on 1.9.89 when water authority assets were formally "rested" in the Authority.

The NRA is a non-departmental public body sponsored by the Department of the Environment. Its overall policy is directed and determined by a board of members. Most of these members are appointed by the Secretary of State for the Environment, although two members are appointed by MAFF and one by the Secretary of State for Wales.

The development of national policy is co-ordinated by the NRA's London head office, whilst the ten regions are responsible for the main operational work of the Authority.

Each region has three statutory committees which advise on: river basin management, fisheries functions, and flood defences and land damage.

The aims of the NRA are:

(a) to achieve a continuing improvement in the quality of rivers, estuaries and coastal waters, through the control of water pollution;
(b) to assess, manage, plan and conserve water resources and to maintain and improve the quality of water for all those who use it;
(c) to provide effective defence for people and property against flooding from rivers and the sea;
(d) to provide adequate arrangement for flood forecasting and warning;
(e) to maintain, improve and develop fisheries;
(f) to develop the amenity and recreational potential of waters and lands under NRA control;
(g) to conserve and enhance wildlife, landscape and archaeological features associated with waters under NRA control;
(h) to improve and maintain inland waterways and their facilities for use by the public where the NRA is the navigation authority.
(i) to ensure that dischargers pay the costs of the consequences of their discharges, and as far as possible to recover the costs of water environment improvements from those who benefit;
(j) to improve public understanding of the water environment and the NRA's work;
(k) to improve efficiency in the exercise of the NRA's functions and to provide challenge and opportunity for employees and show concern for their welfare.

The NRA has statutory duties to promote recreation. It produces leaflets and booklets that explain waterside amenities and encourages the development of riverside pathways.

Recreational activities which it encourages include:

(a) angling,
(b) nature study,
(c) walking,
(d) waterway or river navigation.

GOVERNING BODIES OF SPORT

A governing body of a sport is an association that represents the interests of a particular sport and the interests of those members who play that sport. Through its committees it may make decisions concerning the rules of that sport, the organisation of competitions and leagues and the selection of teams of players to represent that sport in regional or international competition. It is usual for schools, clubs and individuals to affiliate to the governing body, often through its county or area association. It is through the committees of these regional divisions that most members have their most immediate representation.

The role of the governing bodies may be summarised as:

(a) the protection of the sport and of participants;
(b) the production of codes of conduct and the framing of rules;
(c) the promotion of sport through the organisation of championships and respresentative teams.

Examples of the initials of governing bodies of sport, together with their full titles, include the following:

AAA	Amateur Athletic Association
ASA	Amateur Swimming Association
BAE	Badminton Association of England
BAGA	British Amateur Gymnastics Association
BAWLA	British Amateur Weight Lifting Association
BJA	British Judo Association
BMC	British Mountaineering Council
BTF	British Trampolining Federation
FA	Football Association
LTA	Lawn Tennis Association

(See page 228-9 — Coaching and Officiating Qualifications)

The National Coaching Foundation

The National Coaching Foundation,
4 College Close,
Becket Park,
Leeds LS6 3QS
Tel: 0532 744802

The National Coaching Foundation is a company with charitable status; it is largely financed by the Sports Council and has been established to provide a service to all coaches. It has fourteen National Coaching

Centres which provide focal points for a full range of education, information and research services. The services offered by the NCF include:

(a) coach education programmes and courses;
(b) information services;
(c) quality resources — videos, books, articles;
(d) conferences;
(e) computer facilities;
(f) applied research programmes.

Full details of all these services and publications may be obtained direct from the NCF.

(This information is taken from the NCF publications "All about the NCF" and "National Coaching Centres — calling all coaches", see Bibliography.)

The National Playing Fields Association

NATIONAL PLAYING FIELDS ASSOCIATION

The National Playing Fields Association,
25 Ovington Square,
London SW3 1LQ
Tel: 071-584 6445

The NFPA was established in 1925 as an independent national charity with the object of providing some form of central direction to the provision of adequate playing fields and recreational facilities and space throughout the country.

In 1933 it was granted a Royal Charter.

The policy of the NFPA is devoted to the preservation, improvement and acquisition of playing fields, playgrounds and play space where they are most needed and for those who need them most, in particular children, young people and the handicapped. The structure of the NPFA consists of a council made up of 15 representatives and individuals from a wide range of recreational and educational bodies.

In addition, there is a network of County Playing Fields Associations, which, although independent bodies, are affiliated to the national organisation. There is also a branch in Scotland.

Policies and decisions are implemented by the Council.

The NPFA provides a number of services for use by local authorities, sports clubs and voluntary organisations. These include:

(a) technical advice on the provision, design, layout, construction and safety of playing fields, playgrounds and play equipment;
(b) publicity and information, publications and drawings;
(c) conferences, and courses;
(d) some grant aid and loans to voluntary groups and organisations together with advice on obtaining grants and loans from other sources.

The majority of the Association's funding comes from subscriptions, donations and fund raising events, as well as receipt of legacies, but it also receives a small grant from the Sports Council to help with its administration costs

The National Trust

The National Trust,
36 Queen Anne's Gate,
London SW1H 9AS
Tel: 071-222 9251

The National Trust is a registered charity. It was founded to protect the best of our heritage for ever and it is now Britain's largest private landowner, administering places of historical interest or natural beauty.

The Trust was founded in 1895 and was later incorporated by a special Act of Parliament, The National Trust Act 1907, with a mandate to promote "The permanent preservation for the benefit of the nation of lands and tenements (including buildings) of beauty or historic interest". Under this Act, the Trust can ensure that its properties can never be sold or taken from it without the express will of Parliament. The Trust has also been given permission, also by Act of Parliament, to hold revenue-producing lands and investments to raise money to maintain its properties.

As a charity, the Trust depends entirely on private support, it receives no direct funds from Government. Its funds come from a number of sources:

(a) membership subscriptions and donations;

(b) legacies and properties which have been handed over by the treasury, having been received in payment of death duties;
(c) fees paid by the public visiting Trust properties;
(d) rents paid by tenants living in Trust properties or who are farming its lands.

The Trust also raises money through special appeals, aiming at particular areas, properties or projects. In 1986–7 these were:

(a) The Lake District Appeal (to maintain existing properties);
(b) Enterprise Neptune (to purchase threatened areas of coastline in Wales, Cornwall and North Yorkshire);
(c) Victorian Garden (to fund the purchase of the gardens of Biddulph Grange).

These appeals give an indication of the types of property that the National Trust now administers.

The types of property owned by the National Trust may be said to consist of:

(a) historical buildings, including—
  (i) furniture, paintings and other treasures associated with particular properties;
  (ii) houses;
  (iii) castles and medieval ruins;
  (iv) windmills and water mills;
(b) gardens;
(c) areas of countryside, including—
  (i) mountains,
  (ii) fens,
  (iii) heaths,
  (iv) downland,
  many of which are specially preserved for the plants and wildlife associated with them;
(d) areas of coastline, including—
  (i) islands,
  (ii) cliffs,
  (iii) beaches,
  (iv) footpaths.

(Much of this information has been collated from National Trust publications, see Bibliography.)
There is also a separate National Trust for Scotland. This was established in 1931 and is also a charity. It owns very similar properties to those owned by the National Trust. Further information may be obtained from: National Trust for Scotland, 5 Charlotte Square, Edinburgh EH2 4DU, tel: 031-226 5922.

English Heritage
(Historic Buildings and Monuments Commission for England)

English Heritage,
Fortress House,
23 Saville Row,
London W1X 2HE
Tel: 071-734 6010

English Heritage (Historic Buildings and Monuments Commission for England) is the largest independent organisation statutorily responsible for heritage conservation in the country. It was established under the National Heritage Act 1983 and began work on 1.4.84, taking over the public functions formerly carried out by the Government through the Department of the Environment.

It is the Government's official adviser on conservation legislation concerning the built environment and provides the major source of public funds for repairs to historic buildings and ancient monuments, town schemes and rescue archaeology. English Heritage is also responsible for the preservation and presentation of some 400 historic properties in its care, including Stonehenge (Wiltshire), Iron Bridge (Shropshire), Housesteads Roman Fort and Lindisfarne Priory (Northumberland). Most of these properties are open to the public. English Heritage's governing body, the Commission, is appointed by the Secretary of State for the Environment and chaired by Lord Montagu of Beaulieu. It has a permanent staff of about 1500 as well as ten expert advisory committees and sub-committees.

It is also possible for members of the public to become members of English Heritage. Members gain free admission to all English Heritage properties where an entrance fee is charged. Other benefits include a quarterly journal, a copy of the "Guide to English Heritage Properties" and other information and publications.

English Heritage also produces a number of videos which are available for purchase or hire.

English Heritage Membership Department and Education Services, PO Box 1BB, London W1A 1BB; tel: 071-973 3000.

LOCAL AUTHORITIES

Local authorities are independant administrative bodies created by Parliament. Their members (councillors) are elected but the officers (employees) are appointed. Their primary purpose is to provide services. The powers and duties of local authorities are determined by Acts of Parliament. Currently, the framework of their responsibilities is provided by the Local Government Act 1972 and the Local Government (Miscellaneous Provisions) Act 1976.

At present there are three levels of local authority, each with specific responsibilities for providing opportunities for recreation and leisure:

(a) parish councils,
(b) district councils,
(c) county councils.

Very often two or more councils will jointly contribute to the provision of a single leisure facility. A frequently encountered example is the provision of a sports facility on a school site where the money has been jointly provided by the education department of the county council and the leisure department of the local district council. Such facilities are frequently referred to as "joint provision" centres.

The influence that local authorities have upon the overall provision made for leisure and recreation in the United Kingdom is immense. Although they only have a *duty* to provide recreational opportunities through educational facilities and libraries, local authorities have very considerable *discretionary* powers to provide for leisure and recreation.

In practice local authorities exercise these powers in a number of ways. They:

(a) provide, staff and maintain a wide range of facilities including—
   (i) parks and gardens,
   (ii) playing fields and sports grounds,
   (iii) libraries, art galleries and museums,
   (iv) theatres and arts centres,
   (v) sports centres and swimming pools,
   (vi) outdoor activity centres,
   (vii) playgrounds;

(b) support, give grant aid and make available equipment to community groups and voluntary associations (including clubs and societies);
(c) may offer expertise and advice and disseminate information;
(d) organise multi-sports events and exchanges;
(e) affect provision by other agencies through planning and making decisions on development proposals.

The effect that compulsory competitive tendering of local authority services may have upon this provision is uncertain, but it is almost certainly going to involve a reduction in the extent to which local authorities will staff and maintain existing facilities and provide new ones in the future. In this event these functions could be taken up by members of the private sector.

COMMERCIAL ORGANISATIONS

The main purpose of any commercial organisation or enterprise is to make financial profit. These organisations are commonly referred to as the private sector. Any interest such organisations may have in recreation and leisure provision will be in terms of the direct and indirect benefit that may be gained by the organisation from involvement in those activities. It is this which determines the types of activity that are provided for.

Leisure and recreation activities which are usually provided for by commercial companies

These include:

(a) eating and drinking in restaurants, clubs, pubs and wine bars;
(b) entertainments such as cinemas, theatres, concerts, dances and discotheques, professional sports competitions;
(c) outings and informal recreational visits to theme parks, safari and wildlife parks, zoos and historic buildings;
(d) certain sports and physical recreations such as aerobics, weight and fitness training, squash, ten pin bowling, ice skating, golf, activity and adventure holidays;
(e) travel and tourism, holidays, staying at hotels, guest houses, caravan and camping sites;
(f) home-based entertainment including television, video, reading, gardening, hobbies and do-it-yourself.

Private sector companies may also provide recreational facilities for their own staff. Such provision may include:

(a) Recreation/club room — video, television, fruit machine, card and board games, darts, snooker and/or pool table.
(b) Bar facilities (often in club room).
(c) Social functions — dinner dances, day trips, cheap holiday opportunities, events.
(d) Sporting facilities/activities — teams, including football pitches; squash/badminton clubs/courts; gymnasium/exercise room, weights, multigym, exercise cycles; changing and showering facilities, sauna.
(e) Restaurant/canteen — meals, snacks, drinks.

Often the same facility may be used to stage very different activities, eg the canteen may be partially cleared of tables and the seating rearranged to stage a dance or disco.

The provision of such facilities will not, however, be the main purpose of the organisation, but be part of the means by which it attempts to maintain a happy and well motivated work force.

Sponsorship

This is another means by which private sector organisations contribute to the provision of recreation and leisure opportunities. By financially supporting sports events the commercial sector hopes to gain financial benefits itself. These benefits will primarily arise from the publicity that results from public attention being focused upon the event being sponsored and the sponsor's name being associated with the success, popularity and values associated with the activity and its participants.

COMMUNITY GROUPS

Community groups are largely made up of very diverse voluntary organisations which, together, offer an immense variety of leisure and recreational opportunities.

These voluntary organisations consist mainly of clubs, societies and associations, but also include charitable trusts. Where a number of local organisations wish to work together collectively, they may form a community association. Once established, these community associations may start new sections (eg playgroups, junior youth clubs, sports clubs or old folks clubs.) Community associations are frequently supported by local authorities.

Members' clubs

Typically these clubs or sections are run by committees, elected by the members. Committees usually include amongst their members the following officers:

(a) the chairman, who directs committee meetings;
(b) the honorary secretary, who deals with correspondence, minutes etc;
(c) the honorary treasurer, who deals with all financial matters.

Sports clubs may also have a fixtures secretary, to deal with fixtures and matches.

Most sport in the United Kingdom, especially at the "grass roots" level, is organised by local voluntary clubs and associations which are usually affiliated to the governing body for that sport, frequently through their local county or regional association.

Youth groups

These are another important group of voluntary organisations who make a significant contribution to the provision of leisure and recreational opportunities for young people. Such groups include:

(a) youth clubs, including those supported or run by the National Association of Youth Clubs;
(b) national organisations, which also offer short and medium-term accommodation, in addition to a range of recreational activities. Such organisations include:
   (i) the YMCA/YWCA,
   (ii) the Youth Hostels Association;
(c) uniformed groups, including:
   (i) the Scout Association,
   (ii) the Girl Guides Association,
   (iii) the Boys' Brigade,
   (iv) the St John Ambulance Cadets.

Although all the local groups are affiliated to national organisations, usually individual groups are initiated locally. All the national organisations listed above are members of the CCPR.

The interrelationship of the providing agencies

The way in which the different national agencies interrelate in order to provide opportunities for people to participate in recreational activities is complex. The following figure gives an indication of some of these interrelationships and the way in which facilities may be financed.

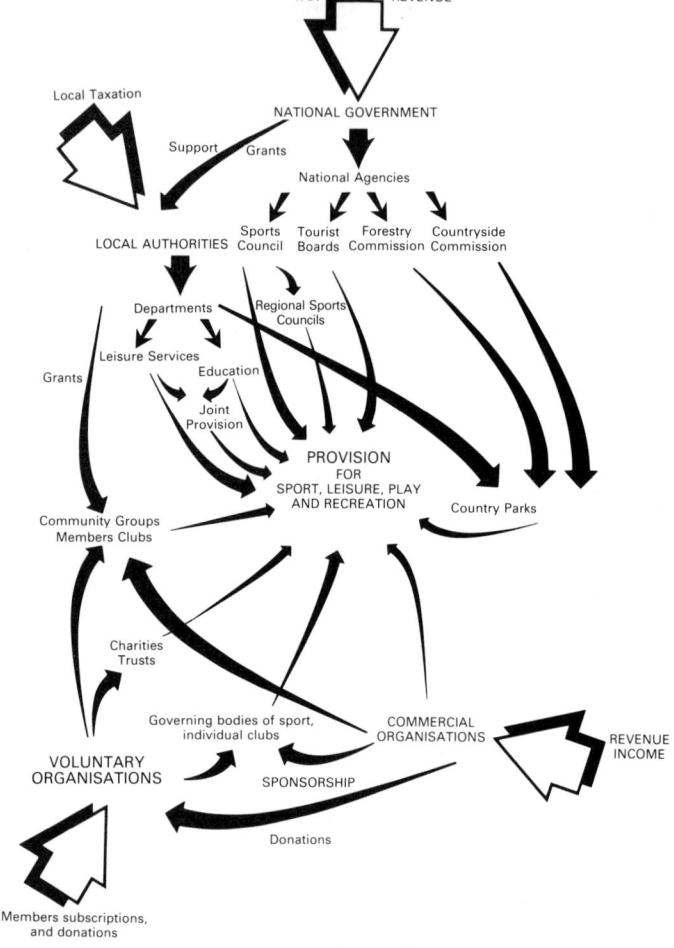

Figure 20 The interrelationship of the different agencies in providing opportunities for participation in recreational activities

481-1 PROVISION AND CONTROL

Exercise 1

(a) List THREE examples of EACH of the main agencies in the following table.
(b) List their main activities.
(c) Analyse the operating principles of these agencies into commercial, social and philanthropic factors.

MAIN AGENCY	MAIN ACTIVITIES	OPERATING PRINCIPLES
NATIONAL ORGANISATIONS (a) (b) (c)		
LOCAL AUTHORITIES (a) (b) (c)		
COMMERCIAL ORGANISATIONS (a) (b) (c)		
COMMUNITY GROUPS (a) (b) (c)		

Exercise 2

(a) Conduct a survey of the recreation and leisure provision made by a local authority.
   Your answer should include reference to:
   (i) sports provision,
   (ii) parks and gardens,
   (iii) libraries, museums and arts centres,
   (iv) playgrounds.

(b) State how the location of the provision is distributed throughout the authority.
   Your answer should include reference to the main population centres and the main shopping and commercial centres.

Exercise 3

(a) Draw a sketch map of a local area near to where you live.
(b) Indicate on the map the main providing agencies to be found.
(c) List the principal services offered by each.
(d) Comment on the reasons for any differences in operation.

An example is given below:

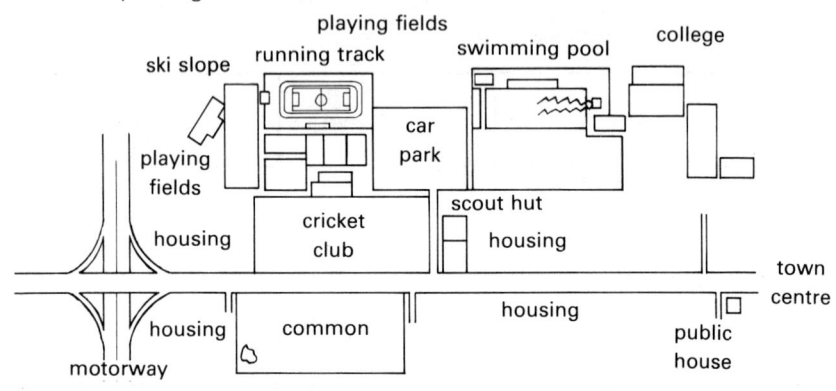

[Sketch map showing: ski slope, running track, playing fields, swimming pool, college, playing fields, car park, housing, cricket club, scout hut, housing, motorway, housing, common, housing, public house, town centre]

Ski slope — ski slopes	Swimming pool — pools flumes children's play area social facilities sauna/solarium weight training martial arts
Cricket club — cricket pitches tennis courts squash courts bowling green social facilities/bar	
Common — informal recreation	College — sports hall all-weather area weight training
Playing fields — informal recreation rugby/football pitches	
Public house — eating/drinking	Scout hut — scouts/guides
Running track —track football pitch	

Exercise 4

(a) Make a list of the LOCAL and NATIONAL agencies that may be involved in the provision of facilities and opportunities for leisure and recreational activities within a Country Park.

(b) List the ADDITIONAL agencies that could be involved if the Country Park was situated within:

   (i) a National Park,
   (ii) a Site of Special Scientific Interest.

Exercise 5

(a) Survey and compare the facilities provided, and the principal activities catered for, by ONE of the following:

   (i) TWO National Sports Centres,
   (ii) TWO National Parks,
   (iii) TWO contrasting commercial organisations.

(b) State how the PROVISION reflects the controlling agencies' OPERATING PRINCIPLES.

481-1 PROVISION AND CONTROL

Past examination questions related to national agencies involved in the provision of recreational and leisure opportunities

Part I Written paper

1. (a) State the most important economic objective of a commercially owned nightclub. (1 mark)
   (b) List FOUR leisure activities which are usually provided for by commercial companies. (2 marks)
   (c) Give TWO reasons why local authority-run leisure/sporting facilities are often allowed to make a loss. (2 marks)
   (December 1984)
2. To which of the FOUR categories of providing agency do the following belong

   (a) Butlin's Holiday World
   (b) Forestry Commission
   (c) Anglian Water
   (d) Scouts and Guides
   (e) English Tourist Board (5 marks)
   (June 1991)
3. (a) List TWO voluntary uniformed organisations for boys. (2 marks)
   (b) List TWO voluntary uniformed organisations for girls. (2 marks)
   (c) Name an organisation running and supporting Youth Clubs, excluding local authorities. (1 mark)
   (December 1987)
4. (a) The Sports Council has encouraged the building of "standard" sports halls in conjunction with a major building firm.
   State the name by which the scheme is known. (2 marks)
   (b) Many local organisations involved in recreational activities are run on a voluntary basis.
   List in EACH case, the honorary official who
   (i) deals with all financial matters;
   (ii) deals with correspondence, minutes, etc;
   (iii) deals with fixtures. (3 marks)
   (June 1988)

5. (a) List THREE functions of a governing body of sport. (3 marks)
   (b) Give the initials of the governing bodies of FOUR of the following sports:

   cricket, ladies hockey, netball, tennis, badminton, rugby union, rugby league, swimming. (2 marks)
   (December 1988)
6. List FIVE National Recreation Centres, in each case stating the activity particularly identified with the centre. (5 marks)
   (June 1991)

481-2 PROVISION AND CONTROL

Past examination questions related to Provision and Control

Part II Paper 2 The organisation of recreation and leisure

1. State the Central Government department to which each of the following are responsible:
   - (a) Arts Council,
   - (b) Sports Council,
   - (c) English Tourist Board,
   - (d) Nature Conservancy Council (for England),
   - (e) Forestry Commission. (10 marks)

   (April 1990)

2. (a) Name FOUR National agencies that receive Central Government funds through the Department of Environment. (8 marks)
   (b) State the Central Government department which provides the Arts Council with funding. (2 marks)

   (April 1991)

3. Name FIVE geographical regions of the Sports Council (10 marks)

   (April 1991)

4. (a) State TWO functions of the Sports Council. (2 marks)
   (b) (i) List FOUR National Sports Centres. (2 marks)
       (ii) From the Sports Centres you have listed above, briefly describe the aims and functions of TWO which are concerned with outdoor pursuits. (2 marks)
   (c) What do the following initials stand for?
       (i) CCPR
       (ii) NPFA (1 mark)
   (d) State and briefly explain THREE major aims of the CCPR.(3 marks)

   (June 1984)

5. (a) State SIX major aims of the Countryside Commission in relation to National Parks as outlined in the Countryside Act 1968.
   (2 marks)
   (b) Name the National Parks of England and Wales labelled 1—10 on the diagram given below. (5 marks)
   (c) List SIX services provided in the National Parks by the National Park Authorities. (3 marks)

   (June 1985)

6. (a) List FIVE Areas of Outstanding Natural Beauty. (5 marks)
      (Extract from June 1989)
   (b) List THREE recreational activities which may be encouraged by water authorities (National Rivers Authority). (3 marks)
   (c) List TWO aims of the National Playing Fields Association.
      (2 marks)
      (Extracts from June 1986)
7. Tourism and the Arts are both important to Britain. State
   (a) TWO aims of the Arts Council. (4 marks)
   (b) THREE aims of the Tourists Boards. (6 marks)
      (June 1990)
8. Name FIVE commercial companies involved in leisure provision nationally. For each company identify their main area of interest.
      (10 marks)
      (June 1990)
9. The commercial sector's interest in recreation is primarily as a source of profit. State FIVE areas of leisure provision of particular interest to the commercial sector. (10 marks)
      (June 1990)

10. Describe FIVE ways in which a community can affect the provision of recreation and leisure opportunity. (10 marks)
(April 1990)
11. A community can have an effect on its recreation and leisure provision in a number of ways.
   (a) State THREE ways this could be done at a local/regional level.
(6 marks)
   (b) Describe TWO ways of achieving this at national level. (4 marks)
(June 1991)
12. Certain groups within the community have particular leisure needs, these include

   (a) elderly
   (b) ethnic minorities
   (c) teenagers
   (d) women
   (e) unemployed.

   State ONE need for each group and give ONE example in each case how that need could be satisfied. (10 marks)
(April 1991)
13. (a) State TWO ways in which the outside area of a leisure centre could be adapted to people with disabilities.
   (b) Identify TWO ways, in EACH case, in which the interior of a facility could be adapted to assist the following

      (i) the physically disabled
      (ii) the partially sighted
      (iii) the elderly
      (iv) women with children (10 marks)
(June 1991)
14. The voluntary sector makes a significant contribution to recreation and leisure.
   (a) Give TWO characteristics of a voluntary organisation. (4 marks)
   (b) Give TWO examples of voluntary organisations in EACH of the following

      (i) sports
      (ii) non sporting recreation
      (iii) arts and entertainment. (6 marks)
(June 1991)

Bibliography, References and Further Reading

About the NCF. National Coaching Foundation, 1988
Annual Report, 1987/1988. English Tourist Board, 1988
Annual report for the year ended 31 March 1988. British Tourist Authority, 1988
Arts Council 43rd annual report and accounts 87–88. Arts Council, 1988
The Arts Council of Great Britain Three-Year Plan 1988/89–1990/91
At work in the countryside, 1988/89. Countryside Commission, 1988
Britain's Tourism — factsheets. English Tourist Board, 1988
The Central Council of Physical Recreation: A Guide: what it is and what it does. CCPR
Colne Valley Park Information Leaflets. Buckinghamshire County Council, NCC
Colne Valley Park Standing Conference Proposals for the Regional Park October 1988. Buckinghamshire County Council, 1988
Education Services in National Parks. Countryside Commission
English Heritage — Aims and Organisation. English Heritage, 1988
English Heritage: Facts and Figures 1987–1988. English Heritage, 1988
English Nature — the Nature Conservancy Council for England — Information sheet 1991
The Forestry Commission and Recreation. Forestry Commission, 1988
The Forestry Commission's Objectives. Forestry Commission, 1988
Historic Buildings and Monuments Commission for England Report and Accounts 1987–1988. HBMCE, 1988
KTG Know The Game series (80+ titles). EP Publishing
Lake District, Coastline, Victorian Garden. National Trust, 1986
National Coaching Centres — calling all coaches. National Coaching Foundation
National Rivers Authority — A Brief Introduction, NRA, 1990
National Sports Centres fact sheet, The. Sports Council
National Trust Membership. National Trust, 1985
National Trust Membership: see what you're saving, National Trust 1984
Nature Conservancy Council Information Leaflet, 1988
Practical approach to The Administration of Leisure and Recreation Services, A. Croner, 1988
Safety in Outdoor Pursuits DES Safety Series Number 1. HMSO, 1979
Safety in Physical Education DES Safety Series Number 4. HMSO, 1978
Safety in Physical Education. British Association of Lectures in PE, 1979
Sport in the Community — the Next Ten Years. Sports Council, 1982

Torkildsen, G. Leisure and Recreation Management. E&FN Spon, 1983
Watch over the National Parks. Countryside Commission, 1985
What is the Sports Council? fact sheet. Sports Council
Who's Who of British Tourist Boards, The. British Tourist Authority, 1986
Work of English Heritage, The. English Heritage, 1986
Your Countryside, Our Concern. Countryside Commission, 1988.

3 Resource Management
PERSONAL PRESENTATION

The recreation and leisure industry is one which is people based. Users of leisure facilities expect to enjoy their experiences and the appearance, attitude and behaviour of the staff will directly affect that experience.

The cliché "You don't get a second chance to make a good first impression" does have a very real ring of truth to it. Visitors often judge leisure facilities by the people who work in them. This places a responsibility on *all* members of staff to be pleasant, smart and cheerful but it particularly applies to staff working on reception.

It is important that staff should be pleasant and cheerful and of clean and tidy appearance.

Reception duties

The most important duties of a receptionist are:

(a) to provide a welcome to the centre;
(b) to be able to give information to customers and visitors;
(c) to be able to deal with problems.

In order to provide an effective welcome members of staff should:

(a) be pleasant and cheerful (a smile can work wonders);
(b) acknowledge the visitor as promptly as possible, especially if busy (eg with a telephone call), using their name if possible;
(c) be of clean and tidy appearance, both in terms of clothing and personal hygiene (hair, nails, etc).

Uniforms and name badges can be particularly useful in that they ensure that the staff are clearly identifiable and they can help form part of a strong corporate image.

Non-verbal communication

Non-verbal communication is the way we convey feelings and attitudes to other people in an unspoken manner. Such communication includes many aspects of appearance, "body language" and personal deportment, including:

The most important duty of a receptionist is to provide a welcome to the facility. Aspects of non-verbal communication such as attitude and behaviour may adversely affect the type of welcome that a visitor receives.

(a) facial expressions (smiles, scowls, etc);
(b) eye contact;
(c) attitudes;
(d) gestures (particularly with the hands, arms and legs);
(e) behaviour.

Notices, signs and posters, etc are sometimes also considered to be aspects of non-verbal communication.

Dealing with people

Although some people are naturally very good at dealing with others, doing it professionally is a skill. It is easier and more enjoyable, however, if you genuinely try to be nice and patient. Visitors frequently ask questions, often the same ones, more as a means of making contact than as a method of obtaining information (which is very often clearly displayed). It is important for the member of staff to be patient and to remember that although the same question may have been asked many times already that day it is the first time that this particular visitor has asked it.

On occasions staff will have to deal with minor problems or complaints. Although each will have to be dealt with on its individual merits, two simple examples may give an indication of how such situations may be approached.

1. A telephone caller wishes to speak to the manager who is unavailable at the time:

    (a) explain the situation and ask if you may be able to help;
    (b) offer to find somebody else who may be able to deal with the matter;
    (c) if this is not possible, offer to take a message, and note the caller's name, telephone number and organisation and find out when it would be convenient to call back;
    (d) indicate when the manager is likely to be available and try to ascertain when the caller is most likely to ring again.

2. A customer comes to reception complaining that he or she has been "double booked" on a squash court:

    (a) Check that this is in fact the case:

        (i) has the customer got the time and date correct?

(ii) did he or she go to the correct court?
(iii) have the people already on the court actually booked *that* court, at *that* time (and not over-run or gone on to an empty court).

Remember that you are trying to solve the problem, not create one! Be polite when establishing the facts.

(b) Check to see if there are any other courts free that might be used.
(c) If this is not possible then another court should be offered to the customer at a different time, preferably free of charge. (If the receptionist does not have the authority to do this, then the matter could be referred to the duty manager.)

Visitors who are difficult must be dealt with in a professional manner. Listen to what they have to say, they may have a genuine grievance. Do not enter into an argument with them, if necessary get help from somebody more experienced.

DATA RECORDING, STORAGE AND RETRIEVAL

The purpose of any system of recording and storing of information and data is to make that information available when it is needed. It is no good storing information if it cannot be found later (ie accessed). Very often the most simple system is the most useful but, when large amounts of data have to be processed and accessed, more complex systems may be necessary.

It is useful to consider the different systems under two main headings:

(a) manual systems;
(b) computer based systems.

Manual systems of recording and storing information

These are often the most simple and easy to operate. Such systems include a large number of forms and sheets which may be filled in directly as information is received and may include:

(a) booking sheets (for squash or badminton courts),
(b) maintenance sheets,
(c) accident forms,
(d) card index systems.

Very often these forms are contained within a single book (which may include duplicates) and, once filled in, act as a storage system in themselves. Alternatively, completed forms may be kept in a filing system.

Filing systems

These may range from a simple card index or ring folders to large filing systems using several cabinets or a large number of box files. Such systems can very rapidly become cumbersome and occupy a large amount of valuable space. The retrieval and updating of information can also become very time consuming, particularly if any form of cross-referencing is required.

Computer based systems of recording and storing information

These are most often used for dealing with large amounts of information, especially where data has to be updated, cross-referenced or accessed on a large number of occasions. Such systems are particularly useful when they are used to monitor the use of large leisure facilities or for stock control (eg for consumable or resaleable equipment and for bar sales) by means of a computerised till.

Computerised systems are also extremely useful when combined with the use of bar codes (eg for dealing with membership and the issue of library books, reminders and circulars). Software is normally available, or can be designed, to suit the specific needs of individual organisations.

Information from computer based systems can be accessed over long distances by means of a central computer to which a number of terminals are connected. This may be done directly (through "hardwiring") or through a telephone or television linkup (eg Prestel, Ceefax).

The speed with which a computer based system can be used will result in cost savings of time, space and accuracy which compensate for the relatively high cost of the initial outlay and the setting-up period.

Once information is held on the computer, the security of the system must become a priority concern. Data may need to be protected from either the interested or nosey "hacker" or from individuals who may wish to change information. The use of security entry codes would normally be sufficient in most leisure and recreation situations.

Unlike manual systems, however, computer based systems must comply with current data protection legislation. This can involve a certain amount of extra time and work for the users of such systems.

The main advantages and disadvantages of manual and computer based storage and retrieval systems are summarised in Figure 21.

SHIFT WORK

To enable most people to use sports and leisure facilities they must be open at times extending well beyond the normal working day, and at weekends, throughout the year. A typical sports centre with a

SYSTEM	ADVANTAGES	DISADVANTAGES
MANUAL	Very cheap to install (especially if simple box files)	If a large amount of information and data has to be stored then the system can become very bulky and take up considerable areas of valuable space
	Very simple to set up and use	
	Very useful and effective where the amount of data to be stored is limited or where the data includes pictorial information (eg photographs, charts, brochures)	It may be difficult and time consuming to cross reference information, especially where the system is large.
		The system can easily become untidy or cluttered with out-of-date or irrelevant information
COMPUTER	Can cope with very large volume of information	Expensive to install
		May require specially written software
	Once stored, information can be retrieved, cross referenced and collated very quickly	May require sophisticated training and skills in order to be used effectively, both by existing and new staff
	Information can be updated easily and tidily	All the information can be irretrievably lost (wiped) if the system is shut down and so back-up systems are essential
	Information, including drawings, can be accessed over considerable distances by linking computers using telephones or television	May be vulnerable to unauthorised use unless security entry access codes are used
		When not starting from scratch it can be very time consuming to convert from one system to another and there may be disrupted access to information while this work is in progress

Figure 21 The advantages and disadvantages of manual and computer based data storage and retrieval systems

93

swimming pool may be open from 07.30 for the early morning swim sessions right through until 22.30 or 23.00 when the bar closes. Clearly it is unreasonable to expect staff to work a fifteen and a half hour day and consequently some form of shift system has to be adopted. This will need to:

(a) provide for sufficient time off work for staff;
(b) ensure that there is always adequate supervision and safety cover;
(c) cater for fluctuations in use.

Shift systems

These will vary considerably with the needs of the particular sports centre. For a typical small sports centre a simple, two-shift system is usually sufficient. Such a centre may close early at weekends which would permit the shift system to be organised, for example, as indicated below:

SHIFT	Mon	Tue	Wed	Thu	Fri	Sat	Sun
A	07.30 14.30	07.30 14.30	07.30 14.30	07.30 14.30	07.30 14.30	08.00 17.30	OFF
B	14.00 22.30	14.00 22.30	14.00 22.30	14.00 22.30	14.00 22.30	OFF	08.00 13.00

Figure 22 An example of a two-shift system

Each shift would then work "earlies" one week and "lates" the next. Obviously the starting and finishing times would vary depending upon the employees' terms and conditions of employment, the needs of the sports centre concerned and the availability of suitable part-time staff.

Where the sports centre is much larger and open for longer hours each week (eg 07.00–23.00 seven days per week) two shifts would be insufficient to cover the entire opening hours of the centre and still provide the necessary days off for the staff. Under such circumstances a three-shift system would need to be used. These too can be organised in different ways but Figure 23 gives one example of how this may be done.

SHIFT	Sat	Sun	Mon	Tue	Wed	Thu	Fri
A	off	off	late	late	early	early	off
B	late	late	early	early	off	off	late
C	early	early	off	off	late	late	early

Figure 23 An example of a three-shift system

Staff would then work shift A one week, shift B the next and shift C the week after in rotation, thus having one weekend off in three.

In both these examples the manager and some clerical staff would almost certainly work an additional middle shift from 09.00–17.00 Monday to Friday (ie "normal" working hours).

The personal advantages and disadvantages of working shifts

Obviously what is seen as a disadvantage by one employee may be seen as an advantage by another (depending upon their personal preferences and individual lifestyles). The following lists, however, attempt to identify some of the more obvious factors and group them accordingly.

Advantages

(a) Time off during the day when shops are open;
(b) enhanced rates of pay (eg for working shifts, unsocial hours, evenings or weekends);
(c) may fit in well with certain family constraints (eg where both parents of young children need to maintain full time jobs).

Disadvantages

(a) Working "unsocial hours" (ie when other people are not) causing some disruption to their social life;
(b) the irregularity of the shifts may make planning ahead difficult and make the following of regular activities (eg evening classes or playing in leagues) almost impossible;
(c) disruption of eating and sleeping habits may have an adverse effect upon health.

An additional disadvantage of shift systems, which affects the management as well as staff, is that their use can result in inadequate communication between staff on different shifts.

HYGIENE

There is a need to be aware of basic hygiene in all recreation and leisure environments including:

(a) swimming pools;
(b) sports complexes;
(c) parks and open spaces;
(d) river banks and outdoor water sports areas.

This is in order to:

(a) limit the spread of disease;
(b) avoid pollution;
(c) avoid aesthetic offence.

Swimming pools

Particular problems associated with swimming pools include:

(a) foot infections (eg athlete's foot, verrucas);
(b) infections and diseases that could be transmitted through the medium of the pool water;
(c) pollution of the pool water.

These problems are discussed in greater detail in the section on swimming pools.

Sports complexes

Problems associated with sports complexes include:

(a) infections and diseases that may be transmitted through personal contact (eg colds, flu);
(b) foot infections (that may be picked up in the changing rooms);
(c) infections and diseases associated with the handling, preparation and sale of food (eg salmonella);
(d) smoking (many people who engage in physical activity do so in order to improve their health and find smoking offensive).

Parks and open spaces

Problems which particularly relate to parks and open spaces include:

(a) infections which may be in the soil (eg tetanus);
(b) infections associated with dog excrement (eg toxocara, hydatid cysts, Canicola fever) which many people also find aesthetically offensive;
(c) litter. (Drink cans and glass, particularly if they have been run over by grass cutting machinery, present particular risks both from cuts and an increase in the risk of infections.)

River banks and outdoor water sports areas

(a) Diseases spread by rats (eg Weil's disease),
(b) stomach upsets.

HYGIENE PRECAUTIONS

These general precautions apply to all those who work in recreation and leisure environments but are especially important for those who are working with food:

(a) Always wash hands thoroughly after using the toilet, after cleaning, using chemicals, or setting out equipment (especially that which is dusty or dirty).
(b) Always cover up any cuts or abrasions.
(c) Those who have a cold, flu or other illness should stay at home, otherwise they may pass on the infection to other staff or to members of the public.
(d) Clothing must be clean and the personal appearance of staff should not be such as to cause offence. Staff working in the leisure industry are in frequent contact with members of the public and a good impression is essential.
(e) If staff are exercising they should make a point of showering before working in other areas (eg reception).

HEALTH AND SAFETY

The main health and safety legislation and controls that apply to leisure and recreation environments are:

(a) the Health and Safety Work, etc Act 1974;
(b) the Offices, Shops and Railway Premises Act 1963;
(c) other relevant Codes of Practice.

HEALTH AND SAFETY AT WORK, ETC ACT 1974

Introduction

Briefly, this is an enabling Act which imposes extra general duties on employers whilst still requiring them to comply with all existing current legislation. Its main purpose is to maintain or improve existing standards of health and safety for employees and members of the general public from risks arising out of work activities.

Main provisions

The main provisions of the Health and Safety at Work, etc Act 1974 are:

(a) the employer's responsibilities with reference to:
 (i) safety in the workplace;
 (ii) safety in working practices and from machinery and plant;
 (iii) hygiene and welfare;
 (iv) electrical and fire safety;
(b) the employee's responsibilities to keep safety rules and observe safe practices.

These main provisions impose specific duties upon both:

(a) the employer and
(b) the employee.

The most important of these duties are summarised below, together with some examples of how they relate to particular leisure and recreation environments.

Employers' main duties

These duties are all to be carried out "so far as is reasonably practicable":

(a) A written statement of the organisation's health and safety policy must be prepared and adequate organisation and arrangements made in order to ensure that the policy is carried out effectively.

(b) Ensure that systems of working are safe and that adequate supervision arrangements exist for monitoring that these are carried out effectively (in leisure centres this will include arrangements for setting out heavy equipment, eg trampolines and gymnastics apparatus, and supervising public use of swimming pools and weight training areas).

(c) Ensure that handling, transport, use and storage of articles and substances is done in such a way as to prevent risks to health and safety arising and to make certain that protective equipment and clothing is provided and used where required. (In leisure centres this will include the lifting and storage of heavy equipment and the use and storage of chemicals used for cleaning, for water treatment in swimming pools, and weedkillers and pesticides used for the maintenance of soft landscapes. This also includes arrangements for ensuring that potentially dangerous equipment and chemicals are securely locked away when not in use.)

(d) Ensure that there are safe means of access and egress at all times. In leisure centres this particularly includes sports hall fire exits which must not be blocked by trampolines, crash mats or five-a-side football goals but also includes ensuring that stairways are free of cleaning equipment, eg mops and buckets, and that fire doors are not locked.

*Ensure that fire doors are **not** blocked and that there is safe access and egress at all times*

(e) Ensure that there are no risks to the health and safety of the public as a result of the working practices of the organisation. In all leisure and recreation environments this is particularly important, especially where there are young children who may have little perception of any dangers that may exist.

(f) Provide information about health and safety to all employees and ensure that all training programmes include appropriate instruction in health and safety.

Employers must provide information about health and safety to all employees

(g) Provide facilities for the welfare and use of employees which are safe and without risks to health.

Employees' main duties

Employees have the following duties:

(a) To take reasonable care that they do not endanger themselves or anyone else through their work activities. In leisure and recreation environments this includes not endangering themselves, eg by attempting to lift or set out equipment that is too heavy for them, by disregarding rules governing the use of safety equipment and clothing, such as when handling chemicals or using lawn mowers that require the wearing of steel-capped boots, and by ensuring that when assigned supervisory duties designed to protect members of the public that these are done conscientiously, eg on poolside or in the gymnasium.
(b) To co-operate with their employers in meeting the requirements of the Act. This means following any laid down procedures and working practices devised by the employer in order to comply with the requirements of the Act.
(c) To not interfere with or misuse any equipment that has been provided in the interests of meeting the requirements of the Act. For example, not "fooling about" with fire extinguishers.

Enforcement

The Act is enforced by inspectors who are appointed by the Health and Safety Executive. These inspectors have powers to enter premises, inspect and remove articles or substances and to require employees to give information and assistance in order to enable them to carry out their inspection.

If an inspector discovers any contravention of the Act the following courses of action can be taken:

(a) a prohibition notice may be issued;
(b) an improvement notice may be issued;
(c) a prosecution may be initiated — instead of or as well as issuing one of the above notices.

Approved Codes of Practice

These may be issued by the Health and Safety Commission, which may also approve suitable codes of practice submitted to them by other bodies.

LIFTING HEAVY WEIGHTS IN LEISURE AND RECREATION ENVIRONMENTS

One of the most common ways in which employees injure themselves at work is by trying to lift objects that are too heavy for them (for example gymnastics apparatus and trampolines).

The main rules to be followed when lifting heavy weights are:

(a) always get trained staff to help whenever possible;
(b) clear objects and people (especially children) from the immediate area;
(c) make sure that the pathway the object is to take is as clear as possible (and that doors are fixed open);
(d) use appropriate equipment when it is available (eg trolleys, hoists);
(e) when lifting use the correct technique:

   (i) *feet close to the object,*
   (ii) *legs bent,*

(iii) back and arms straight,
(iv) head back,
*(v) lift with the legs, **not** the back,*
(vi) lift together.

OFFICES, SHOPS AND RAILWAY PREMISES ACT 1963

The Offices, Shops and Railway Premises Act 1963 is concerned with ensuring that the general standard of cleanliness, hygiene and working conditions is acceptable. This also includes ensuring that heating, lighting, ventilation and sanitary conveniences are all satisfactory. The Act relates in particular to work in the ancillary support areas and corridors and stairways of sports and leisure facilities.

OTHER RELEVANT CODES OF PRACTICE

These include a very large number of statutes. For those studying at this level, however, the following should be sufficient for the purposes of providing examples:

Fire Precautions Act 1971

Fire Safety and Safety of Places of Sport Act 1987

Food Hygiene (General) Regulations 1970 (SI 1970 No. 1172)

Health and Safety (First Aid) Regulations 1981 (SI 1981 No. 917)

Local Government (Miscellaneous Provisions) Act 1982

CALLING THE EMERGENCY SERVICES

This may be necessary for a number of reasons. The nature of the emergency will determine which of the emergency services is summoned:

EMERGENCY	SERVICE
physical accident	ambulance
fire	fire brigade
theft	police
disturbance	police
coastal or seaside emergency	coastguard
mountain accident	mountain rescue

Figure 24 Emergency services

Whichever service is needed the basic procedure is the same:

(a) dial 999 and state which service is required;
(b) state the telephone number from which the call is being made (in case of being cut off);
(c) give the name and address of the place where the emergency has occurred (eg sports centre, swimming pool or playing fields) together with any other information that will help to locate the place quickly;
(d) give an idea of the nature and seriousness of the incident;
(e) give an indication of the number of casualties or persons involved.

RECORDING ACCIDENT DETAILS

Following an accident it is important that detailed information is recorded accurately as soon as possible after the event whilst the details are still fresh in people's memories. Usually this information will be recorded either in an accident book or on accident forms designed for the purpose. These forms will vary from organisation to organisation but the essential information will almost always include the following:

(a) details of the casualty —
   (i) name and address (including telephone number),
   (ii) age, sex;

(b) details of the incident —
   (i) date, time, place;
   (ii) brief account of what happened and, if possible, the cause;
   (iii) apparent nature of injuries as far as is possible to judge (indicate right or left as appropriate);
(c) names and addresses of any witnesses;
(d) action taken including —
   (i) the nature of any first aid given,
   (ii) whether the casualty was taken to hospital or advised to seek medical advice,
   (iii) to whom the incident was reported.

It is important that the details are recorded for a number of reasons. It allows management and health and safety officers to monitor safety, compile statistics and identify trends or remedial action. If there is a claim for negligence then the facts are available.

CHEMICALS COMMONLY USED IN RECREATION ENVIRONMENTS

A number of different chemicals are used in the leisure and recreation industry. These are mainly used for:

(a) cleaning purposes;
(b) disinfection of toilets and associated areas;
(c) swimming pool water treatment;
(d) garden, soft landscape and playing field maintenance;
(e) control of pests.

Chemicals used for cleaning purposes

These are many and varied. They are usually selected to deal with the cleaning problems associated with:

(a) a particular type of surface, eg glass, thermoplastic tiles, carpet;
(b) a particular type of problem, eg chewing gum, felt tip markers.

The *type of use* that indoor surfaces are put to can also cause some special cleaning problems. For example, the fine dust left behind when roller skates with "non-marking" nylon wheels have been used can leave sealed floors slippery and dangerous for sports like badminton and five-a-side football. Simple "V" mopping may be insufficient unless a mop dressing chemical is also used.

Examples of chemicals used for cleaning purposes include:

(a) wax based polishes;
(b) detergents;
(c) solvents, eg white spirit.

When handling or using these substances it is important to note that some, particularly solvents, give off fumes which:

(a) may be inflammable;
(b) may be dangerous if inhaled.

When using such chemicals make sure that the area is well ventilated and that there are no naked lights or flames anywhere nearby.

Chemicals used for the disinfection of toilets

The most commonly used chemicals for the disinfection of toilets and associated areas are bleaches such as sodium hypochlorite. Other chemicals are available which are also effective but it is very important to note that *bleach must not be mixed with acids, other toilet cleaners or cleaning products* as this may cause dangerous chlorine gas to be given off. For this reason bleach should not be left in toilets when there is a possibility that children may use the toilet without flushing it first.

It should also be emphasised that many cleaning chemicals are *corrosive and can burn*. Others are irritants and therefore great care should be taken when handling them. Always wear gloves and protective clothing where possible and especially where these are provided.

Chemicals commonly associated with swimming pool water treatment

The principal types of chemical used are:

(a) bleach, to disinfect the pool water;
(b) acid, to maintain acceptable pH levels in the pool water;
(c) flocculants to assist with the filtration of pool water;
(d) chemicals used for the testing of the pool water.

When handling swimming pool chemicals it is important to take great care. Pay attention to, *and carry out*, all safety procedures as laid down, use the safety equipment and clothing provided and get assistance when heavy quantities of chemicals have to be moved or lifted.

Chemicals used in garden, soft landscape and playing field maintenance

Chemicals will be used for a variety of purposes in this area. These will include:

- (a) fertilisers,
- (b) weedkillers,
- (c) insecticides,
- (d) chemicals used for the control of plant diseases,
- (e) chemicals used for the marking of pitches.

Many of these are poisonous or corrosive and, in consequence, must be stored securely and, when in use, not left around unsupervised. This is particularly important when young children may be playing nearby.

Control of pests

In addition to garden pests, leisure facilities, especially those housed in old buildings, may suffer from problems which require the use of pesticides (eg ants, cockroaches, mice). Again, these substances must be stored securely and not used in any place where they may accidently poison young children or pets.

STORAGE OF CHEMICALS

Because of the dangers associated with chemicals it is important that they are stored where accidental or unauthorised contact with them is avoided. Children, particularly, could be at risk. Chemicals should, therefore, be locked away in a separate storeroom.

They should *never* be put or stored in a different type of bottle or container to that in which they belong and labels should *never* be removed from those containers.

Heat tends to make those chemicals which give off a vapour do so more readily and also increases the risk of fire. It is therefore important that chemical stores are cool, fireproof and, to prevent the build up of fumes, well ventilated.

Swimming pools

Swimming pools have two additional problems:

(a) the large amounts of chemicals that may have to be stored;
(b) the importance of making sure that the acid and bleach cannot accidently come into direct contact with each other.

In order to overcome these problems most pools have smaller day tanks, which contain just enough chemicals for one day, separated from the main bulk storage tank by taps. This is to prevent the accidental release of very large quantities of chemicals into the pool water. The bleach and acid tanks are then separated from each other by two bund walls which prevent the chemicals mixing in the event of leakage or accidental spillage. The layout is illustrated in Figure 25 below.

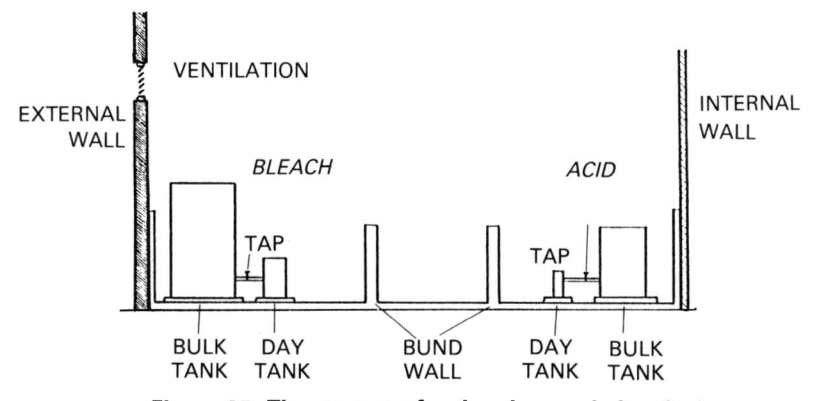

Figure 25 The storage of swimming pool chemicals

Note: Many of the problems associated with the storage of dry or wet acid have been overcome by the use of carbon dioxide gas for the treatment of pool water.

Summary

The principal requirements of a chemical store are that it should be:

(a) separate,
(b) secure,
(c) cool,
(d) well ventilated,
(e) fireproof.

Treatment of chemical burns and poisoning

In all cases, when handling chemicals, contact with the skin and eyes should be avoided.

If any chemical comes into contact with the eyes, they should be rinsed immediately with plenty of water. Medical advice should then be obtained promptly. The casualty should not be allowed to rub the eye.

If chemicals come into contact with the skin, it should be washed immediately with plenty of running water. Any contaminated clothing should be removed promptly whilst washing the affected area. Seek medical advice.

If chemicals have been swallowed *do not* attempt to make the casualty sick. He or she may be given water or milk to drink. The casualty should be conveyed to hospital immediately.

In all cases where medical attention is sought, it is helpful if the harmful chemical can be identified and, if swallowed, some idea of the amount taken can be given.

SUPPORT (NON-ACTIVITY) AREAS AND FACILITIES

Any recreation and leisure environment will require a number of support areas in addition to those designated for activities. Such areas may include:

(a) reception areas,
(b) changing rooms,
(c) toilets,
(d) showers,
(e) plant room,
(f) storage areas, including;

    (i) cupboards for sports equipment,
           bar and vending stock,
           chemicals and cleaning materials,
   (ii) wall or office safe for cash and valuables,
  (iii) separate team changing rooms for clothing during matches,
  (iv) individual lockers for personal belongings and clothing,
   (v) supervised areas for basket and hanger storage of clothing,

(i) committee/meeting rooms,
(j) licensed bar/lounge,
(k) snack bar/cafe/restaurant,
(l) vending machine area,
(m) shop,
(n) crèche,
(o) first-aid room.

Other areas, that might be alternatively classified as either activity areas or support areas, include:

(p) sauna,
(q) solarium,
(r) spectator areas.

All of these areas will require regular maintenance and cleaning.

The support areas listed above will make use of a wide range of different materials for the different surfaces that will exist within them. Examples of the surfaces that may be encountered include:

(a) composition block (including "breeze" block and composite mineral tiling),
(b) wood,
(c) thermoplastic tiles,
(d) carpet,
(e) glazed tiles,
(f) concrete,
(g) brick,
(h) quarry tiles,
(i) rubber,
(j) plastic and polymeric,
(k) glass.

Cleaning processes and materials

For each of these surfaces there is a limited range of different cleaning processes and materials that may be suitable but, given the range of surfaces, the total number of different cleaning materials, equipment and methods available is considerable.

If there is any concern or doubt about materials or methods it is best to check the labelling on the cleaning fluids and chemicals carefully or seek advice.

For some surfaces and areas, however, identifying the most suitable method of cleaning and maintenance is relatively straightforward:

(a) toilets and showers — all surfaces, but particularly the floors, need to be washed and disinfected at least once a day;
(b) changing areas — floors, especially when the changing rooms are used for outdoor changing, must be swept thoroughly before they are washed and disinfected;
(c) carpeted areas, eg bar, lounge and offices, need to be cleaned daily with a vacuum cleaner, and may, in addition, require brushing on a regular basis.

(Note: see "Chemicals used for cleaning purposes" page 104).

MAINTENANCE

Factors affecting maintenance

These may be described as consisting of:

(a) the original choice of materials;
(b) the design of the facilities;
(c) the pattern and type of use that the facilities are subjected to, together with the degree of users' expertise;
(d) the extent and the quality of supervision;
(e) proper scheduling of planned maintenance.

Original choice of materials

This is important for a number of reasons. It is not always the best policy to use the cheapest materials in the construction of sports halls, for a number of reasons:

(a) cheap materials are likely to wear out more quickly and require replacing much sooner than would otherwise be the case;
(b) they may be more difficult to keep clean and attractive;
(c) they may be less effective in terms of insulation, resulting in increased energy costs for many years;
(d) there may be increased risks to health and safety, especially if the materials are particularly prone to breaking easily;

(e) cheap materials may not perform as well — this may particularly be the case with mats and surfaces.

Design of the facilities

Good design can help reduce the maintenance problems of facilities. This may be achieved primarily in three ways:

(a) by avoiding the creation of areas which will be difficult to keep clean and maintain, or which will cause extra work (eg where indoor and outdoor facilities share the same changing area);
(b) by avoiding the creation of areas which will be difficult to supervise, where vandalism (eg graffiti or breaking into lockers) may occur;
(c) by the provision of suitable and secure storage spaces within the facility (thus helping to reduce damage to equipment).

The Sports Council/Bovis Standardised Approach to Sports Halls (SASH) design has been quite effective in this respect by taking into account the factors described above and by facilitating the use of mass produced replacement parts.

Pattern and type of use

This primarily affects maintenance in two main ways:

(a) increased use tends to result in increased need for maintenance;
(b) the pattern of use may largely determine the times when scheduled maintenance may be carried out.

Increased use of sports facilities may be expected at certain times of the day, week or year, in particular during the school holidays.

School holidays

These may cause particular maintenance problems:

(a) Increased use by children will result in a need for greater supervision.
(b) The increased use is likely to result in more wear and tear, damage and general maintenance.
(c) Maintenance work is likely to be more difficult whilst large numbers of children are using the facilities.
(d) Less time is available for maintenance work to be done.

Users' expertise

Generally speaking, the more skilled or experienced the users of facilities and equipment are, the less damage or extra maintenance is likely to result from that use. For example, novice squash players may be unaware of the difference between marking and non-marking balls and shoes, and, as a result, use inappropriate equipment. They are also more likely to strike the side walls with their rackets, damaging both the walls and the rackets (which may have been borrowed from the centre) in the process. (Similarly, judo mats may be damaged as a result of being carried by the ends, instead of by the sides and consequently being folded in the middle which may cause them to split).

Inexperienced users of equipment may be unaware that it can be damaged by incorrect handling

Scheduling of planned maintenance

Although much maintenance is carried out on a day to day basis (eg cleaning, checking of equipment) it is important that there is, in addition, a properly planned, long term maintenance schedule. This is necessary for a number of reasons:

(a) It is cost effective in that —
   (i) early, preventative maintenance is likely to be much less expensive in *materials and labour costs* than those repairs that would ultimately be necessary once a complete breakdown has occurred;
   (ii) it helps prevent breakdowns and equipment failure from

actually occurring, thus minimising the loss of *revenue income* that results when these do happen (eg when a sports hall or swimming pool is completely out of action);

(iii) planned maintenance can be scheduled to take place at times when it will cause minimum inconvenience to customers, staff and the facility management and, again, result in minimum loss of revenue income.

(b) It improves health and safety as it ensures that —

(i) the facilities and equipment will have been thoroughly checked recently.

(ii) that all areas of the facility are cleaned regularly and to a daily, weekly or monthly timetable.

(c) It makes the centre or facility more attractive to use and to work in.

In order for scheduled maintenance to be effective, it is essential that records of *all* maintenance work should be kept. These records should state clearly what work has been carried out and who has done it, the materials used, the cost and the labour involved.

The use of daily/weekly maintenance sheets can be effective in that:

(a) it helps to ensure that routine tasks are not overlooked;
(b) it aids communication between shifts where these tasks are shared;
(c) it provides a record of the routine maintenance work that has actually been carried out.

Figure 26 is an example of the form that such a maintenance sheet might take for a small sports centre with a sports hall, weights room and bar.

Extent and quality of supervision

The importance of good supervision has already been covered to a great extent. The benefits may be summarised as follows:

(a) deliberate vandalism (eg to lockers, grafitti) will be reduced;
(b) wear and tear and accidental damage will be reduced;
(c) cleaning problems will be alleviated (eg those associated with chewing gum, litter, toilets).

Supervision need not be overbearing. A recognisable staff presence is often sufficient to have an effect. In this respect uniforms are particularly

Daily/weekly maintenance sheet

DATE..

DUTY MANAGER (SHIFT A)   DUTY MANAGER (SHIFT B)
....

DUTY CENTRE ASSISTANTS   DUTY CENTRE ASSISTANTS
....
....
....

DAILY JOB CHECKLIST INITIAL BOX WHEN JOB COMPLETED	REASON FOR ANY JOB NOT DONE/ COMPLETED	MAINTENANCE NEEDS
SPORTS HALL V-mopped ☐		
CHANGING ROOMS		
Men: swept ☐		
mopped ☐		
Ladies: swept ☐		
mopped ☐		
TOILETS Mens: mopped ☐		
Ladies: mopped ☐		
toilet rolls/paper towels ☐		
RECEPTION swept and mopped ☐		
CORRIDORS swept and mopped ☐		
WEIGHTS ROOM tidied ☐		
swept and hoovered ☐		
equipment checked ☐		
BAR hoovered (evenings) ☐		
BINS emptied ☐		
ELECTRIC LIGHT BULBS checked ☐		
blown blubs replaced ☐		
WEEKLY JOB CHECKLIST		
Mondays: Shower walls washed ☐		
Sports hall floor buffed ☐		
Tuedays: ground floor windows washed ☐		
Wednesdays: shower walls washed ☐		
Sports hall floor buffed ☐	(Trampoline	
Trampolines checked ☐	coach)	

Figure 26 Daily/weekly maintenance sheet

useful. Staff should, however, patrol all areas of the facility regularly, especially those where problems may occur. All staff must also be prepared to intervene in order to prevent damage occurring.

SASH centres are particularly well designed with regard to allowing for good sight-lines, particularly from reception, to areas of the sports centre that may require constant, informal supervision.

STANDARDISED APPROACH TO SPORTS HALLS (SASH)

During the early 1970s there was a rapid expansion in the provision of new sports facilities. Many of these were designed and built at considerable expense and then it was found that certain management, maintenance and running-cost problems had, inadvertently, been built into them. As a result of these problems and the obvious need for a good basic design to be made available to the new local authorities, in 1981 the Sports Council invested in research and technical expertise to develop a good value-for-money sports centre design using a sports facility already built at Tamworth as a basis.

The result was the Standardised Approach to Sports Halls. A design and construction package was developed jointly by the Sports Council and Bovis Construction. By using mass production and fast-build techniques the average construction time for a SASH centre is 35 weeks. Although the basic design is standard, it allows for a number of extra optional facilities to be added.

In addition, the external finish of the centre may be chosen from a range of materials which include horizontal profile steel sheeting, brick cladding and combinations of brick, stone, concrete and insulated steel cladding. By 1987 there were 24 SASH schemes in operation. Examples of SASH centres include the Bitterne at Southampton (the first to be opened), Barnsley, Kings Lynn and the St John's Centre at Worcester.

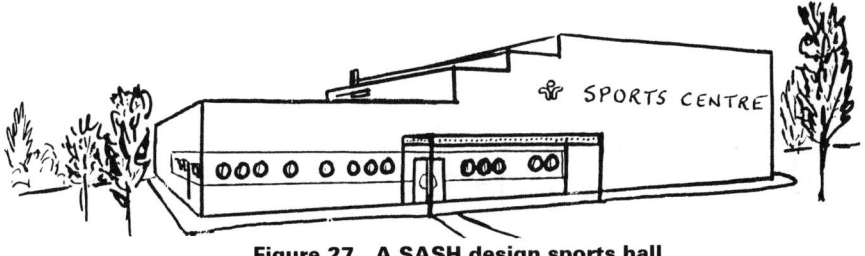

Figure 27   A SASH design sports hall

Technical details

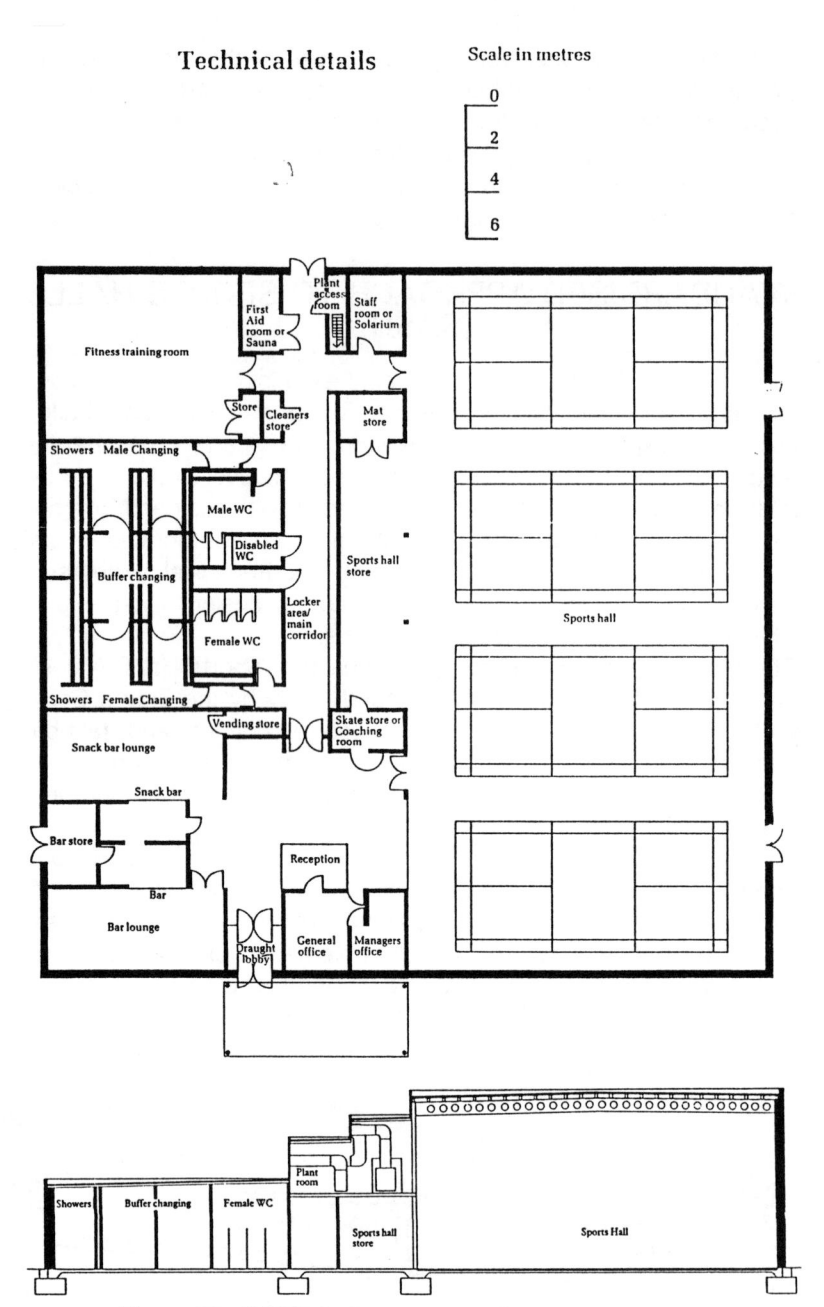

Scale in metres

0
2
4
6

Figure 28 SASH design sports hall — technical details

SWIMMING POOLS

TYPES OF SWIMMING POOL

Swimming pools come in a wide variety of different shapes and sizes, depending largely upon the purposes for which they were designed.

Rectangular tank pools

These are the traditional, basic design pools — deep at one end, shallow at the other (although hydrotherapy and learner pools tend to have a constant depth of about one metre). The majority of pools today are of this type (see Figure 29). These pools are particularly good for serious recreational swimmers (who swim to keep fit), competition swimmers, specialist clubs (eg sub-aqua, water polo) and teaching (eg swimming, life saving, canoe rolling).

Leisure pools

A more recent development has been the concept of the leisure pool, which has gained in popularity since the early 1970s. The main features of leisure pools include:

(a) a free form tank pool incorporating a shallow beach;
(b) wave machine, with the waves breaking on to the beach;
(c) water slides or flumes;
(d) the use of bright colours;
(e) the extensive use of plants, which help soften tiled areas;
(f) large amounts of natural overhead lighting combined with quality artificial lighting.

These leisure pools vary in size and complexity, from the simple 12.5 m pool in Shetland to the large complex leisure pools at Gorton, Manchester, at Windsor, Berkshire and The Coral Reef at Bracknell, Berkshire.

Leisure pools, although very popular, only account for a small proportion of the total number of public swimming pools in the United Kingdom. At present there are still less than 100 leisure pools amongst a total of almost 2000 pools open to the public. However, a significant number of these have been completed since 1986.

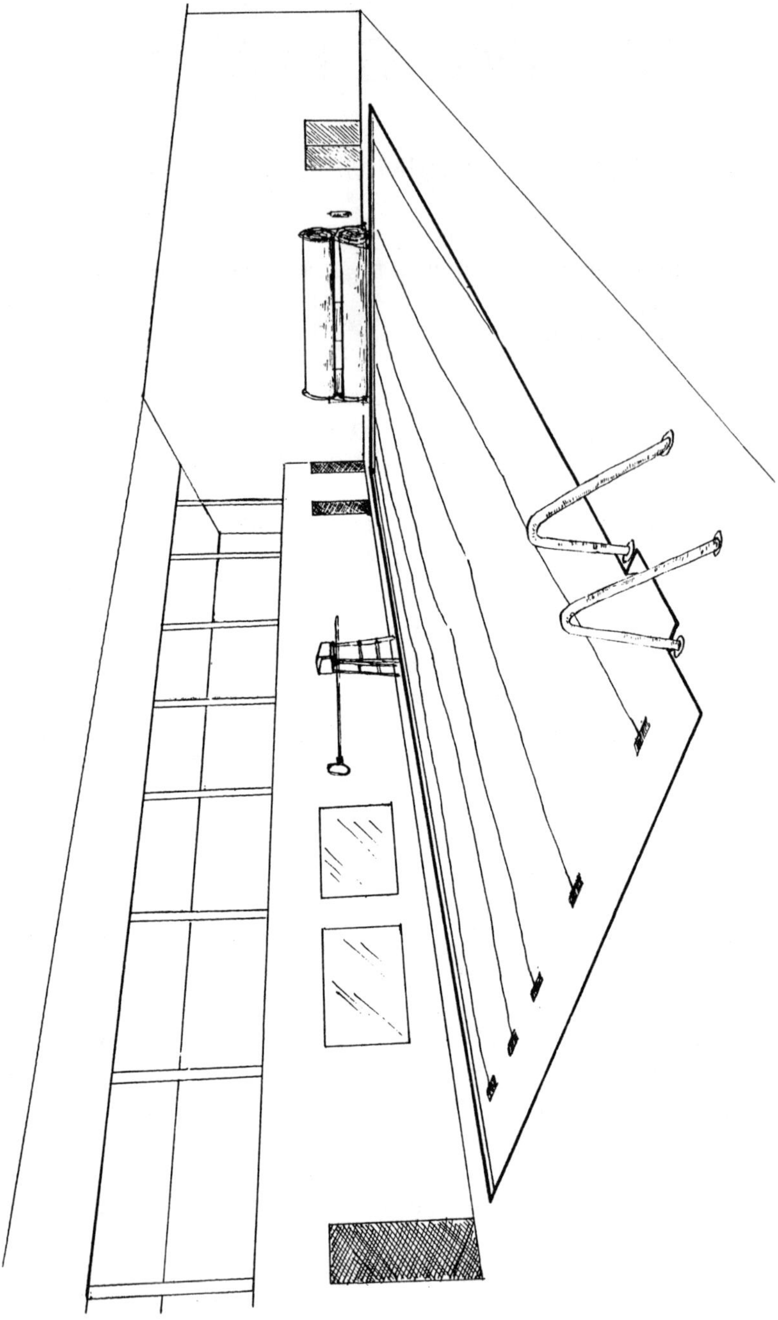

Figure 29 A traditional rectangular tank pool

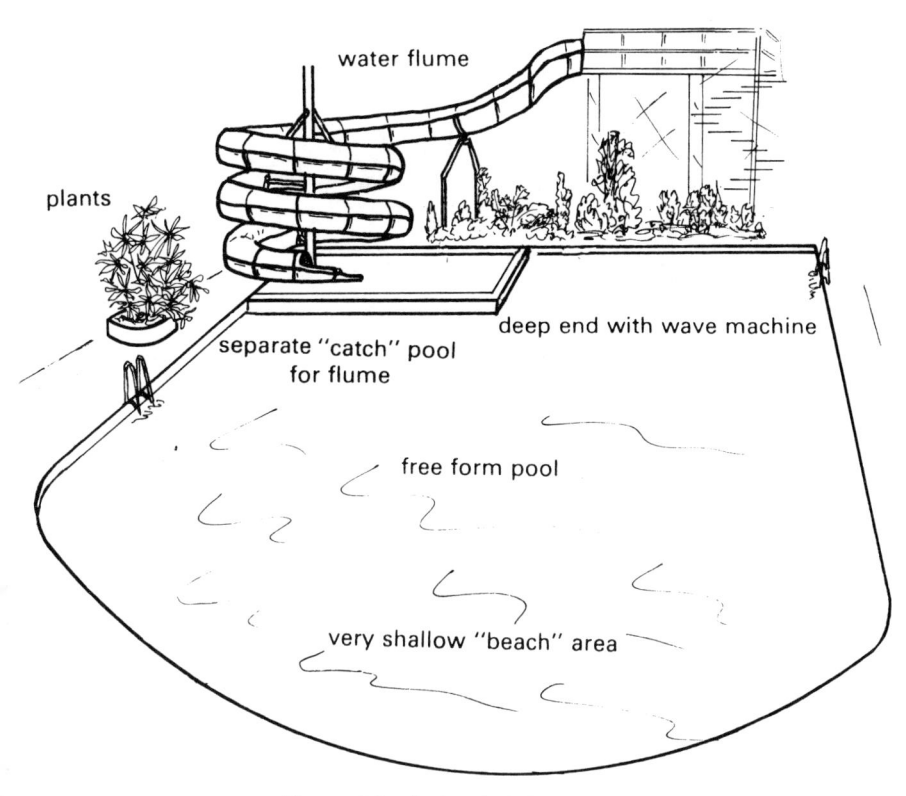

Figure 30 A simple leisure pool

Leisure pools are not, however, ideal for many regular swimmers, who prefer the traditional rectangular tank pools.

The ideal, but most expensive, solution to this problem is to provide separate pools for different types of swimmer, as they do at the Gurnell Pool, West London, the Crown Pool, Ipswich and Watford Springs, Hertfordshire.

An alternative is to attempt to incorporate into the design of a free form leisure pool a rectangular tank which could still be used by serious swimmers at particular times, as has been done at the Cocks Moor Woods Leisure Centre, Birmingham. The way in which these alternative solutions might be arranged is indicated in Figure 32.

At present approximately 50 per cent of all leisure pools still have competition tank pools incorporated into the building or the free form pool design.

120

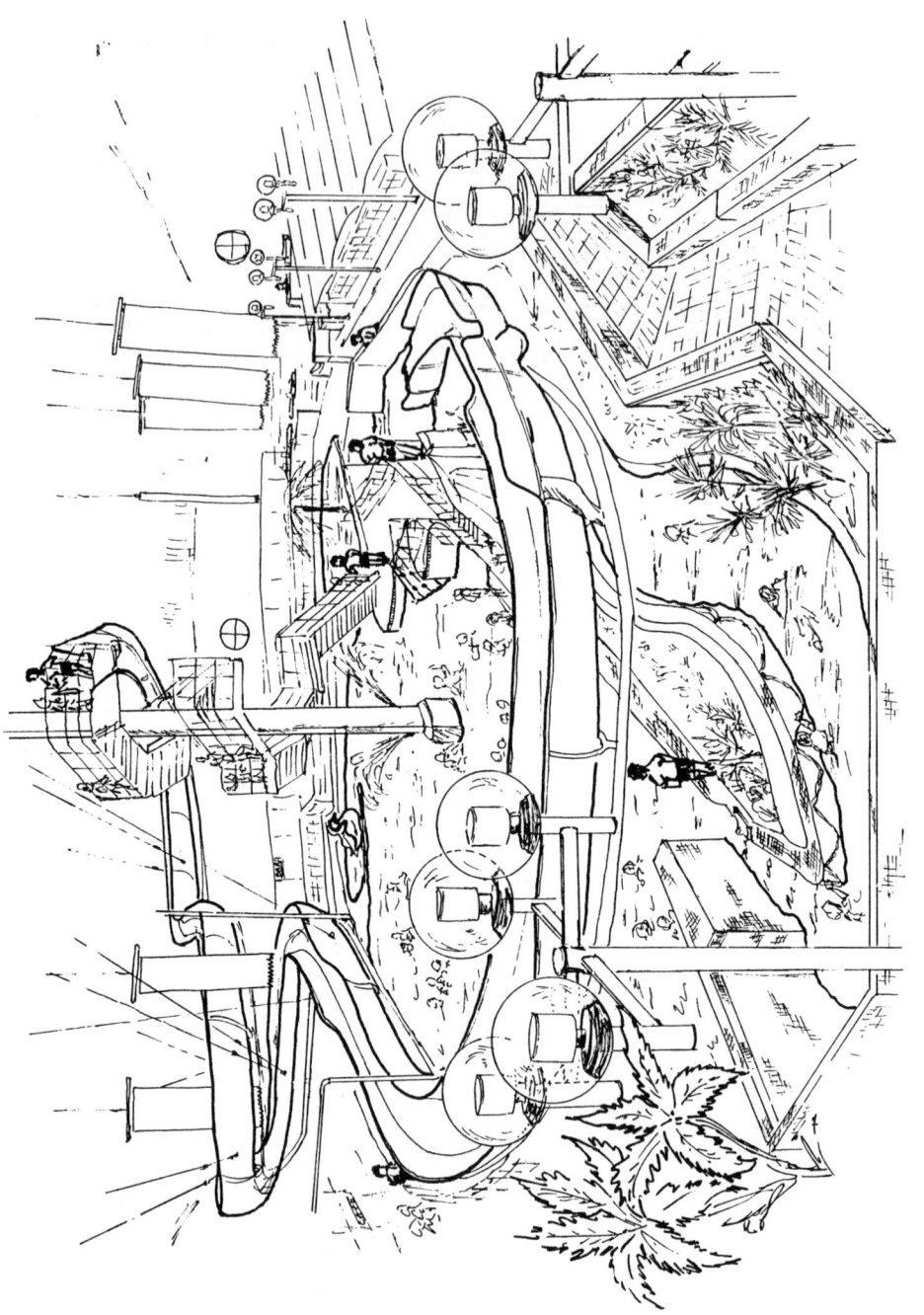

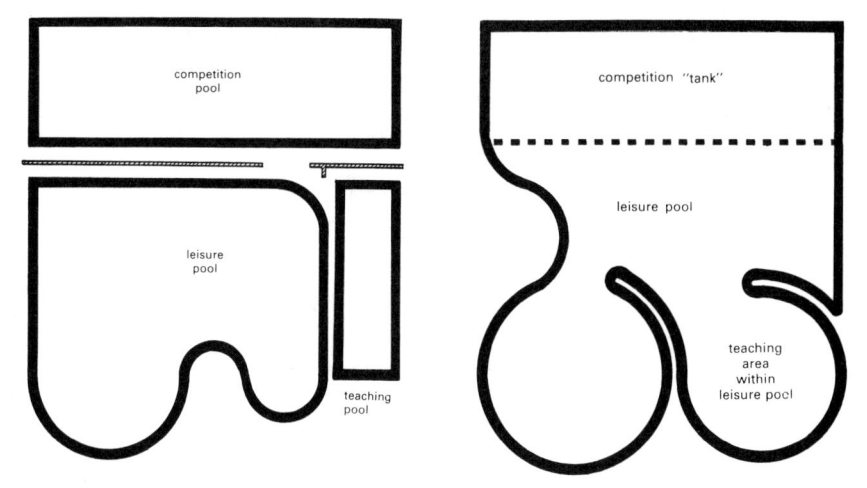

Figure 32 Ways in which a competition pool or "tank" might be incorporated into a leisure pool complex

HYGIENE REQUIREMENTS — SWIMMING POOLS

All swimming pool establishments have special requirements in respect of hygiene. The main reasons for this are as follows:

(a) A large number of bathers in close proximity to one another may be sharing a relatively small volume of water, which is an ideal medium for the transferance of many diseases and infections.

(b) Bathers wearing minimal clothing and walking around in bare feet are —

(i) particularly likely to pass on any infections that they may have;
(ii) particularly vulnerable to catching infections themselves.

(c) Pool water kept at a temperature which is comfortable for bathing, the warm, moist poolside and changing areas, and the humid atmosphere of swimming pool establishments are ideal environments for bacteria to multiply in.

There is, therefore, great potential for the creation of high levels of pollution and the transmission of diseases and infections from one bather to another, unless swimming pools can meet special hygiene requirements through their plant and filtration systems.

PLANT AND FILTRATION SYSTEMS

Swimming pool plant and filtration systems vary from pool to pool, but all have to perform the same basic functions. Very simply, these are:

```
STERILISE ──→ FILTER ──→ HEAT
     ↖         │         ↗
         CIRCULATE
```

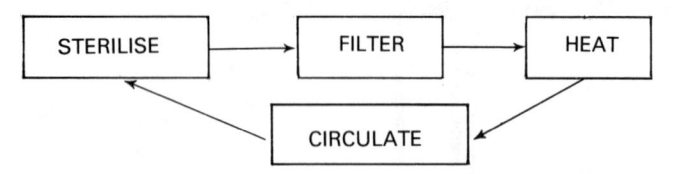

Figure 33 Swimming pool plant functions

Before discussing the processes in more detail it is necessary to define some basic terms:

(a) *Sterilise* — the process of killing off any living germs or bacteria in the pool water.
(b) *Filtration* — the process of purifying a fluid of solid matter by pouring it through porous material.
(c) *Solvent* — a liquid which is capable of dissolving a solid (eg water, white spirit).
(d) *Solute* — a solid which is capable of being dissolved, or is actually dissolved, in a liquid (eg salt, sugar, calcium hypochlorite).
(e) *Solution* — a liquid with solids dissolved in it.

pH values

pH values are numbers used to express the degree of acidity or alkalinity of a solution (eg swimming pool water).
  Low values are acid; neutral is seven; high values are alkaline.
  The pH of a swimming pool must be correctly controlled to ensure the effectiveness of disinfection, comfort of bathers and protection of pool hardware.
  The pH of a swimming pool should be within the range 7.2–7.8, ideally 7.2–7.6. The natural pH of the eye is 7.4.
  Lower values (acid) will cause smarting eyes and turn the pool water green.
  High values (alkaline) will turn the pool water green and cloudy and reduce chlorine effectiveness.

Sources of pollution

The principal sources of pollution in a swimming pool are the bathers themselves.

Other sources include spectators (especially where they have access to, or overlook, the poolside), airborne pollution, dirt from maintenance work carried out adjacent to the poolside area and particles produced by chemical reactions involving the water treatment chemicals. Examples of pollutants include:

- (a) sweat
- (b) urine
- (c) faeces
- (d) skin
- (e) saliva
- (f) cosmetics and make-up
- (g) suntan oil
- (h) food
- (i) dust and dirt
- (j) articles dropped from viewing areas.

These pollutants are not distributed evenly throughout the pool water. Much is concentrated near the surface of the water, especially in the top 5–10 cm, and consists of floating matter. Dissolved and suspended pollutants are more evenly distributed throughout the pool water with the heavier, insoluble materials sinking to the bottom of the pool.

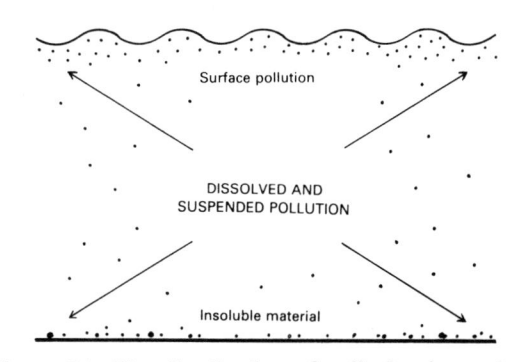

Figure 34   The distribution of pollution in pool water

Principal causes of eye irritation

If there are any problems with the quality of the pool water this is often very quickly indicated by soreness (redness) in the eyes of the pool users. The principal causes may be summarised as follows:

(a) incorrect pH levels in the pool water;

(b) reaction to the sterilising chemical (eg chlorine);
(c) sensitivity to pollutants in the water;
(d) water washing away tears from the eye allowing water to enter the epithelium (due to the lower salt concentration).

THE TREATMENT OF SWIMMING POOL WATER

Sterilisation

A wide range of chemicals are available for this purpose. Since most of the alternatives have their respective advantages and disadvantages, the final choice may depend upon a number of factors. These may include the degree of water hardness, whether it is an indoor or an outdoor pool and the cost and availability of supplies. The chemicals most commonly used are chlorine based bleaches. Examples include:

(a) sodium hypochlorite,
(b) calcium hypochlorite,
(c) chlorine gas.

Since bleaches are strong alkalis some acid, usually carbon dioxide gas or hydrochloric acid, has to be added to the water in order to re-establish an acceptable pH level before it is returned to the pool. (It should be noted, however, that hydrochloric acid *must not* be added to sodium hypochlorite, otherwise chlorine gas fumes will be produced.)

Filtration

This is, essentially, a very simple process. Most people have a basic understanding of filtration from their early school science lessons — separating an undissolved solid, usually sand, from a simple solution by pouring the mixture through a filter paper as shown in Figure 35.

A swimming pool filtration system works on exactly the same principle. Chemicals dissolved in the pool water pass through the filter, whilst undissolved and suspended pollutants are removed.

The most common types of filter in regular use are graded sand and layered sand and gravel media filters, although cartridge units containing a porous membrane may be used in some systems.

The effectiveness of the graded sand and gravel media filters is improved by the use of a flocculant which forms a floc or gel on the

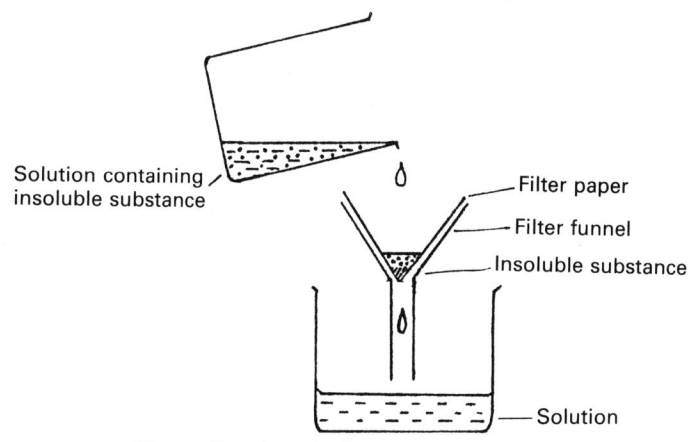

Figure 35 Simple filtration of solids

surface of the sand. Alum is a commonly used flocculant. In general, the longer that the water is in the filter the cleaner and clearer it will be. An example of a slow-rate sand and gravel media filter is shown in Figure 36.

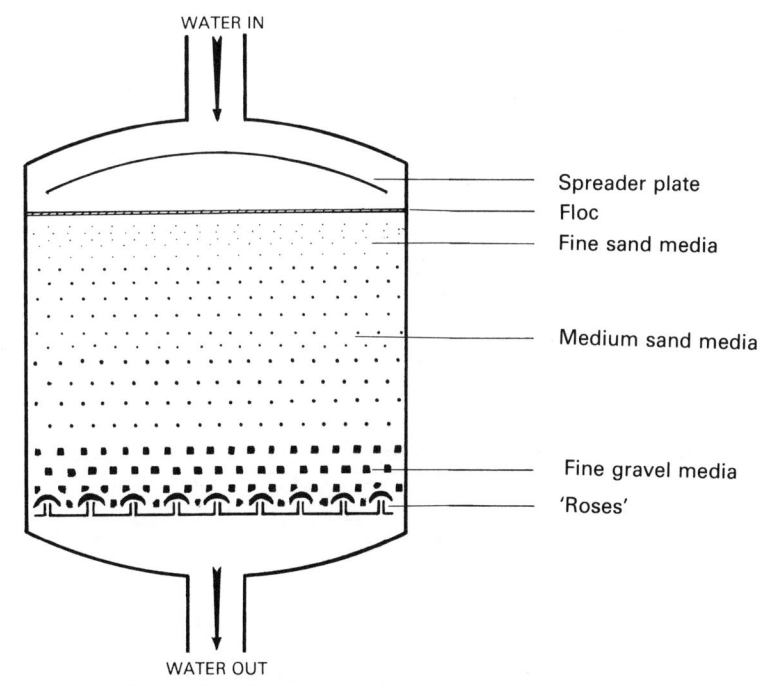

Figure 36 Slow rate sand and gravel media filter

The plant and filtration system may also need to be supplemented by the use of a pool suction cleaner to "hoover" the pool bottom in order to remove insoluble materials from the bottom of the pool. For large objects a net may also be used for this purpose.

Heating

A wide range of methods and many fuels are currently employed in the heating of pool water. However, whether gas, oil or solar panels are used the aim is the same — to bring the pool water to an acceptable temperature for bathing, usually between 27°–30°C, in a manner which is as cost effective and energy efficient as possible.

Circulation

Swimming pool water circulation systems are designed to ensure that all the pool water is purified and returned to the pool on a regular cycle, the frequency of which is determined by the type and size of the pool, the amount of use being made of it and the type of filtration system in that particular pool. Turnover rates may need to be as frequent as every 15–20 minutes where there is very heavy usage. Most public pools will work on a turnover of once every 3–4 hours.

In many pools the main flow is out from the deep end main drain, through the plant system, returning at the shallow end. Surface level draw-offs or scum channels compliment this main system and take out some of the most heavily polluted water for more frequent purification.

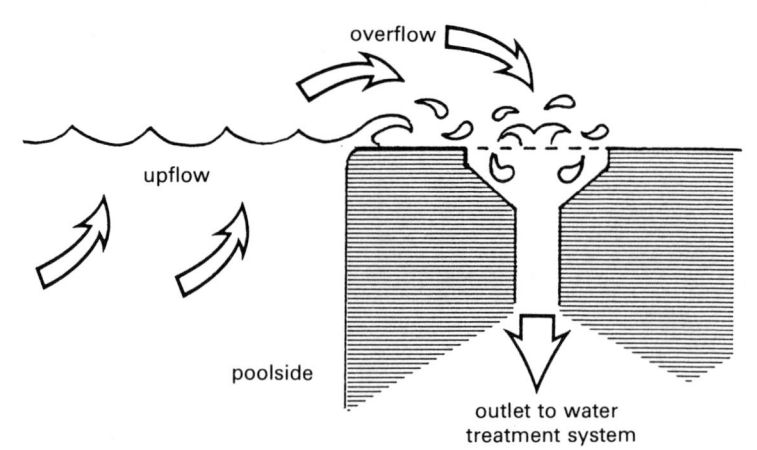

Figure 37 Surface level detail of upflow/overflow circulation

The flow of water around the system is maintained by one or more pumps. These are usually protected from damage by a strainer basket which prevents large solid objects (eg stones or rings) entering the pump. The water is then sterilised and filtered. Sterilising chemicals may be added either before or after the pool water has been filtered but if added before they reduce the likelihood of bacteria building up within the filter. Additional pipes and valves are included in the system to allow water to be pumped through the filter in the opposite direction in order to clean it. This process is known as a backwash. The frequency of backwashing will depend largely upon the size of the filter and the heaviness of pool use. It may vary by as much as once every few months to once every few hours. Most public pools will backwash once or twice a week.

The water is then passed through a heater or calorifier before being metered or tested and returned to the pool. The following diagram shows such a swimming pool and plant installation.

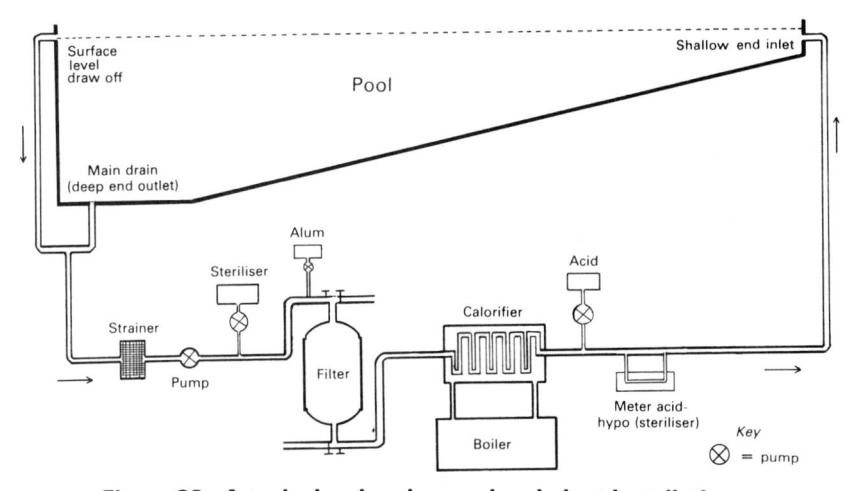

Figure 38 A typical swimming pool and plant installation

VENTILATION SYSTEMS

All sports buildings, but especially swimming pools, need continuous supplies of fresh air. A good ventilation system is essential for this. Fresh air clears moisture and smells and is necessary for the health of staff and customers but can also result in the unwanted loss of heat.

It is important for the safety of buildings to avoid cycles of cold and hot, dry and moist, otherwise the structure, particularly of roofs, can seriously deteriorate.

When used in conjunction with dehumidifers and heat recycling equipment considerable energy savings can be made.

COMMONLY USED TESTS OF SWIMMING POOL WATER

Although much metering, testing and analysis of pool water is now done automatically, some manual testing of the pool water is still necessary. Details of some commonly used tests and procedures are given below.

Collection of pool water samples

For all tests it is important that samples being tested are representative of the entire body of water. Samples should be taken from as far below the surface as possible and should not be taken adjacent to the inlet pipe unless it is for the express purpose of checking the composition of the water being returned to the pool.

The collection container, or comparison tube, should be rinsed several times with the water to be tested. The water sample should then be tested promptly after collection.

Testing for total and free chlorine

Total chlorine is the total amount of chlorine dissolved or suspended in the water. Free chlorine is that chlorine which is available to kill bacteria.

Different tests and kits exist. The one described using orthotolidine (OT), an organic compound, is only representative. Always read the kit instructions carefully; usually they will include most or all of the following:

(a) rinse the test cell in the water to be tested;
(b) fill the test cell to the graduation mark with the water to be tested;
(c) add the orthotolidine reagent in the amount specified in the kit instructions;
(d) cap the test cell and mix the contents;

(e) allow the specified time for maximum colour development, eg three minutes, and compare the colour with colour standards of known value.

At normal pool water temperatures OT reacts with the total chlorine content to produce a series of light yellow to deep orange colours as indicated in the figure below:

COLOUR	light straw colour	yellow shades	amber to orange-red
ppm	0.1–0.2	0.8–1.2	5.0–20.0
TOTAL CHLORINE	low levels		high levels

Figure 39 Scale for assessing total chlorine levels in swimming pool water

This is the *total* residual chlorine reading. For the *free* chlorine content, chill the sample to 1°C before testing. Free chlorine levels can also be tested using another organic compound, diethyl-p-phenylene-diamine (DPD).

Testing for pH

This test is conducted in a similar manner to the above by using an extremely sensitive organic dye on the water sample. Phenol red (pH range 6.8–8.2) is the commonly used pH indicator for swimming pool water testing.

Other tests

Other tests that are carried out on swimming pool water include:

(a) test for alkalinity;
(b) testing for hardness (total dissolved solids);
(c) testing for cyanuric acid (this is used as a chlorine extending agent).

FOOT INFECTIONS

Although effective pool water treatment considerably reduces the risk of most infections being passed from one pool user to another, prevention of the transmission of foot infections continues to be a problem.

The two most common foot infections are:

(a) verrucae (plantar warts);
(b) athlete's foot.

The reason why foot infections continue to be a problem is that, generally, they are picked up on the soles of the feet in either the changing room areas or the pool side and that both these infections thrive in warm moist conditions.

The most common methods of combating these infections are as follows:

(a) regular "mopping down" of the areas most at risk using a sterilising chemical (some pools use high pressure water hoses or steam hoses for cleaning changing room floors);
(b) the maintenance of as dry a changing room floor surface as possible;
(c) the provision of footbaths, usually between the changing areas and the pool side.

Modern leisure pools, with upflow/overflow circulation systems, have a relatively large amount of pool water, containing sterilising chemicals, constantly splashing over the poolside area, thus dispensing with the need for frequent mopping down. (See Figure 37, page 126.) Some pools use high pressure water hoses or steam hoses for cleaning changing room floors.

New pools may also have good underfloor heating in the changing areas which helps to keep these floors dry and relatively free of infection. The effectiveness of footbaths, however, is very much open to question.

Probably the most effective precaution is that which bathers can take for themselves — the simple one of just drying their feet very thoroughly before they put on their outdoor footwear.

SAFETY REQUIREMENTS

Safety requirements for swimming pools will initially be considered under two main headings:

(a) the safety of bathers and other users;
(b) the safety of personal property and belongings.

THE SAFETY OF BATHERS AND OTHER USERS

This is the area which causes most public concern, especially with respect to apparently preventable drownings. Consequently there has been considerable official interest in swimming pool safety, particularly with respect to the obligations of local authorities and others providing facilities for swimming, under the Health and Safety at Work, etc Act 1974. Responsibility for enforcing the Act rests with the Health and Safety Executive or the relevant local authority, depending upon the "main activity" on the site at which the pool is located.

An analysis of swimming pool drownings, based on a report published by RoSPA, shows that the numbers involved are very low in relation to:

(a) total deaths by drowning (between 500 and 900 per annum between 1975–1985);
(b) the number of visits to swimming pools (roughly estimated as 150 million per year by the Association of District Councils).

However, the actual number of drownings (between 18 and 55 per annum between 1975–1985) still gives cause for concern and, consequently, has a considerable influence on supervision and safety practice in swimming pools on a day to day basis.

However, an analysis of all accidents in swimming pools shows that the most common cause of accidental injury is, in fact, slipping on wet floors — frequently as a result of running on the pool side.

This clearly means that supervision and safety considerations must go beyond just the prevention of drownings and include a much wider range of possible hazards that might put bathers at risk.

Safety measures should be reflected in:

(a) pool design;
(b) rules of conduct and safety precautions for bathers;
(c) safety equipment provided;
(d) emergency procedures.

Pool design

Safety factors which should be included in pool design include:

(a) non-slip floor tiles on the pool side and in the changing areas;
(b) gently graduated pool depths, especially in leisure and teaching pools;
(c) the provision of specially designed diving pools with diving stages and springboards separate from the main pool;
(d) separate, or reserved, areas of the pool for waterslides, chutes and flumes to discharge into;
(e) such measures as may be necessary to ensure that glare from the windows does not prevent lifeguards from seeing bathers.

Safety precautions for bathers

Safety precautions for bathers can be said to fall into three main categories;

(a) safety on the poolside;
(b) safety in the pool;
(c) safety with regard to other users.

Rules of conduct

Examples of rules of conduct which fall within these categories include:

(a) do not run on the poolside;
(b) do not take breakable containers, eg glass, on to the poolside;
(c) do not swim after a heavy meal or after drinking alcohol;
(d) those suffering from a medical condition such as heart disease, epilepsy or asthma should be especially careful;

(e) do not push other people into the water or splash or duck others;
(f) avoid shouting and screaming;
(g) do not "bomb" into the water from the diving boards.

Safety equipment

The range of safety equipment commonly found and used in swimming pools is extensive, varied and constantly being updated. Examples include the following:

(a) safety hooks, throwing ropes, rings and floats;
(b) first aid and resuscitation equipment;
(c) raised observation chairs for the lifeguards;
(d) whistles and alarm buttons for the lifeguards;
(e) video equipment — this may be of particular value for regulating the use of waterslides and flumes where the full length of the slide cannot be supervised from a single vantage point;
(f) warning notices, eg "no diving", "deep end", etc;
(g) rails around the side of the pool where there are diving areas to prevent bathers jumping in from the side under divers.

Emergency procedures

In addition to the safety measures already discussed it is essential that staff are familiar with the procedure for dealing with other emergencies that could occur in any leisure environment. These include:

(a) disorderly behaviour;
(b) drowning, serious injury or illness;
(c) outbreak of fire and bomb scares;
(d) structural failures;
(e) emission of toxic gases;
(f) failure of the pool lighting.

THE SAFETY OF PERSONAL PROPERTY AND BELONGINGS

This is an area of greater concern for bathers than it is for users of other leisure facilities, largely because bathers have little option but to trust that their belongings will be safe either in the lockers provided or in the care of the swimming pool staff. It is very difficult for them to take care of their belongings on the pool side. This can place a considerable burden of responsibility upon the swimming pool staff.

Clothes storage

The main factors that need to be considered in clothes storage are:

(a) security of the belongings;
(b) supervision of the changing areas;
(c) the need to be able to regulate the time spent in the pool by bathers at peak use periods;
(d) the capacity of the storage spaces to cope with the number of bathers at peak use periods.

The two most commonly encountered methods of clothes storage are:

(a) basket and hanger,
(b) individual lockers.

Basket and hanger

This, the traditional method of storing clothes and personal belongings, has several particular advantages and disadvantages. These may be summarised as follows:

Advantages
(a) cheap and simple to install;
(b) economical in terms of space;
(c) very easy to regulate the time spent in the pool by bathers during periods of peak use;
(d) very often swimmers do not have to pay a deposit to use this system of storage.

Disadvantages
(a) requires a high degree of staff supervision;
(b) it is easy for items of clothing or personal effects to fall from the baskets or be stolen from them;
(c) bathers may hold members of the swimming pool staff responsible for the "loss" of items of personal property from baskets when they were not actually put there in the first place. Such incidents can very easily lead to unpleasant confrontations between staff and members of the public.

Individual lockers

Advantages
   (a) They require a much lower (relatively) level of staff supervision;
   (b) there is much less likelihood of accidental loss of property;
   (c) they can be much more secure;
   (d) lockers do not need to be situated in the changing area and may be sited adjacent to the pool.

Disadvantages
   (a) Good quality lockers can be very expensive to install;
   (b) cheap lockers are very susceptible to vandalism;
   (c) loss of keys and the subsequent need to change the locks can be a problem;
   (d) sufficient numbers of lockers to cope with peak levels of use may require very large amounts of space;
   (e) regulation of the amount of time spent in the pool by bathers at times of peak use may need careful organisation.

Notwithstanding these difficulties, attractive, good quality, vandal-proof lockers have now largely superceded the basket and hanger system of clothes storage. Furthermore, leisure pools are now attempting to encourage people to spend much greater lengths of time in the pool and its associated areas which has greatly reduced the need to attempt to regulate the amount of time spent actually in the water at these centres. This, combined with the use of colour coded armbands issued on entry, now tends to make any disadvantages associated with lockers in this respect irrelevant.

MAINTENANCE OF CHANGING ROOM AREAS

Swimming pool changing areas can present some particular problems when maintenance work has to be carried out. The principal difficulties, if the changing rooms are not to be taken out of use completely, are as follows:

   (a) the wet environment, coupled with an absence of power points, means that great care must be taken when using electrical tools;
   (b) bathers with bare feet are particularly vulnerable to injury by any sharp materials that may find their way on to the floor;

(c) the wet environment may increase the amount of time required for fixing compounds and cement to dry thoroughly;
(d) the predominance of the number of men currently employed in the carrying out of maintenance work may entail some reallocation of changing areas when it is those areas that are normally used as female changing rooms that are involved.

ENERGY SAVING IN SWIMMING POOLS

Swimming pools use considerable amounts of energy, primarily in heating the pool water and the air in the pool hall and, consequently, much attention has been focused upon modern methods of achieving high levels of cost and energy efficiency.

Areas where energy savings can be made include:

(a) ventilation,
(b) dehumidification,
(c) heat recovery.

Suitable economy measures include ensuring that:

(a) ventilation is matched to activity and occupancy levels;
(b) temperature and heating levels are carefully regulated throughout the day;
(c) existing energy is efficiently recycled and redistributed.

Other measures include:

(d) using pool covers where possible (these must be kept clean, however, as they can become an ideal medium for bacteria and micro organism growth);
(e) the use of lower ceilings;
(f) the reduced use of glass in order to minimise heat loss through windows.

COMMERCIAL INTEREST IN SWIMMING POOLS

In the past there has been a lack of commercial interest in swimming pools. This has been the result of a combination of factors:

(a) the high cost of building, staffing and maintaining swimming pools;

(b) the expense of treating the swimming pool water and maintaining comfortable levels of heating and humidity within the building;
(c) the relatively low price that bathers have expected to pay for the use of heavily subsidised local authority "swimming baths";
(d) the fact that all local authority swimming pools ran at a considerable financial deficit.

The advent, and considerable success, of the new leisure pools which make use of features such as waterslides, flumes, wave machines, water cannon and inflatables, and have good quality catering facilities, has meant that a much wider market interest has been generated and the public has been shown to consist of market sectors prepared to pay rather more than previously for the use of pools of this type. This, combined with modern plant and building systems, which are now much more cost and energy efficient, has meant that swimming pools can now be run much more cost effectively and, in consequence, there is currently a much greater commercial interest in building and running leisure pools in conjunction with other facilities. Future developments should continue to be both innovative and exciting.

SOFT LANDSCAPES

BASIC DEFINITIONS

Hard landscapes

Those relatively permanent brick and concrete structures and buildings that usually form the central feature of the site, eg the sports centre, swimming pool or office buildings.

Soft landscapes

The trees, shrubs, soil contouring, rock gardens and pathways, grassed areas and flower beds that are used to make the site look pleasant and attractive. These often serve a useful purpose as well, eg hedging.
The hard landscape in Figure 40 is the leisure centre itself which comprises the central feature of the site. The soft landscape consists, in this instance, of the trees, shrubs, rocks, soil contouring, pathways and fencing in the foreground.

Figure 40 Hard and soft landscapes

THE DESIGN, PLANTING AND ESTABLISHMENT OF SOFT LANDSCAPING

The stages involved in the design, planting and establishment of soft landscapes include:

(a) planning,
(b) design,
(c) costing,
(d) ordering materials,
(e) layout,
(f) cultivation of ground and soil area,
(g) seeding and planting,
(h) tidying of site,
(i) establishment.

} THE MAIN STAGES OF PLANTING

Planning

Successful landscaping depends on careful planning at an early stage before permanent site features have been built or erected, a thorough assessment of the site and the taking of the necessary precautions to retain valuable existing features, eg mature trees.

Plots may look alike but there are always subtle differences, either in the surroundings, contours, differing soil types or need for screening. The first duty, therefore, is to consider carefully one's aims and weigh these against the characteristics of the plot and the surrounding landscape.

An outline of the site and its existing features needs to be drawn, with the shape of any proposed buildings or features included and then any changes to the surroundings can be decided upon.

Design

There are a number of important principles to remember when designing a landscape. These include the following:

(a) Have a theme and carefully follow the ideal in the design wherever possible; for example, contemporary or classical layout. The theme may be the continuation of an existing one on the site but a naturalistic approach to urban open spaces is a current trend in landscape management.
(b) Achieve proportion and strive for a pleasing relationship between dimension, shape and height. By working in three dimensions added height may be achieved through the use of structures, contouring and planting.
(c) Consider the overall composition and aim for a balance of the site features; ie not all set to one side or with a heavy dependence upon one single feature.
(d) Find a focal point, define it as the centre of interest and draw the eye towards it.
(e) Develop mood, possibly by the use of local materials and stonework and by considering colour and shape.
(f) Consideration of the form, shape and proportion of the area to be soft-landscaped will, together with a knowledge of the soil and local climate, affect the choice of trees and shrubs to be used. These should include a good proportion of evergreens to ensure all year round balance, and the use of plants that will provide a variety of shapes, colour and texture to both give and maintain interest.
(g) Any barriers or enclosures that may be required can be constructed from a wide range of alternatives, including fencing, walls, hedges and shrubs.

Costing

Priorities are very often influenced by economics, particularly during times when tight financial budgets are being enforced. It is essential to make every effort to get good value for money whenever possible. One should still design and build the best all-purpose scheme within the budget allocated, even if it has to be carried out in several phases over a period of time.

Before obtaining a number of quotations from different suppliers visit as many as possible and check the quality of their products, especially nurseries (where the way in which they treat and handle their plants may have a critical effect upon their quality). By doing this it may be possible to reduce costs and allow a greater degree of development at each stage than would otherwise be possible.

Ordering materials

Once quotations have been received then materials can be ordered, preferably well in advance. This avoids delays and may mean that prices are lower than they might be later in the year. It also helps to ensure that stock will still be available when required.

Be *precise* and state, very clearly, *exactly*, what is required and whether there are any special delivery instructions.

When ordering state exactly what is required

Layout

This will include the initial site preparation and major landscaping, ie the actual contouring of the site, building of any permanent structures (eg walls) and siting of any major features (eg heavy stone or rocks) that will take place before any planting is done.

Cultivation of ground and soil area

Cultivation of the soil is, simply, the process of moving the soil particles, usually by digging, in order to increase aeration and improve drainage. These are essential requirements for any fertile soil.

Preparation of the site should begin at least two or three months before sowing takes place. More time will be needed if the site also needs levelling or special drainage.

First, any rubble or debris should be removed and cleared to one side. This can often be used as hard core for the foundations of paths or walls that may be built later.

Old tree stumps and roots have to be removed and weeds may need to be destroyed by the use of an appropriate weedkiller. Since soft landscaping will very frequently take place on sites that have been heavily disturbed by machinery (eg where building work has taken place) additional problems are likely to arise:

(a) Levelling, or grading, may be needed. (This is the process of removing the top soil, levelling the sub-soil and then replacing the top soil.)

(b) The soil may have become heavily compacted, in which case the sub-soil will also need to be thoroughly broken up.

(c) The top soil may have been heavily disturbed and unevenly distributed about the site and it may then be necessary to establish what the depth of the remaining top soil actually is — 20 cm or more is ideal. It it is less than 15 cm then additional top soil will have to be brought in for those areas that are to be planted.

(d) Very wet sites may also need to have some form of drainage system installed.

Depending upon the nature of the soil, whether sandy, clay or loam, some form of fertiliser or humus may need to be added (eg compost, peat, or well-rotted manure) and heavy soils may also need some very course sand or gravel to be dug in at the same time. Soils with severe pH problems may need some additional correction. Whenever practical, dig as deeply as possible in the autumn, thus allowing the winter frosts to break up the clods. Spring cultivation should be kept to the absolute minimum required for the plants that are to be grown, with the final preparation done when the soil is fairly dry.

Seeding and planting

Seeding

Bearing in mind local climatic conditions, there are several general rules that apply to all outdoor sowing:

(a) sow at the correct time of year;
(b) sow at the correct depth;
(c) do not sow the seed too deeply.

Failure to follow these rules will result in poor germination and thin, weak seedlings which may also be more susceptible to disease.

Planting

It is also possible to draw up a list of general rules that will apply to almost all planting situations:

(a) Always carefully check the condition of the plants on arrival in order to make sure that they have not been damaged during lifting, handling or transportation.

Always carefully check plant condition on arrival

(b) Check the plants delivered very carefully against the original order and make sure that any specific delivery instructions have been carried out.
(c) Do not plant out during hard weather, especially when the ground is frozen.
(d) Plant at the correct time of year (as a general rule, for perennials October is ideal for evergreens, although planting may be continued through until late February or early March, whilst November is ideal for many deciduous plants but this, again, may be continued through until late April or early May. Bedding plants are usually planted in October for spring display and during late May or early June for the summer).
(e) When planting, ensure that a hole has been dug which is large enough to accommodate all the roots comfortably and allow them to be spread out in all directions.
(f) The soil around the sides and bottom of the hole should be loosened and peat or compost mixed in with it so that this can be incorporated into the roots.
(g) Any pot grown plants must be thoroughly moist before planting (this may involve soaking the roots in a bucket of water).
(h) Do not insert the plant too deeply into the hole (for shrubs this usually means that there should not be any more than 2.5 cm of

When planting out do not insert the plant too deeply into the hole

soil above the top of the root ball, whilst for trees the soil should go no higher than the original soil mark on the stem).
(i) The soil around the roots must be made very firm when filling the hole, making use of full body weight (trees need support and should be tied to a stake whilst they are establishing themselves).
(j) Any damaged growth should be cut away after planting.
(k) Finally, a mulch can be applied around the base of the plants; this should be about 5cm deep and should help keep down weeds, but it should not touch the stem of the plant itself.

Tidying the site

This should be an on-going process. To leave weedkillers, in particular, where young children could gain access to them is inexcusable, but tools and cuttings, dead wood and rubbish must all be cleared away. It is good practice to have compost heaps sited close to where any tools are stored in order to reduce time spent walking between the two.

Establishment

Effective establishment requires carefully planned aftercare, particularly during the first growing season after planting. Obviously plants, especially trees and shrubs, may take several years to mature and they will do so at different rates according to the particular variety of tree or shrub, the soil, environment, climate and degree of maintenance provided.

As a rule, it is during the first year that a tree or shrub will establish itself and in many cases, dependent upon species, it will not grow much. During the next year, subject to appropriate maintenance, it may be expected to make more progress.

Hard frosts can loosen the roots of plants and lift them. In this event they should be made firm again by treading. Cultivation of the area around newly planted stock should be avoided and kept to the minimum required to control weeds. Any weeding must be done with care in order to avoid damaging surface roots. This is another good reason why the use of mulches to suppress weeds is desirable (they also help to conserve moisture). Weedkillers may be used but considerable care is needed. Hedges, depending upon their variety, may need careful pruning, cutting back or may need to be left alone and it is important to check upon the needs of the particular plant at the outset.

Trees, especially if required for screening, may take up to seven years to make a serviceable head and during this period, particularly in the first year or two, they are vulnerable to vandalism. Consequently it has been common practice initially to plant several trees close together in small clumps to form barriers (mainly for mutual protection) and then select a single healthy tree once they are established (the remainder are discarded). This is not always possible, however, and quite badly vandalised trees often recover fairly well and form a serviceable head.

It has been found that it is often much better to use single, large, container-grown trees instead. They give an instant effect and are more resistant to vandals.

Whichever method is used, some aftercare will still be necessary. Stakes should be renewed, if necessary, until the tree is wind-firm and the ties adjusted to allow for stem growth. The soil over the roots of newly planted young trees should be kept free of grass and weeds otherwise this will severely affect establishment. Only once the trees are well established may they be undersown with a rough durable grass. This often requires little maintenance and may need relatively few mowing cuts per year.

Watering should not be necessary for the establishment of trees unless drought conditions are encountered.

PLAYING SURFACES FOR INDOOR AND OUTDOOR RECREATIONAL ACTIVITIES

Today there is an increasingly wide range of different types of playing surface available for indoor and outdoor recreational activities. They all have different characteristics, which include:

(a) the degree and type of routine and specialised maintenance that is required to keep them serviceable;
(b) the ways in which pitches and courts may be marked on them;
(c) the effect that they may have upon the way a particular game is played.

BASIC DEFINITIONS

It is therefore necessary to attempt to categorise the different surfaces in some way, in order to simplify the process of comparing them and considering their respective advantages and disadvantages. To begin with the simplest, and most commonly used, distinction to make is to determine whether the surface may be regarded as being either "natural" or "artificial". This is not necessarily as obvious a distinction as it may first appear, as it depends more upon how the surface is put together and maintained than it does upon the materials from which it is constructed. The most useful and commonly applied definitions are those provided by the Sports Council (from "Specifications for Artificial Sports Surfaces", see Bibliography).

Natural sports surface

". . . a sports surface formed by the suitable preparation of an area of land; this may be taken to include loose mineral layers."

Such loose mineral layers would include all-weather pitches of the "red-gras" type, popular in the early 1970s, and still in common use today. Grass turf, obviously, is regarded as a natural surface but so are water, snow and ice, no matter how artificially created or manipulated they may be.

The loose particulate surfaces used as safety areas below outdoor climbing walls and children's play equipment (eg sand, gravel, bark chippings and even synthetics) are also regarded as natural surfaces.

Artificial sports surface

". . . a sports surface formed by a layer or layers of suitably processed and formed material laid so as to produce an essentially continuous and bound-together surface."

Such a definition also includes those essentially continuous surfaces produced from natural materials that have undergone a manufacturing process. This, therefore, will include sprung wooden floors as well as those surfaces that are clearly synthetic (eg produced from plastic, rubber or textiles).

NATURAL	ARTIFICIAL
(a) grass turf (b) water (c) ice (d) snow (e) sand (f) gravel (g) loose bark chippings (h) particulate mineral layer (shale)	(a) concrete (b) asphalt (c) composition block (d) textiles (e) rubber (f) plastic (g) wooden floor (h) polymeric (i) sprung floor

Figure 41 Examples of natural and artificial sports surfaces

Advantages and disadvantages of artificial surfaces

Advantages
- (a) Usable in almost any weather conditions.
- (b) Will withstand almost constant use and, provided that they are well lit, may be used 24 hours a day, 52 weeks a year (subject to the needs of local residents).
- (c) Usually require much less routine maintenance and remarking.
- (d) Usually give a truer and faster playing surface with consistent bounce.
- (e) Where existing ancillary facilities are already of a high standard, the additional use that can be made of these (eg stadium, bar and catering facilities) may help to make the artificial surface cost effective.

Disadvantages
- (a) Very expensive to install and, when necessary, to repair. It may, consequently, take a very long time for the surface to break-even financially, if, indeed, it is possible at all.
- (b) The high rebound resistance and high speed of a ball off many surfaces may be undesirable for some sports.
- (c) Some governing bodies (eg EUFA) may not accept artificial surfaces as appropriate for some of their competitions.
- (e) The nature of the surface may cause a high incidence of friction burns or stress related injuries.
- (f) It may be necessary to purchase special footwear to protect either the surface or the participants from damage or injury.

These may be alternatively classified as:

(a) heavy duty indoor/outdoor;
(b) medium duty indoor/outdoor.

Examples of these are given below.

HEAVY DUTY SURFACES (Class A)	USE
concrete	multi-purpose indoor and **outdoor general use** eg netball, tennis, five-a-side **football**
coated macadam (asphalt, bitumen)	multi-purpose **outdoor general use** eg netball, **tennis**
composition block tiles	multi-purpose indoor general use eg sports halls; badminton, five-a-side football
MEDIUM DUTY SURFACES (Class B)	USE
sprung floor	multi-purpose indoor general use eg badminton, aerobics squash, judo, gymnastics
polymeric (rubbers and plastics)	multi-purpose indoor and outdoor general use eg basketball
timber	indoor multi-purpose eg dance floors, basketball, table tennis, badminton martial arts

Figure 42 Uses of heavy and medium duty surfaces

When comparing the characteristics of the different surfaces it is now necessary to consider their performance parameters and in order to be able to do this a much wider range of terms and definitions must be considered.

PERFORMANCE PARAMETERS OF SPORTS SURFACES

These may be regarded as consisting of the following:

(a) rebound resiliance —
    (i) ball/surface,

(ii) person/surface;
(b) substrate effects;
(c) stiffness;
(d) friction;
(e) rolling resistance;
(f) spin;
(g) resistance to set;
(h) wear and weathering;
(i) comparison with natural surfaces.

Other factors which are important and may affect the choice of surface, particularly in indoor sports halls, are the extent of the range and nature of the activities that are to be catered for, and the quietness of the surface in use (sprung wooden floors can be particularly noisy).

Finally, the surface should be of a colour that is restful to the eye and does not distract from the court markings made on it. A matt finish avoids, or reduces, glare from sunlight or artificial light.

Rebound resiliance

This is the ratio of the *energy returned* after impact to the *energy put in*.

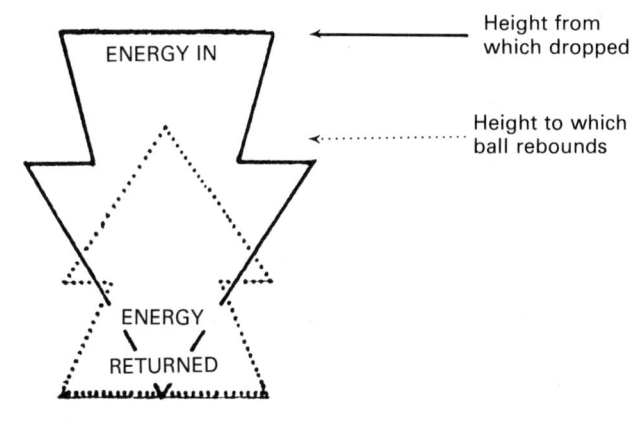

Figure 43 Rebound resiliance (i) ball/surface

Ball/surface

This can be measured by dividing the height to which a ball rebounds by the height from which it was dropped. Different surfaces will have different rebound resiliance.

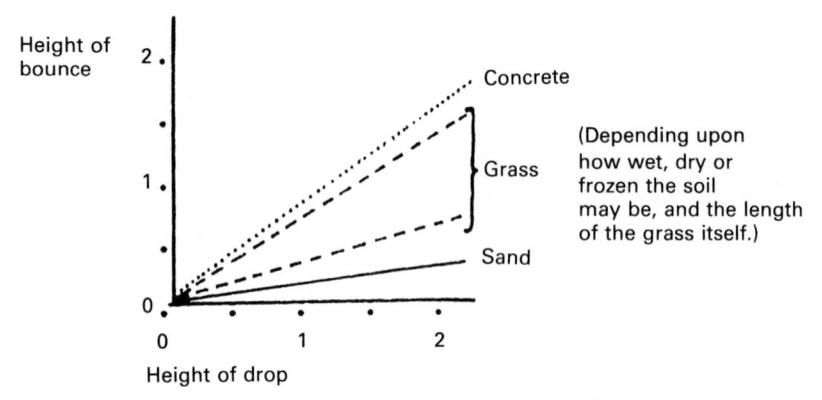

Figure 44 Rebound resiliance (ii) person/surface

Person/surface

This is more difficult to objectively measure but it is of importance as, together with stiffness, it will have a considerable bearing upon the extent of any risk of injury, especially in contact sports.

Substrate effects

These are the effects that the layer or layers of material below the top playing surface have upon the performance of the top surface. These layers are referred to as *substrata*. They may be an essential component of the surface or merely its base. The substrata particularly affect rebound resistance and stiffness, eg the same artificial cricket matting

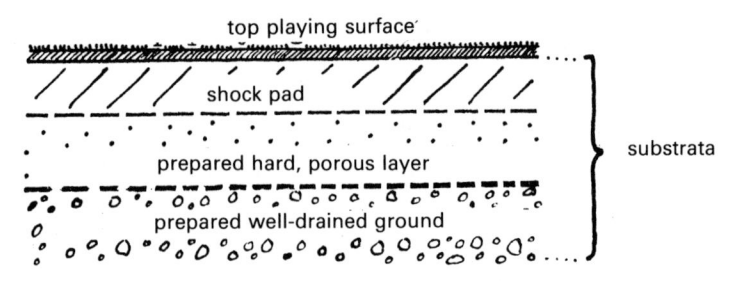

Figure 45 Substrata — outdoor synthetic surface

may be made to produce a bounce conducive to either fast or spin bowling dependent upon the nature of the pad it is placed upon. The substrata also affect the resistance of the top surface to damage and its drainage qualities. These may be seen in Figure 46.

Stiffness

This is measured by the ratio of applied force to the deflection of the surface, ie the degree of "give" that it has for a specified force. In simple terms it refers to how hard or soft the surface is.

Friction

This is the extent of the force that opposes movement between any two surfaces in contact with one another. In the context of sports playing surfaces this contact is likely to be between the player, or the player's footwear, and the floor. It is commonly referred to as traction and is necessary to allow for free movement without a substantial risk of accidental slipping (except in sports such as skiing or ice skating, where particularly low levels of friction are essential). Low levels of friction reduce the risk of friction burns (a complaint often levelled against a number of artificial surfaces). The presence of water significantly alters the level of friction and many surfaces are artificially watered to maintain optimum levels (eg artificial ski slopes and synthetic turf pitches).

Rolling resistance

This is the degree to which a surface slows down a ball rolling across its surface. It is particularly important in sports like hockey, Association football and bowls. Synthetic turf pitches have had a rather mixed reception in Association football (where the ball has a tendency to move very quickly over the surface) whilst in field hockey, international matches are now seldom played on grass turf at all (largely due to the high degree of consistency and evenness of synthetic pitches).

Spin

The degree to which a ball will spin on any given surface is determined by the friction between the ball and the surface and the stiffness of the surface.

This is particularly important in sports such as cricket and tennis and synthetic surfaces for these activities are designed with this in mind. Artificial cricket wickets frequently have reverse pimples under the synthetic turf in order to improve the spin of the ball off the wicket. This is illustrated in the figure below:

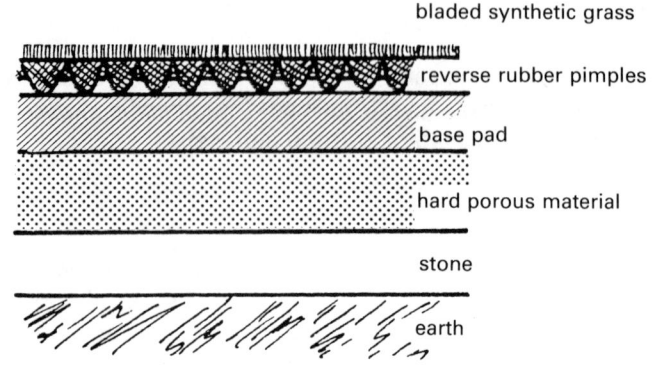

Figure 46 Synthetic cricket wicket

(Layers shown: bladed synthetic grass, reverse rubber pimples, base pad, hard porous material, stone, earth)

Resistance to set

This is the ability of the surface to withstand repeated local impacts without becoming permanently deformed. It is especially important where a smooth surface is required (eg the area where the ball pitches on a cricket wicket).

Wear and weathering

Due to the quite considerable initial financial outlay involved in the installation of almost all playing surfaces it is important that they represent good value for money. This means that they must have a long life and, consequently, must be able to withstand heavy use and, if outdoors, exposure to the elements.

Comparison with natural surfaces

This usually refers to a comparison between the playing characteristics of an artificial surface and those of natural grass turf or the surface upon which a particular sport or activity is traditionally played (eg artificial ski slope matting and snow).

The aim, of course, is to produce a surface that matches the essential playing characteristics of the natural surface in virtually all respects so that the essential characteristics of the game, and the way that it is played, are not adversely affected or altered.

Sprung floors

These are installed where there is a need, for example in sports like gymnastics and judo, for the floor to have good qualities of *shock absorption* (ie be able to absorb impact).

Most mats and many playing surfaces are what is known as *point elastic* (ie they give at the point of contact but there is no elasticity in the surface away from that point). However, sprung floors are mounted on wooden joists which act as springs and allow a large area of the floor to give, or deflect, under heavy impact. This is often termed *area elastic*. The figure below illustrates the difference between point elasticity and area elasticity.

Point elastic at mat under small force

No movement of sprung floor

Point elastic at mat and area elastic deflection of sprung floor under heavy impact

Figure 47 Point and area elasticity

153

EXAMPLES OF APPROPRIATE SURFACES FOR VARIOUS RECREATION ACTIVITIES

Firstly it must be stated that any judgement of what is an appropriate surface for any given recreational activity will be a subjective one. Ideas on what is appropriate will also change with time, technological advances and improvements to existing and new surfaces. However, a traditional surface will, for many people, continue to be the most appropriate one for their chosen activities. The following are listed only to give a starting point:

Recreational Activity	Surface
Association football and Rugby football	Natural grass turf
Bowls (outdoor)	Natural grass turf
Bowls (indoor)	Carpet, preferably green, laid on a specially designed base
Cricket (outdoor)	Natural grass turf wicket
Dance and aerobics	Sprung wooden floor
Gymnastics	Specially designed mats on a sprung floor
Martial arts	Usually a sprung wooden floor with tatame (mats) for judo and aikido
Squash	Sprung wooden floor

Figure 48 Surfaces appropriate to different recreational activities

Many sports are now played on such a wide variety of surfaces that it is difficult to reach agreement about which type may be regarded as appropriate to a particular activity.

Lawn tennis is a good example. Traditionally played on grass turf, it is now played on many other types of surface all around the world, both indoors and outdoors, and all are considered appropriate for major international competition.

Field hockey, again traditionally played on grass turf, is now played almost exclusively on synthetic surfaces at international level.

Handball, volleyball and basketball are all other activities that may take place on many different types of surface and for which no single surface is obviously appropriate.

COURT AND PITCH MARKINGS

Indoor court markings

Indoor courts may be marked in a number of different ways. The principal methods are:

(a) taped markings;
(b) painted lines;
(c) inlaid sections;
(d) pre-marked polymer mats and carpets.

The relative advantages and disadvantages of these methods may be summarised as shown in Figure 49.

Outdoor court and pitch markings

Outdoor courts and pitches present a rather different set of problems with regard to marking as there is a much wider range of surfaces to be considered, each with very different characteristics, and the additional problems that are associated with weathering also have to be considered. Surfaces that will require marking include:

(a) grass,
(b) tarmac (asphalt),
(c) concrete,
(d) shale,
(e) synthetics, including artificial turf.

The principal methods available for marking these surfaces are:

(a) wet lime,
(b) creosote,
(c) paint,
(d) tape.

The relative uses, advantages and disadvantages to these methods are summarised in Figure 50.

METHOD	ADVANTAGES	DISADVANTAGES
TAPED MARKINGS	(a) Easy and quick to lay/correct (b) Suitable for temporary markings (c) May be used immediately after laying (d) Good range of colours available	(a) Not very durable and can soon look untidy (b) Not as effective on walls or rough surfaces (c) More expensive than paint (d) Usually requires two people to lay.
PAINTED LINES	(a) Easy to lay by one person (b) Quite durable and easy to remark or retouch (c) Cheap (d) Effective on walls and rough surfaces	(a) Difficult to correct or remove (b) Need for remarking when floor is sanded (c) Need to allow ample time for paint to dry.
INLAID SECTIONS	(a) Very durable — will withstand vigorous cleaning and sanding (b) The quality of the lines is maintained throughout its lifetime (c) The lines can still be overlaid using other methods	(a) Are permanent and must be laid accurately first time (b) Expensive to install (c) Require specialists to install them (d) Very expensive to repair or alter (e) Only suitable for certain types of flooring (d) Only a limited range of colours is available
PRE-MARKED POLYMER MATS AND CARPETS	(a) Both court and lines are very boldly indicated (b) There is no possibility of confusion with other markings (c) Particularly suitable for televised events (d) Can be laid over other markings	(a) Very expensive to buy and repair (b) Only one court can be marked on each mat (c) They are bulky to store and awkward to transport (d) Time consuming to lay out and must be laid with great care to avoid rucking

Figure 49 Advantages and disadvantages of different methods of marking indoor courts

METHOD	ADVANTAGES	DISADVANTAGES
WET LIME	(a) Suitable for grass and shale (b) Safe and attractive (c) Cheap, quick and easy to lay (d) May be used dry (e) Easy to remove	(a) Frequent remarking needed, especially after heavy rain or grass cutting (b) Unsatisfactory on other surfaces
CREOSOTE	(a) Suitable for grass (b) Semi-permanent (c) Creates good guidelines for lime	(a) Takes 2–3 seasons to grow out (b) Can burn if it gets in contact with the skin and is unpleasant to handle (c) Is unattractive (d) Is unsuitable for any other surface
PAINT	(a) Suitable for tarmac, concrete and synthetic surfaces (b) Resistant to weathering and wear	(a) Relatively expensive (b) Relatively time-consuming to lay
TAPE	(a) Suitable for tarmac, concrete and synthetic surfaces (b) Quite resistant to weathering and wear	(a) Relatively, even more expensive (b) Adhesion of some types of tape to certain synthetic surfaces is questionable

Figure 50 Advantages and disadvantages of different methods of marking outdoor pitches

The advantages and disadvantages stated above are additional to those already listed for indoor courts.

Inlaid sections could be used for outdoor synthetic courts and the use of plastic cones and discs, sand and sawdust to provide quickly set out temporary courts and markings should not be overlooked.

Although line marking may be done by hand there are several machines available which simplify this task. Some examples are shown in Figures 51, 52 and 53.

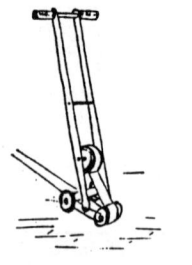

Figure 51 Line marking machine for laying floor tape

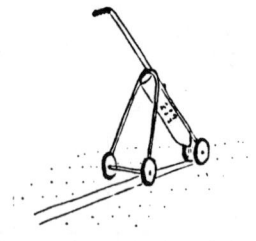

Figure 52 Line marker for spraying lines on to hard surfaces (eg asphalt tennis courts)

Figure 53 Line marker for laying wet lime on grass pitches. Machines of a very similar type which spray the lime, instead of using the central wheels, are also suitable for marking loose mineral surfaces

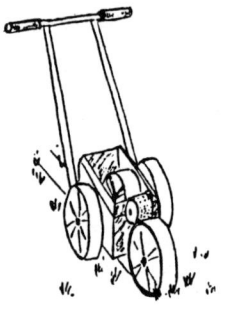

PLAY AREAS FOR CHILDREN

"Play" revisited

For the purpose of looking at the principal factors affecting the design and siting of children's play areas, a broader view of what constitutes play is required than has been used so far.

It is broadly agreed that play is about, and provides opportunities for, those activities and games that children engage in:

(a) of their own free choice;
(b) in the way that they want to;
(c) solely for their own reasons and the value of doing the activity for its own sake.

158

Play forms a crucial role in children's learning and development. It is very much a natural process and part of normal "growing up" and is every bit as creative and imaginative as it is social and physical. These factors must be taken into account when assessing children's play needs.

Although parents are generally held to be the main influence on children's lives, the idea that local authorities should be involved in the provision of play areas and play equipment has long since gained acceptance. Increasingly the private and commercial sector is also recognising the value of providing quality play provision as a means of encouraging families to visit leisure attractions and facilities. This, coupled with concern about the effect that the built environment is having upon children and concerns over the safety of playgrounds and the type of equipment provided within them, has led to a considerable amount of thought and discussion of the issues involved. As a result of this the range and quality of equipment available has increased considerably over recent years.

FACTORS AFFECTING THE DESIGN AND SITING OF PLAY AREAS

The principal factors affecting the design and siting of play areas designated for use by children are:

(a) safety from physical hurt;
(b) ease of supervision;
(c) appropriateness of furniture and equipment in terms of size, texture and material;
(d) availability of adequate toilet facilities;
(e) safe distance from moving equipment or adult sports areas.

Safety from physical hurt

This is the most obvious and immediate consideration for those who are concerned with providing for children's play and for parents whose children may be using the facilities provided. There are, potentially, very many possible dangers and sources of physical injury:

(a) impact with the play equipment (eg being struck by a swing);
(b) falling from the play equipment to the ground (eg from the top of a

slide) or on to other play equipment lower down (eg bars across the bottom of a climbing frame);
(c) being caught in, or crushed by, the play equipment (eg getting fingers caught inside the mechanism of a see-saw, or being caught underneath a roundabout that has insufficient ground clearance);
(d) impact with the floor (eg as a result of stumbling);
(e) collisions with other children (particularly those on skateboards and cycles or playing football);
(f) vandalised equipment and equipment in a poor state of repair is an additional source of risk (particularly where there are sharp or jagged edges or where equipment may give way under stress). Consequently there is a need for regular inspection and maintenance.

Certain health risks can also be considered within this section. Animals, particularly stray dogs, could represent a danger to children. Apart from the obvious risk of being bitten there are also risks associated with their excrement fouling the playground, the most serious being toxocara and hydatid. Cats too, can also be a problem, especially if sand or bark cuttings have been used as a safety surface. These surfaces may also be prone to infestation by insects, particularly ants. If such safety surfaces are to be used then a suitable dog-proof fence should be erected and self closing gates installed. These are also useful in keeping bicycles out and small children in. There is an excellent range of safety surfaces already available and more are being developed all the time. Many can also be painted or marked, in much the same way that school playgrounds are, to give additional play opportunities.

Supervision considerations

Even if playgrounds themselves are safe, there is still a need for supervision. Children, especially younger ones, may be attracted away from the play areas on to roads, railway lines, building sites or open water (eg canals, rivers or lakes). The dangers of bullying or molestation also have to be considered.

Some play provision is directly supervised by teachers, playleaders, or parents but many playgrounds rely upon indirect supervision from passers-by and nearby residents whose homes overlook the play area. This clearly has implications with regard to the design and siting of play areas:

(a) they should be sited well away from main roads, canals and other sources of danger;
(b) consideration should be given to "sight lines" from nearby houses (ie siting play facilities where they may be overlooked, and therefore supervised, by adults from inside their own homes);
(c) they should be sited close to footpaths regularly used by local residents;
(d) seating and, if possible, shelter should be provided for adults accompanying children;
(e) the area should have adequate lighting at night.

Choosing the type of play equipment to be provided

When considering the appropriateness of equipment in terms of size, design and materials, the needs of the community for whom the play area is intended must be taken into account. The number of children, their probable age profile, the proximity of existing play and recreation facilities and the type of housing around the area all help to determine needs.

Existing provision may include parks, open spaces, playgrounds, adventure playgrounds, playcentres, leisure centres or playbuses. However, in the past insufficient attention has been paid to what children's play needs really are. Much existing provision is actually inappropriate. Children's play provision must be child-orientated and, clearly, children have different needs at different ages.

Physical activities that children may wish to engage in include swinging, sliding, hanging, climbing, balancing, going round and round and up and down. It is possible to design play equipment that caters for

161

many of these activities in such a way as to include basic "box-like" shapes and spaces that could, imaginatively, be anything that the child wishes.

Play areas are also used as meeting places for children, including older ones who may go on to play elsewhere; it is therefore desirable that the play area is attractive. The use of bright colours, murals, flora and landscaping should be considered.

The biggest constraint on the choice of equipment, once needs have been established, is likely to be that of finance. Tight budgets may mean that careful consideration has to be given to ensuring that the equipment purchased not only gives value for money but also good play value. The two are not necessarily mutually exclusive. Play value is concerned with the quality and variety of play experience available to the child. Some ill-chosen equipment has very quickly been vandalised because, from the child's point of view, there is very little else that can be done with it. Some phasing of provision over a relatively long period of time may be necessary and, consequently, careful long-term planning is essential.

Provision of toilet facilities

Where the play area has been provided within an existing public park it is almost certainly going to be the case that toilet facilities will already be provided. However, public toilets are, all too frequently, unsuitable places for young children. Private sector toilet facilities tend to be both cleaner and more closely supervised and maintained. Theme parks, motorway service areas and public houses hoping to encourage families to make repeat visits tend to have the resources to ensure that this is the case and recognise the commercial value in doing so. This is not to say that there are not many examples of good quality facilities provided by local authorities but, especially when budgets are tight, it should be remembered that if play areas are sited close enough to children's homes then adequate toilet facilities will already exist there.

Siting of play areas and adult sports areas

This area has already been largely covered in the earlier section when safety was considered. Two further points are, however, worthy of mention:

    (a) areas intended for the use of older children, such as kick-about spaces, represent a source of danger to smaller children;
    (b) cricket balls are potentially lethal when struck firmly by an adult.

Figure 54 An example of a small well-designed play area

It is important that there is sufficient distance between such areas or, if this is not possible, that those areas designated for the use of young children are adequately protected, if necessary by fencing.

This small play area is based upon one situated within a countryside park near Lightwater, Surrey. It has used natural materials in order to be compatable with the countryside surrounding it. It is situated close to the main footpath, has some seating provision for adults accompanying children and a fence with a gate in it to keep dogs out and little children in.

Natural bark chippings have been used to provide a safety surface that is both effective and appropriate to the surroundings. Apart from the swings, which have a low barrier between them and the rest of the play equipment (to prevent children running into them), the equipment is well integrated and offers opportunities for climbing, sliding and imaginative play on a relatively modest budget.

RESOURCE MANAGEMENT

Exercise 1 Shift work

Visit a local leisure centre and find out what shift systems are in operation and how they work. In particular try to find out:

(a) if the same shift system is in operation for all parts of the centre (there may be a different system for the swimming pool to that worked on the "dry" side or in other parts of the centre, eg in the snooker hall);

(b) whether staff are able to easily calculate when their duties and days off are going to be well in advance (ie is the shift system simple or complicated?);

(c) what the contribution of part-time staff is and how this affects the hours of the full-time staff;

(d) how does the shift system cope with periods of intense use (eg school holidays);

(e) compare the system(s) in use in the leisure centre that you have visited with either those described earlier or those in operation in another leisure centre that you know of, and comment upon any differences and try to give reasons for them.

Exercise 2 Health and safety

Produce a plan of a particular recreational environment. The recreational environment should be one of the following:

(a) an indoor recreation centre or sports club;
(b) a restaurant, cinema or night club;
(c) a stadium or professional football club ground.

On the plan indicate all items and features installed in the interests of health and safety, including:

(a) emergency telephones;
(b) fire alarms, fire exits and assembly points;
(c) first aid boxes and equipment.

Exercise 3 Swimming pools

Make a visit to a local swimming pool. Draw a diagram of the pool hall and pool shape. On the diagram indicate the following:

(a) all items of equipment provided in the interests of health and safety;
(b) areas of the pool where bathers may be at particular risk (eg under diving boards);
(c) indicate those positions around the poolside taken up by lifeguards during periods of intensive use, giving reasons or explanations as appropriate.

Exercise 4 Soft landscapes

Visit a number of different types of local leisure facilities and note the extent to which the buildings and any other hard landscaping features have been landscaped softly, and the ways in which this has been achieved.

If possible include reference to a modern shopping mall or retail development within this study.

The report should be illustrated by sketches or photographs and include some comment on the effectiveness of the soft landscaping in attracting customers to the facilities.

Extensive indoor use of trees, shrubs and bedding plants at the Mediterranean Village Gateshead MetroCentre

Exercise 5 Play areas

(a) What factors need to be taken into account when considering the design and siting (location) of areas designed for use by children? List them under the following headings together with examples:

DESIGN	LOCATION

Note

It is often useful to list the main problems and hazards that may arise from use, or misuse, of play areas and to then consider ways of avoiding or minimising these problems at the design stage.

(b) On the diagram opposite consider where you might site areas for the use of children and recommend the equipment you would place in those areas.

(c) Visit and survey a local play area. You should note the following:

   (i) the location of the play area and the area it serves
   (ii) the proximity of any potential hazards
   (iii) the size, nature, integration, safety and play value of the equipment provided.

Include sketch maps/diagrams in your answer and make comments and recommendations.

167

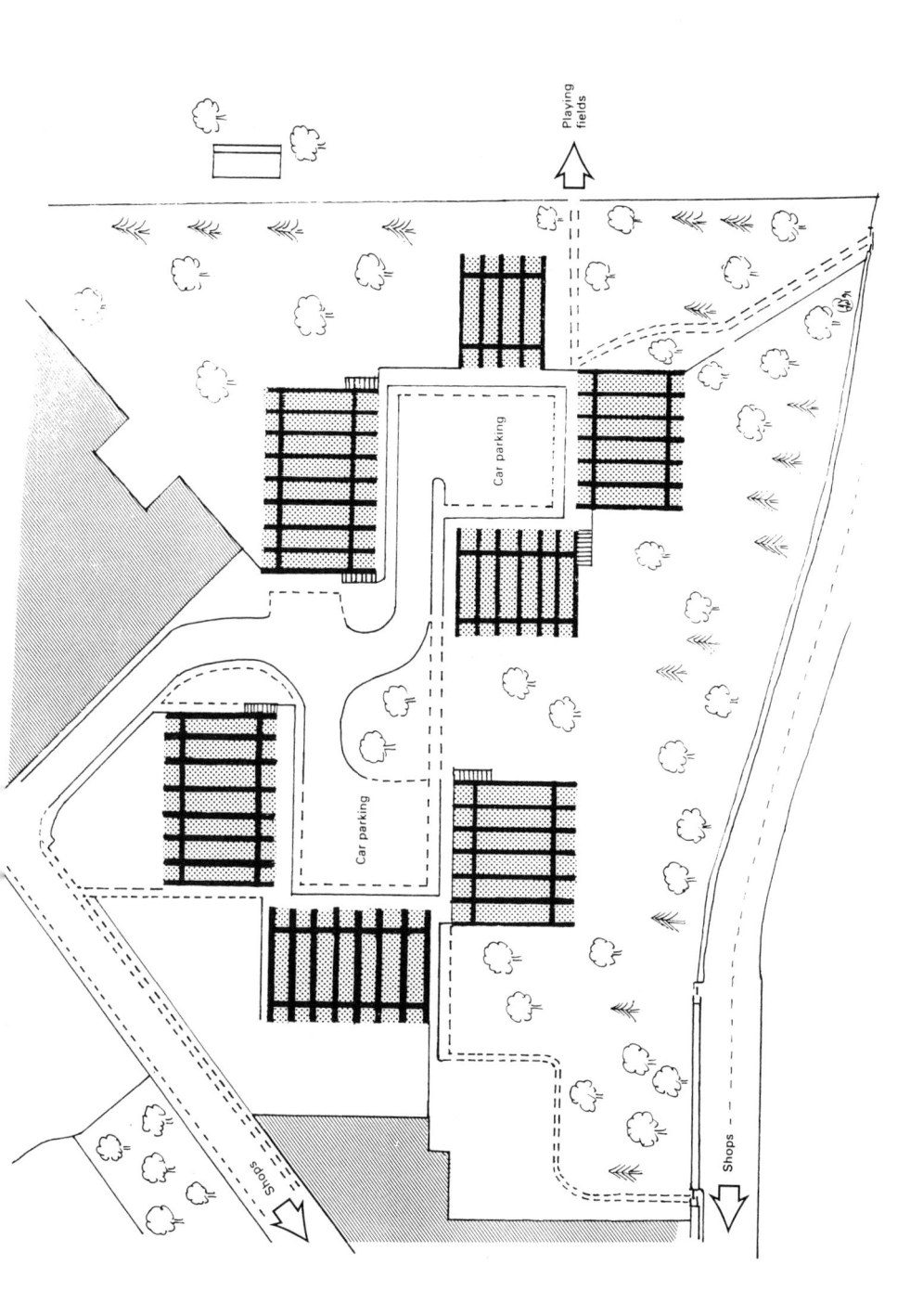

481–1
RESOURCE MANAGEMENT

Part 1 Written paper
Past examination questions related to personal presentation

1. (a) The local leisure centre has advertised for a new receptionist. List the personal qualities to be expected of the applicant by the job description. (4 marks)
   (b) How would a receptionist convey a welcome to a customer through non-verbal communication? (1 mark)
   (April 1990)

2. (a) A customer has telephoned the leisure centre to speak to the manager who is out. List THREE acceptable ways the receptionist could deal with the problem. (3 marks)
   (b) Suggest TWO ways in which information can be conveyed by the manager to the public using a visual format. (2 marks)
   (April 1990)

3. (a) You have recently moved into a new area and have booked a game of squash at the local sports centre over the telephone. As you enter the centre for the first time you are impressed by the receptionist. List TWO aspects of personal presentation that are most important in creating this good impression. (2 marks)
   (b) You have been double booked on the squash court. You complain about the apparent inefficiency of the booking system. List THREE steps you would expect the receptionist to take in dealing with your complaint. (3 marks)
   (December 1984)

4. (a) What is meant by "non-verbal communication"? (1 mark)
   (b) How could "non-verbal communication" be important in the reception area of a leisure centre? (1 mark)
   (c) Suggest TWO ways in which employees could make the customer's visit to the leisure centre more enjoyable. (2 marks)
   (d) Suggest a way by which the management could make staff in the leisure centre more identifiable. (1 mark)
   (June 1988)

Past examination questions related to shift work

1. (a) List THREE disadvantages of working a shift system from an employee's point of view. (3 marks)
   (b) List TWO advantages of shift working from an employee's point of view. (2 marks)
   (June 1987)
2. (a) Explain what is meant by "unsocial hours" in the leisure industry. (2 marks)
   (b) List THREE provisions of a shift system in a typical leisure centre. (3 marks)
   (June 1988)
3. (a) State TWO reasons why shift work is necessary in the leisure industry. (2 marks)
   (Extract—December 1988)

Past examination questions related to health and safety

1. (a) Name TWO Acts concerned with safety in the work place. (2 marks)
   (b) List THREE responsibilities of the employer under safety legislation. (3 marks)
   (June 1990)
2. (a) List TWO main responsibilities of the EMPLOYEE under the Health and Safety at Work, etc Act 1974. (2 marks)
   (b) Which body appoints the inspectors who enforce the Health and Safety at Work, etc Act 1974? (1 mark)
   (c) List TWO other relevant Acts of Parliament dealing with safety. (2 marks)
   (December 1990)
3. (a) List TWO common foot infections associated with swimming pools. (2 marks)
   (b) Name an infection against which precautions must be taken by people undertaking outdoor games or activities. (1 mark)
   (c) Name an infection associated with river banks and water sports. (1 mark)
   (d) State the major cause of accidents on the side of a swimming pool. (1 mark)
   (April 1991)

4. As a visitor to a local leisure centre you discover a fire in a changing room. List FIVE actions to be taken. (5 marks)
(December 1990)

5. (a) Give TWO reasons why a regular fire drill is important in public buildings. (2 marks)
   (b) List the THREE emergency services available through a 999 call. (1 mark)
   (c) State TWO requirements for emergency exit doors in a public building. (2 marks)
(June 1985)

6. (a) Describe the procedure for summoning the emergency services to a fire in your local leisure centre. (3 marks)
   (b) State the further action that should be taken by an employee in the event of a fire at a leisure centre. (2 marks)
(December 1987)

7. (a) Name the emergency services apart from police, fire and ambulance at
      (i) the seaside
      (ii) in mountain areas. (2 marks)
   (b) List the major items of information required on an accident report form. (3 marks)
(April 1990)

8. (a) List THREE principal aims of a first aider. (3 marks)
   (b) Name two organisations providing first aid qualifications. (2 marks)
(June 1990)

Past examination questions related to maintenance

1. (a) "From the point of view of maintenance it is not always advisable to use the cheapest materials in the construction of sports halls." Give TWO reasons why this might be so. (2 marks)
   (b) List THREE reasons why a maintenance schedule is necessary to the leisure industry. (3 marks)
(June 1987)

2. (a) State THREE effects on a maintenance programme of the increased use of a leisure centre by school children in the summer holiday. (3 marks)
   (b) Give TWO reasons for carrying out maintenance according to a regular schedule. (2 marks)
(December 1987)

3. (a) Give THREE examples of how strict supervision can reduce the need for maintenance. (3 marks)
   (b) State TWO reasons why the original choice of building materials may affect the maintenance programme. (2 marks)
   (December 1988)

Past examination questions related to play provision

1. List THREE safety factors important in the DESIGN of a children's play area. (3 marks)
   (Extract—June 1986)
2. The local council wishes to open a new outdoor children's playground for younger children. List FIVE factors to be taken into account when choosing a SITE for the playground. (5 marks)
   (December 1990)
3. An accident has occurred at the local children's playground. In checking the EQUIPMENT after the accident, what points should be noted? (5 marks)
   (June 1990)

481-2
RESOURCE MANAGEMENT

Part II Paper 1   Technical aspects, health and safety

Past examination questions related to data recording, storage and retrieval

1. Give TWO examples of computer based systems in recreation and leisure environments. (5 marks)
(April 1990)

Past examination questions related to health and safety

1. List FIVE essential requirements of chemical storage. (5 marks)
(April 1990)
2. List FIVE items of safety equipment found in a DRY leisure environment. (5 marks)
(June 1991)
3. With reference to the Health and Safety at Work, etc Act 1974, identify

    (a) THREE duties of the employer
    (b) TWO duties of the employee. (5 marks)
(June 1990)
4. List FIVE principles that should be observed when lifting and carrying a heavy object in a recreation environment. (5 marks)
(June 1991)

Past examination questions related to swimming pools

1. Identify THREE reasons for strict hygiene in swimming pools and give TWO ways in which hygiene conditions are maintained.
(5 marks)
(June 1990)
2. (a) Name the TWO most common foot infections. (1 mark)
   (b) State the hygiene requirements to counter these infections.
(2 marks)
   (c) State the most common cause of accidental injury in pool areas. (2 marks)
(Extracts June 1984)

3. (a) Name the THREE main categories of safety precautions for bathers. (3 marks)
   (b) List SIX items of safety equipment commonly used in swimming pools. (3 marks)
   (Extract June 1984)
4. Identify FIVE sources of pollution in swimming pools. (5 marks)
   (April 1990)
5. With reference to swimming pool maintenance, define the following terms and give an example of each:
   (a) solute
   (b) solvent
   (c) solution
   (d) solubility
   (e) pH (5 marks)
   (April 1991)
6. With reference to swimming pools identify:
   (a) THREE sources of pollution. (3 marks)
   (b) TWO methods of clothes storage. (2 marks)
   (April 1991)
7. (a) State the meaning of the term "filtration". (1 mark)
   (b) State TWO types of water filter in common use. (2 marks)
   (c) State THREE causes of eye irritation in swimming pools. (2 marks)
   (amended extracts June 1985/April 1990)
8. State and briefly describe TWO commonly used tests of swimming pool water. (5 marks)
   (June 1991)
9. State and briefly describe TWO methods of removing pollution in swimming pool water. (5 marks)
   (June 1990)
10. State FIVE stages in the water flow cycle of a swimming pool. (5 marks)
    (June 1991)

Past examination questions related to support areas and maintenance

1. (a) List FOUR non-sporting recreational facilities. (4 marks)
   (b) Describe
      (i) the activities that take place (3 marks)
      (ii) the dominant client groups. (3 marks)
   (June 1986)
2. List TEN support areas to be found in a typical leisure complex.
   (10 marks)
(June 1987)
3. List FIVE types of surfaces found within indoor recreation and leisure environments. (10 marks)
   (December 1986)
4. Explain the most suitable process of cleaning and maintaining TWO specified surfaces found within an indoor recreation and leisure environment. (10 marks)
   (December 1986)
5. (a) List the FIVE different areas requiring maintenance in a recreation centre. (5 marks)
   (b) State FIVE different types of surfaces found in indoor recreation environments. (5 marks)
   (June 1988)
6. (a) List SIX accommodation areas needed in a typical leisure centre. (3 marks)
   (b) Identify SIX non-sporting community facilities which a leisure centre could provide. (3 marks)
   (c) State the essential requirements of a chemical storage area. (4 marks)
   (June 1985)
7. List FIVE methods of changing and clothes storage in a typical leisure centre. (5 marks)
   (April 1990)
8. State THREE advantages and TWO disadvantages of a locker system of clothes storage in a typical leisure centre. (5 marks)
   (June 1991)
9. State TWO reasons why a ventilation system is necessary in a typical recreation centre. (5 marks)
   (June 1990)

Past examination questions related to soft landscapes

1. (a) Define the term SOFT LANDSCAPE. (2 marks)
   (b) Identify the planting season. (3 marks)
   (c) List in sequence the stages of planting. (5 marks)
   (June 1989)
2. Name, in sequence, FIVE stages in the planting of soft landscapes.
   (5 marks)
   (April 1991)

Past examination questions related to sports surfaces

1. Define the following terms
   (a) natural sports surfaces
   (b) artificial sports surfaces. (5 marks)
   (June 1990)
2. Identify
   (a) THREE artificial sports surfaces
   (b) TWO natural sports surfaces. (5 marks)
   (June 1990)
3. Name FIVE types of recreation surfaces found naturally. (5 marks)
   (April 1990)
4. Identify TWO sporting activities normally performed on the following
   (a) heavy duty sports surfaces
   (b) medium duty sports surfaces. (5 marks)
   (April 1990)
5. Identify a suitable surface for each of the following recreational activities
   (a) bowls
   (b) squash
   (c) tennis
   (d) badminton
   (e) gymnastics. (5 marks)
   (June 1990)
6. List FIVE performance parameters of any surface. (5 marks)
   (April 1991)

175

7. With reference to sports surfaces, define the following terms
   - (a) substrate
   - (b) stiffness. (5 marks)

   (June 1990)

8. List FIVE advantages of using artificial sports turf. (5 marks)

   (June 1991)

9. (a) List THREE different methods of marking indoor surfaces.

   (3 marks)

   (b) List TWO different methods of marking outdoor surfaces.

   (2 marks)

   (June 1991)

10. Identify the most suitable method of marking each of the following OUTDOOR sports surfaces
    - (a) tarmac
    - (b) grass
    - (c) shale
    - (d) concrete
    - (e) water. (5 marks)

    (April 1990)

11. State THREE advantages AND THREE disadvantages of EACH of the following
    - (a) painted court markings (3 marks)
    - (b) inlaid sections (3 marks)
    - (c) taped markings. (4 marks)

    (June 1985)

BIBLIOGRAPHY

SASH

John G The SASH Update. The Leisure Manager, June 1986
SASH Standardised Approach to Sports Halls design guide. Sports Council/Bovis.

Swimming pools

Energy data sheet number 1 swimming pool disinfection. Sports Council, 1984
Energy data sheet number 2 filtration and water circulation. Sports Council, 1984
Energy data sheet number 4 ventilation. Sports Council, 1985
Energy data sheet number 6 heat recovery. Sports Council, 1985
Energy data sheet number 16 double glazing. Sports Council, 1987
Faust, JP and Waldvogel, RL Water book for pool professionals. HTH/Olin, 1976
HSE draft proposals for Commission guidelines on standards of supervision in swimming pools, 1987
Professional pool handbook. Chlor-Chem, 1983
Purification of the water of swimming pools. HMSO

Soft landscapes

Becket, KA (Ed) Ward Lock's Complete Home Gardener. Ward Lock, 1982
Midgley, K Garden Design. Mayflower, 1979
Pearson, R (Ed) The Wisley Book of Gardening. Collingridge, 1981

Artificial surfaces

Better Results from Sports Turf. East Midlands Sports Council, 1978
Fyfe, L Who's Surfacing What? Sport and Leisure Sept–Oct 1988. Sports Council.
Hawkey, R Sport Science. Hodder and Stoughton, 1981
Indoor Surfaces — A Guide for Specifiers, Leisure Management December 1985
Multi Purpose Non-Turf Surfaces. East Midlands Sports Council, 1979

Specification for Artificial Sports Surfaces. Sports Council, 1978
Synthetic Surfaces for Outdoor Sport and Recreation. Greater London Council/South East Sports Council, 1975
Tipp, G and Watson, V Artificial Surfaces for Outdoor Games Areas. Greater London Council, 1978

Play

Dufton, K Specification for Play, The Leisure Manager January, 1988
Field, C and Bryant, D Play Services, Leisure Management February, 1986
Fyfe, L The National Children's Play and Recreation Unit, Sport and Leisure March/April 1988
Hughes, B Play and the Environment, The Leisure Manager January, 1988
Kerten, V Exposing the Myths of Children's Play, The Leisure Manager December 1988
Kerten, V Play Safe — Relating Provision to Needs, Leisure Management July 1988, September 1988, December 1988
Williams, M Planning for Play, Leisure Management September 1987, November 1987

4 Product Knowledge

Food and Diet for Recreational Activities

FOOD GROUPS

There are five food groups which together make up a balanced diet:

(a) carbohydrates,
(b) fats,
(c) proteins,
(d) vitamins,
(e) minerals.

In addition to the above food groups the other essential component of a balanced diet is water.

Carbohydrates

Carbohydrates are the most important source of energy for the body (energy can also be derived from fats and proteins). These are broken down into glycogen, which is stored in small quantities in the muscle for instant energy, and glucose, whch is transported in the blood to the liver and muscles by the circulatory system.

The three main forms of carbohydrates are starches, cellulose and sugars. Foods which are good sources of carbohydrate include cereals (eg wheat, rice, pulses and foods made from them) potatoes, dried fruit and sugar.

Fats

Fats are an essential part of a balanced diet. They contain and provide a number of essential substances as well as being a very good source of energy. Although the body does need to take in a significant proportion of fat in the diet, care needs to be taken to ensure that too much is not eaten. Modern convenience foods tend to contain a very high proportion of fats, particularly the so-called "fast foods", and unless a varied diet containing plenty of different sources of nutrients is eaten then the consumption of too much fat is likely to be a problem. Over-consumption of fats has been linked with a number of illnesses including heart disease and disorders associated with being overweight.

It is generally accepted that *saturated fats*, contained in foods such as dairy products (eg cream, cheese, butter) and red meat are much more likely to be harmful than *unsaturated fats*, contained in fish, nuts and many types of seeds.

Proteins

Proteins are used in the body for repairing tissues and for growth. In addition they are essential components of *enzymes* and *hormones* which, in turn, are essential to life. Proteins also help to keep the immune system effective. Proteins are made up from substances called *amino acids*. Over twenty different amino acids are required by the human body but, although most can be made within the body, ten essential amino acids cannot and these must be taken into the body as part of our diet. The easiest way to ingest these essential amino acids is through animal, or first-class, protein. However, if a sufficiently wide and varied number of vegetable, or second-class, proteins are eaten then all these essential amino acids will be obtained. Since a varied diet is also recommended in order to obtain the full range of other essential nutrients, particularly vitamins and minerals, this should present no problems.

Foods whch are good source of first-class proteins include lean meat, fish, eggs and dairy products (eg milk, cheese). Good sources of second-class proteins include nuts, cereals (eg rice, wheat) and foods made from them.

Vitamins

Vitamins are essential in the diet in that many chemical reactions that occur in the body will not take place unless certain vitamins are present. Vitamins are either water or fat soluble and combine with other chemicals (including amino acids) to form enzymes.

Vitamins also help to protect the body. Lack of a particular vitamin leads to deficiency diseases associated with a lack of that specific substance.

Vitamins are needed in small *regular* amounts as the body has no way of storing them. (Excess vitamins pass out in the urine.) A normal varied diet containing plenty of fresh fruit and vegetables will provide an adequate supply. Vitamins are destroyed by over-cooking, therefore raw fruit and vegetables are much better.

Good sources of vitamins include fresh fruit, vegetables, fish, eggs and dairy products (eg milk, butter). Some examples are given below:

VITAMIN	SOURCES	USES
A	• cream, milk, cheese, fish oil, egg yolk	healthy eyesight resistance to infection
B_1	• meat, eggs, nuts, yeast	healthy nervous system control of water balance
B_2	• milk, eggs, liver, yeast	oxidation of all foods
C	• fresh fruit and vegetables oranges, lemons	healthy bones and teeth antibody production
D	• eggs, cheese, butter, fish liver oils	healthy bones and teeth
K	• fruit and green vegetables, fish liver oils	blood clotting

Figure 55 Vitamins — sources and uses

Minerals

Minerals are inorganic substances found in the body. About fifteen are known to be essential but minute amounts of others are also necessary.

The main functions of minerals are:

(a) constituents of the bones of the skeleton;
(b) soluble salts which help to control the way in which the fluids and cells of the body are made up;
(c) essential parts of many enzymes.

Although minerals are very important it should be emphasised that they are only needed in small amounts.

Minerals which are particularly important include iron, sodium, potassium, chloride, calcium and phosphorous.

Good sources of minerals include fish, dairy products (eg milk, cheese) meat, liver, eggs and green vegetables.

Again, the key to obtaining sufficient minerals in the diet is *variety*.

The table below gives some examples:

MINERALS	SOURCES	USES
Calcium	• milk, cheese, eggs, green vegetables	hardening of bones and teeth, blood clotting, healthy nervous system
Phosphorous	• cheese, liver, oatmeal milk	hardening of bones and teeth balance of body fluids
Sodium	• milk, fish, meat, eggs table salt	muscle contraction healthy nervous system
Potassium	• almost all foods, including dairy products	muscle contraction healthy nervous system
Iron	• red meat, eggs, cereals, green vegetables	formation of haemoglobin in the red blood cells
Iodine	• fish, vegetables	essential thyroid function

Figure 56 Minerals — sources and uses

Summary

The essential food groups are summarised in Figure 57:

ESSENTIAL FOOD GROUPS		
GROUP	PURPOSE	SOURCE
CARBOHYDRATES	Energy providers	Cereals (bread), rice, dried fruit, sugar
FATS	Energy conservers	Butter, cheese, red meat
PROTEINS	Building body tissues; producing enzymes	Meat, fish, eggs
VITAMINS	Aiding body metabolism; preventing diseases	Fresh fruit, vegetables
MINERALS	Strong bones and teeth; producing enzymes	A wide range of whole and natural foods

Figure 57 **Essential food groups — summary**

DIET AND PHYSICAL ACTIVITY

A normal healthy diet is ideal for most leisure and recreational activities. However, if a large amount of physical activity or training is being engaged in then more energy is being used and consequently more high energy foods (ie carbohydrates) must be consumed.

Training also involves increased wear and tear on the body and this will require an increased intake of protein in order that this may be repaired. Extra muscle bulk will also need protein.

The extra intake of protein and carbohydrate should be obtained through eating a wide range of foods containing these nutrients. If this is done then the extra vitamins and minerals that the body needs will be taken in naturally. The taking of large doses of vitamin and mineral supplements is unnecessary, expensive and may even be harmful.

It is essential that sufficient fluids are taken. If the body is even slightly dehydrated then this can cause a sharp drop in performance.

Deliberate loss of body weight, especially if undertaken over a very short period of time, can result in poor sports performances. If an athlete is overweight then weight should be lost gradually over a period of time by reducing the intake of fats and refined sugars, whilst increasing the amount of exercise that is done and continuing to eat an otherwise balanced and varied diet. Under these circumstances some vitamin supplements, taken in accordance with the instructions, may be of value.

DISORDERS THAT CAN TROUBLE AN OVERWEIGHT PERSON

An unbalanced diet is one of the factors that can lead to a person becoming overweight which, in turn, can make them prone to certain physical disorders.

 (a) Illnesses connected with the heart and circulatory system; these may include—
  (i) hypertension (high blood pressure),
  (ii) atherosclerosis ("furring-up" of arteries),
  (iii) coronary thrombosis (heart attack).
 (b) Injuries to joints and ligaments, caused through the extra strain placed upon them, which may be a contributory factor in the development of arthritis.
 (c) Back pain.
 (d) Accidental injuries (overweight people generally move more slowly than slimmer people due to their extra bulk and consequently tend to be involved in more accidents).
 (e) General health can also be affected; overweight people can feel lethargic and sleep badly.

It should be stressed that being overweight probably does not *cause* most of these disorders directly but data collected by life insurance companies has shown that people who are overweight do have a greater chance of dying earlier. In addition, normal medical examinations are hampered by excess fat and surgeons may be less keen to operate on overweight people because even ordinary operations carry greater than normal risks.

PHYSICAL AND MEDICAL CONDITIONS AFFECTING PARTICIPATION IN EXERCISE

The physical and medical conditions affecting exercise and participation in recreation and leisure activities may be stated as being:

 (a) proximity and size of meals taken;
 (b) general physical condition;
 (c) minor illnesses and infections;
 (d) conditions requiring qualified medical advice.

Proximity and size of meals taken

This can affect participation to a very considerable extent. If an athlete has not eaten for several hours before taking strenuous exercise then his or her blood sugar may be low and consequently he or she may feel faint during or immediately after training. However, immediately after eating a heavy meal tiny fat globules in the blood have an effect similar to gluing the red blood cells together. This places an increased load on the heart which must push the blood through the capillaries as well as to the small intestine, via the hepatic artery, in order to transport the digested food stuffs around the body. One should not, therefore, run or swim within two hours of a heavy meal. This can lead to strain on the heart and digestive system (which may cause the meal to be vomited up) and it can cause muscular cramps (which are particularly dangerous if one is swimming).

It is clearly important to consider very carefully how much food needs to be taken, and when, if one is training or competing.

General physical condition

This is what most people regard as "fitness". It is essential that people have an appropriate level of fitness for the activity that they are engaged in and the level at which they intend to pursue it. The maxim is "get fit to play sport" not "play sport to get fit". It should also be remembered that fitness is specific (ie being fit for one activity does not make you fit for another) and some supplementary training or conditioning may be necessary for even the fittest of players if they are to engage strenuously in a different sporting activity.

Minor illnesses and infections

Minor illnesses and infections may not actually prevent participation in sport and recreational activities but it is quite possible that such conditions will adversely affect performance and enjoyment. It is also possible that athletes will be more susceptible to injuries as their concentration, timing and reactions may be affected.

The most commonly encountered examples will be colds and flu. Athlete's foot and verrucae could also be considered to fall into this category (especially where these are painful).

Lack of sleep or fatigue could similarly affect sports participation.

Conditions requiring qualified medical advice

There are certain conditions where, although activity could be very beneficial to the person's health, qualified medical advice should be sought first. Such conditions include:

(a) heart disease and circulatory disorders;
(b) asthma;
(c) obesity;
(d) back pain.

In most cases, especially if the person has done very little exercise recently, any activity should be done gently to begin with.

EXERCISE

It is widely accepted that exercise is good for the body. A wide range of beneficial effects have been attributed to it over the years, including:

(a) improvement of the health of the heart and lungs;
(b) improvement in muscle tone, strength and stamina;
(c) improvement in body posture and self confidence;
(d) reduction of stress and tension through the enjoyment that may be experienced;
(e) improvement in physical fitness and health.

In many ways these claims are true, but it very much depends upon the nature of the exercise, its duration and its intensity. Some forms of exercise can be positively harmful and could result in illness, injury or even death. In order to fully consider the degree of risk or benefit that a particular type of exercise may have for an individual it is useful to consider what is meant by fitness and the effects of different intensities of exercise and training:

(a) moderate exercise;
(b) strenuous exercise —
    (i) short-term effects,
    (ii) long-term effects.

Sports injuries will be dealt with separately.

FITNESS

Fitness is a term widely used and understood by most people. However the term tends to mean rather different things to different people. The way that an individual sees fitness will depend very much upon the level of activity, or effort, that is required by the body to perform the tasks asked of it.

Fitness is a term that expresses the suitability of an individual's physique and preparation for a particular activity or sport, performed for the duration and intensity required.

Components of fitness

The overall fitness of an individual for a particular activity will depend upon the extent to which a number of different components are combined. These factors are frequently referred to as the "S" factors. The most important of these are:

STAMINA (endurance)
STRENGTH
SPEED (including reactions and reflexes) } power
SUPPLENESS (flexibility).

Other "S" factors which also contribute towards fitness are:

SPIRIT (psychological factors)
SUSTENANCE (diet)
SLEEP (rest)
SKILL (technique).

All these factors may be influenced by systematic exercise and practice, otherwise known as *training*.

TRAINING

Moderate exercise

Moderate exercise is steady, low intensity activity. It is both safe and suitable for almost everyone. Walking, cycling and swimming are perhaps the best examples of this type of activity. It is possible that for many people all the beneficial effects of regular exercise listed earlier may be experienced, particularly if they have previously done little regular exercise. For the competitive athlete, however, moderate exercise alone is most unlikely to be sufficient.

Strenuous exercise

The aim of strenuous training is to bring about an increase in physical performance or fitness for a particular activity as the body adapts to the increased physical demands placed upon it. This process of adaptation takes place over a period of time and sufficient rest must be taken between training sessions to allow the body to recover.

There are a number of principles that must be considered when designing training programmes:

(a) Specificity of training — training programmes must be designed to meet the specific demands of the sport or activity and the particular needs of the individual within that activity.

(b) Intensity — training must be sufficiently strenuous to subject the body to higher work levels than those normally encountered. This is frequently referred to as *overload*. As the body adapts to cope with these increased work levels then these, in turn, should be increased. This process is referred to as *successive overload*.

(c) Reversibility — although the body adapts quite quickly to increased work levels much of the adaptation is reversible (ie fitness can very quickly be lost). Training should be considered as a continuous process, and the *frequency* of training sessions per week or month should be sufficient to maintain the benefits of previous training.

Short-term effects of strenuous exercise on the body

Some of these have been summarised in Figure 58. It can be seen from this table that some of the short-term effects of strenuous exercise could be harmful to people suffering from certain medical conditions. Moderate exercise, however, could be very beneficial.

Long-term effects of strenuous exercise on the body

Some of the most important of these have been summarised in Figure 59.

BODY SYSTEM	SHORT-TERM EFFECTS OF STRENUOUS EXERCISE
Circulatory system	Increased heart rate Increased blood supply to the muscles of the heart itself Increased cardiac output Dilation of the arteries, arterioles and capillaries Redirection of blood supply to the muscles Increase in blood pressure
Respiratory system	Increased rate of breathing Increase in the depth of respiratory movements There is an increase in the rate at which oxygen is taken up by the blood in the lungs; ie an increase in oxygen uptake — largely as a result of the increased cardiac activity
Muscular system	Increased blood supply to the muscles Increased temperature within the muscles There may be a build up of lactic acid in the muscles and blood Fatigue

Figure 58   Short-term effect of strenuous exercise on the body

BODY SYSTEM	LONG-TERM EFFECTS OF STRENUOUS EXERCISE
Circulatory system	The heart becomes larger (ie there is an increase in stroke volume) and stronger The resting heart rate is lowered There is an increase in the size and number of the blood vessels to the muscles
Respiratory system	There is an increase in the size of the lungs (ie an increase in total lung capacity) There is an increase in the maximum rate at which oxygen can be taken up by the blood in the lungs
Muscular system	There is an increase in muscle tone Lactic acid extraction is improved and enzyme presence is increased Depending upon the nature of the training there is likely to be an increase in strength, endurance or both There is likely to be a reduced percentage of body fat

Figure 59   Long-term effects of strenuous exercise on the body

In short, these long-term training effects of exercise upon the heart, lungs, circulatory and muscular systems bring about an increase in *physical work capacity* (ie the body's ability to engage in increased or improved physical performance).

THE MAJOR BODY SYSTEMS THAT AFFECT EXERCISE

The major body systems that affect exercise, and are themselves affected by exercise, may be listed as follows:

(a) the skeletal system;
(b) the muscular system;
(c) the circulatory system;
(d) the respiratory system;
(e) the nervous system.

THE SKELETAL SYSTEM

The skeletal system is made up of just over two hundred separate bones. These bones vary widely in their individual shapes and sizes which allows the skeleton to fulfil a wide range of functions.

Functions of the skeleton

The bones of the skeleton have developed and adapted to perform three separate major functions:

(a) They provide a *rigid supporting structure* within the body which has points for the attachment of muscles, ligaments and tendons (this structure also gives the body its shape).
(b) They provide a *system of levers* upon which the muscles can act in order to produce a large range and variety of movements.
(c) They help *protect* certain vital organs within the body, for example:
  (i) the bones of the skull protect the brain;
  (ii) the spinal column protects the spinal cord;
  (iii) the bones of the spinal column, ribs and sternum protect the heart and lungs.

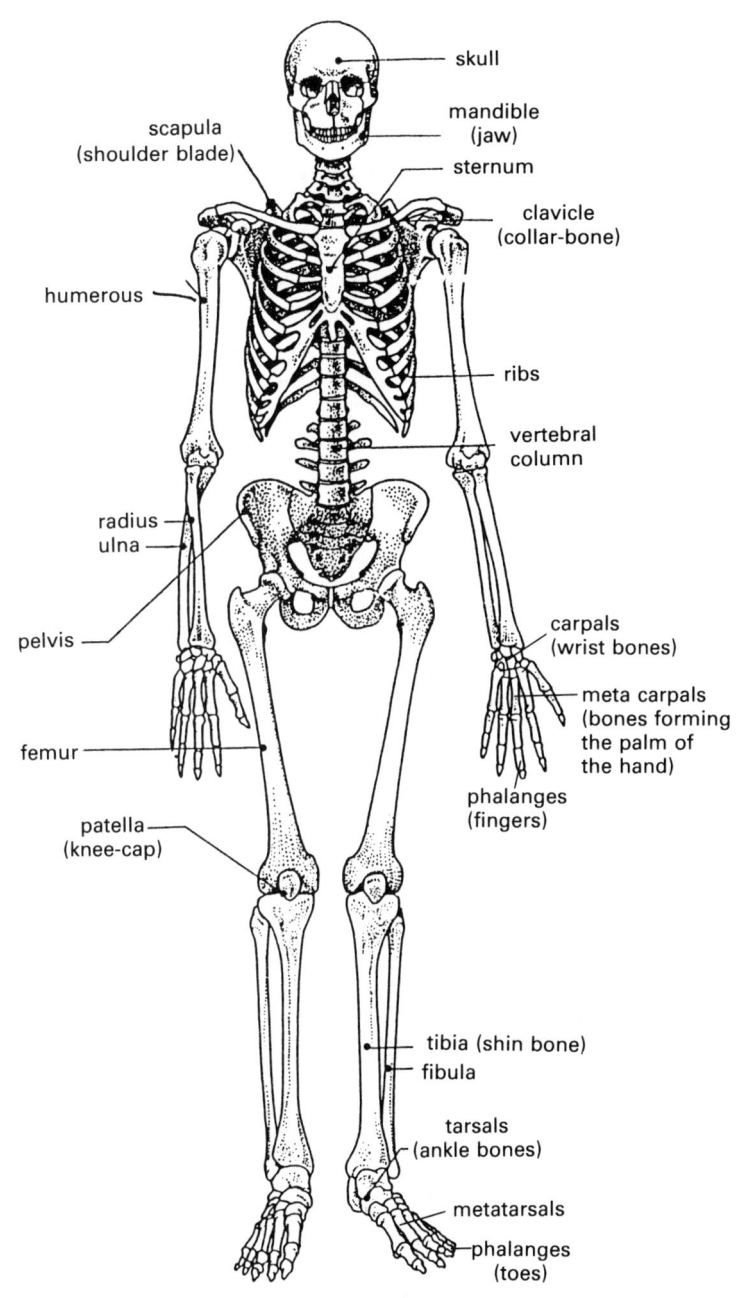

Figure 60　The human skeleton

The bones of the skeleton also act as a storage depot for calcium, and in addition blood cells are manufactured in the marrow within the bone.

Types of joint found within the skeleton

There are three main types of joint:

(a) Fibrous or immovable joints — these occur between joints that do not move (eg between the fused bones of the skull);

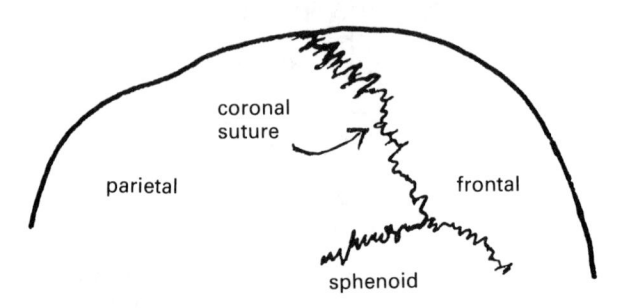

Figure 61 The fused joints between the frontal, parietal and sphenoid bones of the skull — an example of immovable joints

(b) Cartilaginous or slightly movable joints. These occur where the bones are connected to each other by a disc of cartilage and ligaments permitting a limited degree of movement (eg between the sternum and the ribs).

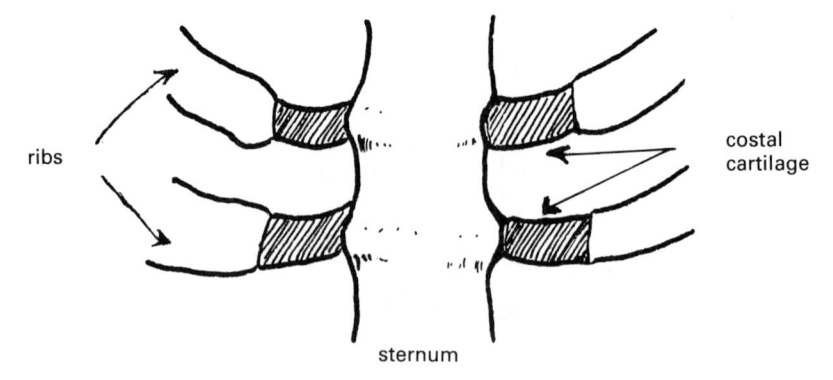

Figure 62 The cartilaginous joints between the sternum and the ribs — an example of slightly movable joints

(c) Synovial or freely movable joints. These are the most commonly found joints in the body; they are both complex and varied in structure and provide for a wide range of movements. The main features of a synovial joint are —
  (i) synovial cartilage, which is very smooth and resilient, covering the articulating surfaces of the bones;
  (ii) a capsule of ligaments holding the joint together, whilst still allowing for a range of movements;
  (iii) a synovial membrane which lines the joint capsule and retains the synovial fluid, a liquid which is formed within the joint and acts as a lubricant.

These, together, allow for friction-free movement within the joint. An example of a synovial joint is illustrated below:

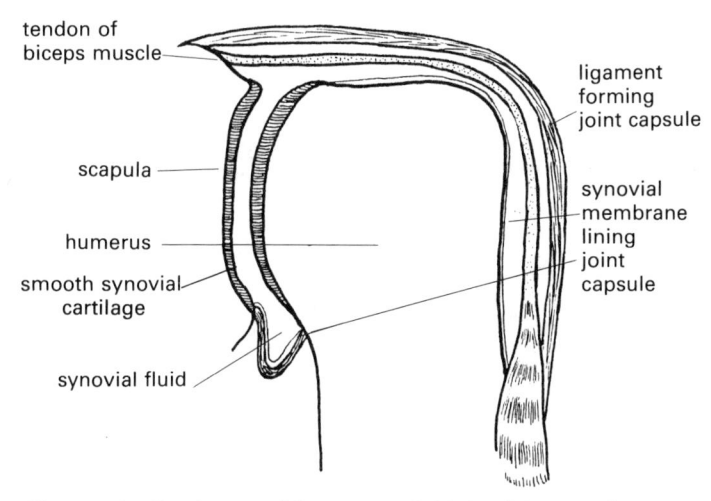

Figure 63 Freely movable or synovial joint (shoulder)

The principal types of synovial joint are:
  (a) ball and socket joints, eg hip and shoulder;
  (b) hinge joints, eg elbow and finger;
  (c) pivot joints, eg between the atlas and axis bones at the base of the skull;
  (d) gliding joints, eg the articular processes of the vertebrae;
  (e) condyloid joints, eg the wrist;
  (f) saddle joints, eg the thumb.

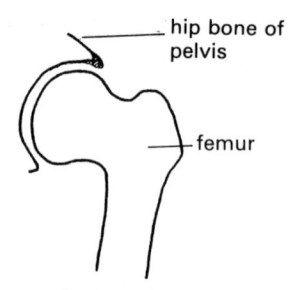

Figure 64 The hip joint — an example of a ball and socket joint

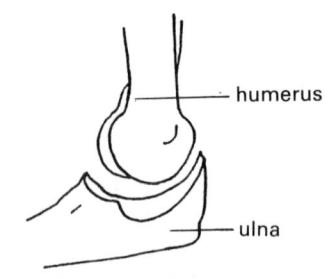

Figure 65 The elbow joint — an example of a hinge joint

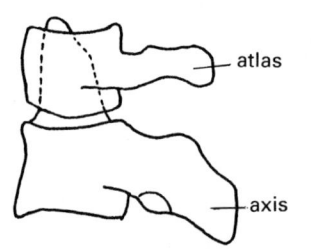

Figure 66 The pivot joint beween the atlas and axis bones in the neck

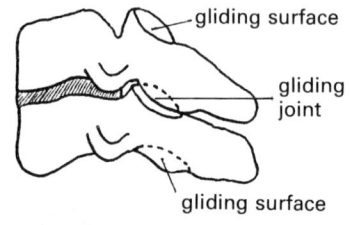

Figure 67 The gliding joint between the articular processes of adjacent vertebrae

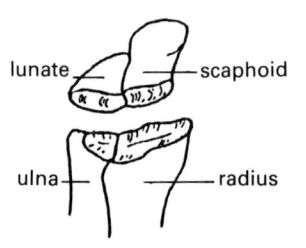

Figure 68 The joint between the bones of the forearm and the wrist — an example of a condyloid joint

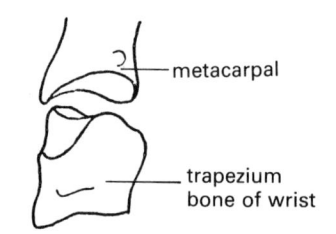

Figure 69 The joint between the metacarpal joint of the thumb and the wrist — an example of a saddle joint

Joint movement

The shape of a joint will determine:

(a) the range and the type or types of movement that are possible;
(b) the strength of the joint and the types of load that may safely be placed upon it.

Other factors will also limit the range of movement that is possible within a given joint:

(a) the restraining actions of the ligaments in or around the joint;
(b) the bulk of the muscles surrounding the joint.

Ligaments and tendons

Ligaments

These are very strong tissues that hold bones together, typically by surrounding the joints. They are not elastic but can be stretched by training to increase the range of movement in the joint.

Tendons

These are tissues that connect muscles to bones. They do not stretch as a result of training.

THE MUSCULAR SYSTEM

The muscular system is made up of over 500 different individual muscles. These are attached to the bones of the skeleton about the joints and together, through the process of contraction, they enable the full range of delicate and powerful movements of the body to be made.

It is this ability to contract that characterises all muscle tissue. There are three kinds of muscle fibres that are found in the body:

(a) smooth muscle, which is found in the walls of many of the organs of the body (eg blood vessels, stomach);
(b) cardiac muscle, which makes up the walls of the heart;
(c) skeletal muscle, which is concerned with the strong contractions that produce movement of the skeleton.

Of these different types of muscle fibre, an understanding of skeletal muscle is the most useful for those involved in conditioning athletes for most leisure and recreational activities.

Skeletal muscle

Skeletal muscle cells are long, cylindrical and have a large number of nuclei. They are bound together into bundles or sheets by connective tissue and these bundles are, in turn, bound together to form complete muscles. The ends of the muscles are then usually attached to bones by white fibrous tissue in the form of ligaments.

When the muscle fibres are stimulated by the nerves they contract, producing either tension or movement between the two ends of the muscle.

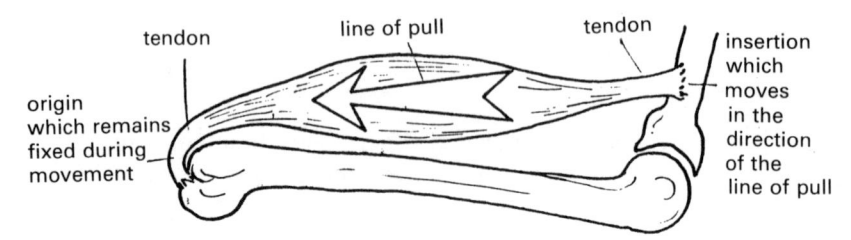

Figure 70 The way in which the attachments of the muscles influence the action of the muscle upon the joint

The following points regarding the action of muscle fibres should be noted:

(a) muscles can only contract and pull along the long axis of their fibres;
(b) when muscles contract the muscle becomes shorter;
(c) individual muscle fibres contract on an "all or nothing" basis (ie they either contract completely or not at all);
(d) the number of individual fibres contracting will determine the strength of the contraction;
(e) whole muscles are made up of a mixture of "fast-twitch" and "slow-twitch" muscle fibres;
(f) fast-twitch muscle fibres are used for fast, powerful movements;
(g) slow-twitch muscle fibres are used where endurance is required;
(h) the proportion of fast-twitch muscle fibres to slow-twitch muscle fibres varies from one athlete to another (this is one of the factors which accounts for individual differences between competitors).

Because muscles can only exert a force when they contract it is necessary that they are arranged in pairs or groups about a given joint, one to flex the joint (eg the biceps at the elbow) and the other to extend the joint (eg the triceps at the elbow). Other muscles steady the bones which give the origin to the contacting muscles — these are known as the *fixators*. Others help to keep the joint about which the movement is taking place steady — these are known as *synergists*.

The principal muscles of the human body are indicated on the following two figures:

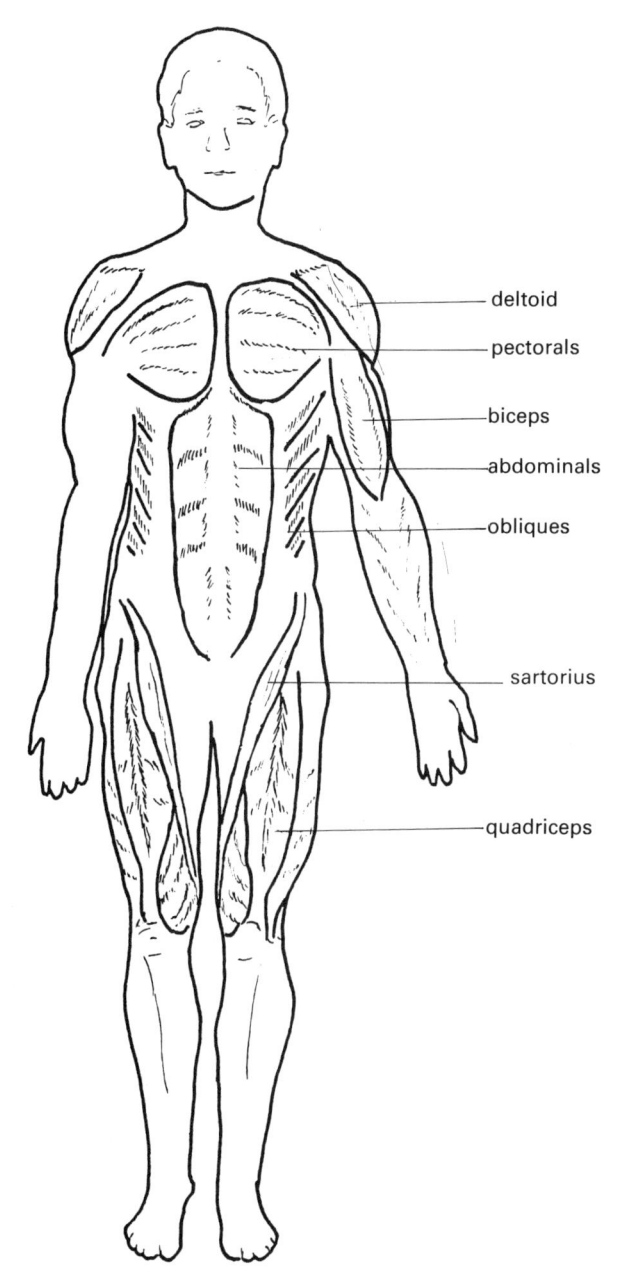

Figure 71 The principal muscles of the human body

198

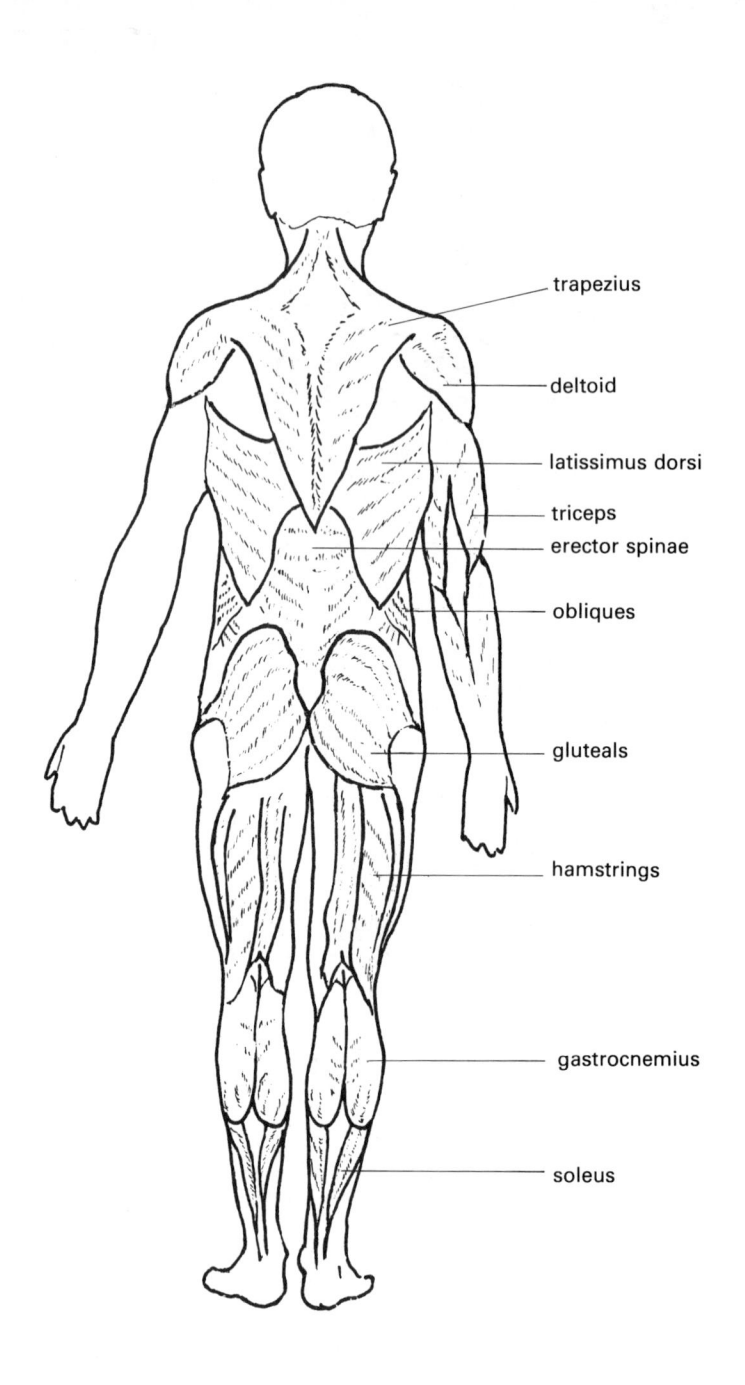

Releasing energy for muscular contractions

In order to contract, muscles need to be able to use the energy available in food (from carbohydrates, fats and proteins), which is stored as chemical energy in the body, and convert it into mechanical, muscular energy.

There are three different systems by which the body releases chemical energy in order to make it available for mechanical muscular contraction:

(a) ATP — CP "instant energy" system
(b) glycogen — LA "short-term extra-energy" system } (without oxygen)
(c) aerobic "long-term energy" system (using oxygen)

ATP — CP system

Stored within the muscle cells is a substance called *adenosine triphosphate* (ATP). This is a chemical compound which provides considerable amounts of energy instantly. However, the amount stored in the muscle cells is only sufficient for a few seconds of activity. The energy is released when the ATP is broken down from adenosine *tri*phosphate to adenosine *di*phosphate and phosphate; ie:

$$ATP \rightarrow ADP + P + \{ENERGY\} \text{ released for muscular work}$$

This process is also reversible:

$$ATP \xleftarrow{\text{is formed from}} ADP + P + \{ENERGY\}$$

Although the amount of ATP available is only sufficient for a few seconds, the ATP can quickly be reformed within the muscle, often using another chemical compound called *creatine phosphate* (CP). This is often referred to as *phosphocreatine* and it is also a high energy compound but much more of it can be stored in the muscles.

By breaking up the creatine phosphate into creatine and phosphate sufficient energy is released to form the ATP from the ADP and phosphate, which then becomes available for more muscular activity, ie:

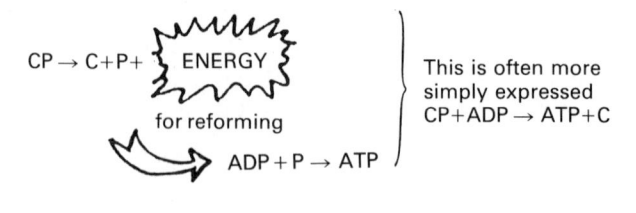

$$CP \rightarrow C+P+ \text{ENERGY}$$
for reforming
$$ADP+P \rightarrow ATP$$

This is often more simply expressed
$$CP+ADP \rightarrow ATP+C$$

this ATP is then available for:

$$ATP \rightarrow ADP+P+ \text{ENERGY}$$

for muscular work

These processes occur whether oxygen is available or not but can only continue in its absence for a very short period of time. If strenuous exercise is to be continued, then other systems of releasing energy are necessary.

The systems which do this are the glycogen–lactic acid system and the aerobic system. These will frequently be used simultaneously; which system is to be most relied upon will depend upon the intensity of the exercise and the availability of oxygen — they are not sequential. The lactic acid system is used to back up any shortfall of ATP not produced by the aerobic system.

Glycogen–lactic acid system

If the intensity of the exercise is high then an additional system to produce energy is required in order to resynthesise ATP. Glycogen (stored in the muscles and liver) is used as the fuel to produce ATP and produces lactic acid as a by-product via the compound *pyruvic acid*, ie:

$$\text{Glycogen} \begin{Bmatrix} \text{which provides} \\ \text{the fuel for} \end{Bmatrix} \rightarrow \text{ENERGY} + ADP+P \rightarrow ATP+LA$$

This process allows the muscles to continue to work at a high level of intensity without oxygen for a further period of time. If the intensity of the exercise continues to remain high then this period of time may only be as much as two minutes. Without oxygen the pyruvic acid is converted into lactic acid which will very quickly cause the muscles to become tired or painful. This same process allows athletes working aerobically to suddenly increase the intensity at which they are working for a very short period of time. Ultimately the body must use oxygen in order to continue with muscular activity and to reconvert the lactic acid back into pyruvic acid which is then oxidised to form carbon dioxide and water. Whilst this is taking place, muscular activity may continue but at a less intense level until sufficient oxygen has been taken in. This situation, where the body has to take in oxygen in order to cope with work already done, is known as *oxygen debt*. This is why an athlete, having sprinted 100 metres without taking more than a breath or two, will need to breathe deeply and rapidly for some minutes afterwards. Where the exercise has been of a low intensity the repayment of the oxygen debt will be much less obvious.

Aerobic system

This is the system that is used if ATP needs to be continuously resynthesised for longer periods of time. It again uses glycogen as the fuel compound, but the build up of lactic acid is prevented by the oxidation of the pyruvic acid which yields a great deal of energy, ie:

$$\text{ADP} + \text{P} + \text{glycogen or glucose} \rightarrow \begin{cases} \text{ATP} \rightarrow \text{ADP} + \text{P} + \text{ENERGY} \rightarrow \text{work} \\ + \\ \text{pyruvic acid} \end{cases}$$

provided ⇓ oxygen is present

oxygen + pyruvic acid → water + carbon dioxide + (from respiration) the *bulk* of the ENERGY for muscular work

This means that, given sufficient supplies of glycogen or glucose and oxygen, muscular activity could be carried on almost indefinitely. In practice aerobic activity can only be carried on at lower levels of intensity than is possible anaerobically, but it can be carried on for much greater periods of time.

THE CIRCULATORY SYSTEM

The circulatory system is made up of:

(a) the heart;
(b) a system of blood vessels consisting of —
   (i) arteries and arterioles,
   (ii) veins,
   (iii) capillaries;
(c) the blood.

Function of the circulatory system

The main function of the circulatory system is to transport blood to all parts of the body via the lungs. Through the medium of the blood, oxygen and other essential substances are carried to the tissues and waste products, including carbon dioxide, are carried away from the tissues to the organs of excretion.

The heart

The heart is essentially a double pump, each pump having two chambers — one to collect the blood in, and the other from which to force it around

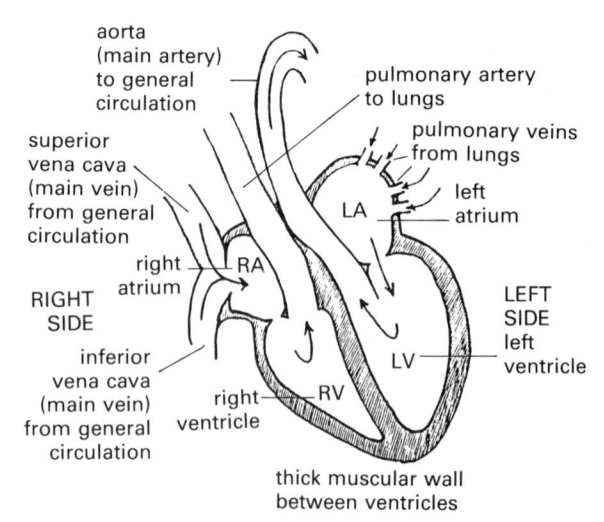

Figure 72 The heart (simplified)

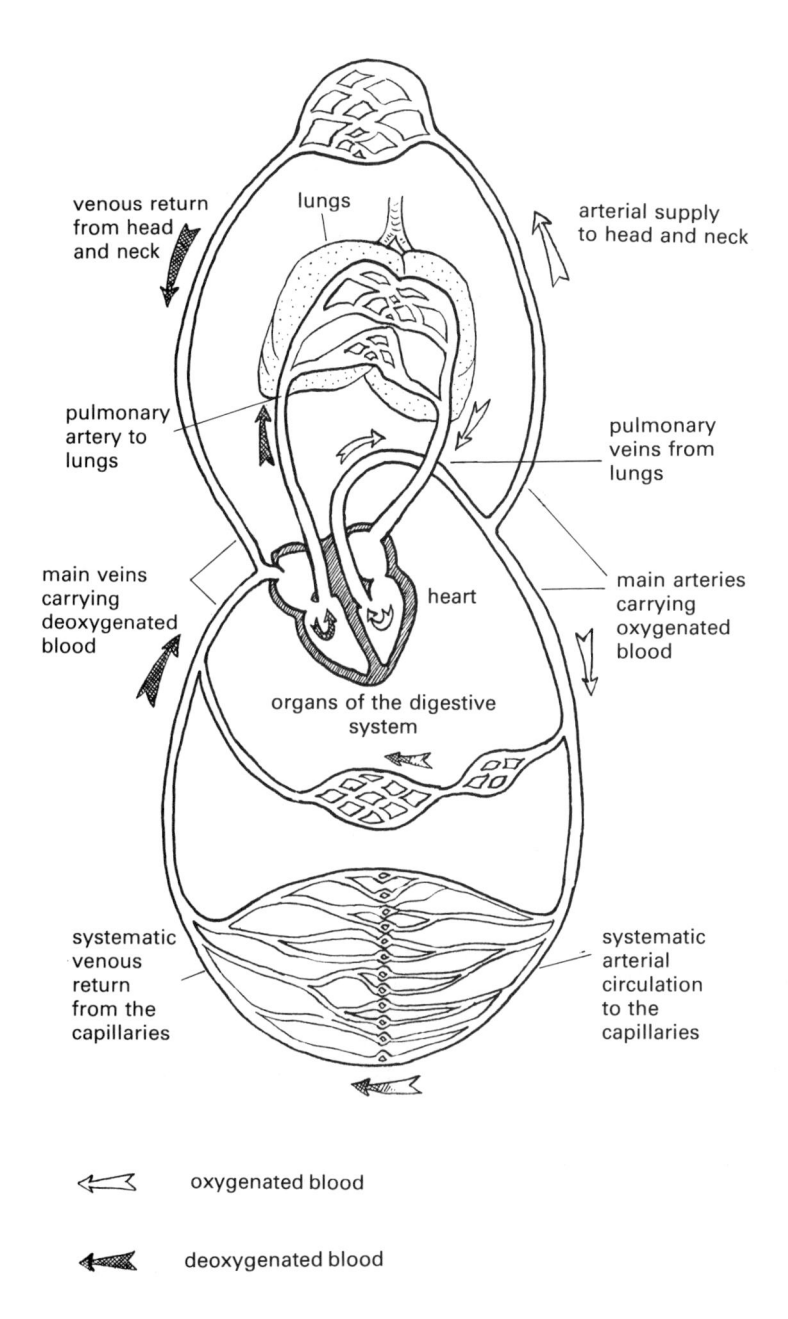

Figure 73 The circulatory system (simplified)

the body. Valves within the heart prevent back-flow. Blood from the right side of the heart is pumped to the lungs where it is *oxygenated* (enriched with oxygen) and then returned to the left side of the heart. It is then pumped from the left side of the heart to the body tissues. Once the available oxygen has been passed to the tissues the blood is said to *deoxygenated*. It is then returned to the right side of the heart and the process repeated. The most important parts of the heart and circulation are indicated and labelled on Figures 72 and 73.

THE RESPIRATORY SYSTEM

The respiratory system is a network of hollow tubes leading from the nose and the mouth to tiny airsacs within the lungs. Whilst in the airsacs (alveoli) the air comes into sufficiently close proximity to red blood cells passing through a network of capillaries to enable gases to pass from one to the other.

Functions of the respiratory system

The main function of the respiratory system is to provide sufficient oxygen to be absorbed by the red blood cells to meet the needs of the body.

Since the body needs varying amounts of oxygen at different times (eg at rest or during exercise) the respiratory system must be capable of responding to this.

In order to draw air into the lungs the intercostal muscles lift the ribs upwards and outwards whilst the diaphram (a sheet of muscle) flattens downwards. This increases the volume of the chest cavity and air is drawn into the lungs. This process is known as *inspiration*.

When the intercostal muscles and diaphragm relax the volume of the chest cavity decreases and air is forced out of the lungs. This is known as *expiration*.

Once in the lungs the air passes along a network of tiny tubes (bronchioles) which end in clusters of alveoli. These alveoli are surrounded by a network of blood capillaries.

Where the blood capillaries and the aveoli come into contact they are only one cell thick. This allows oxygen to pass into the red blood cells and carbon dioxide to pass from the red blood cells into the alveoli.

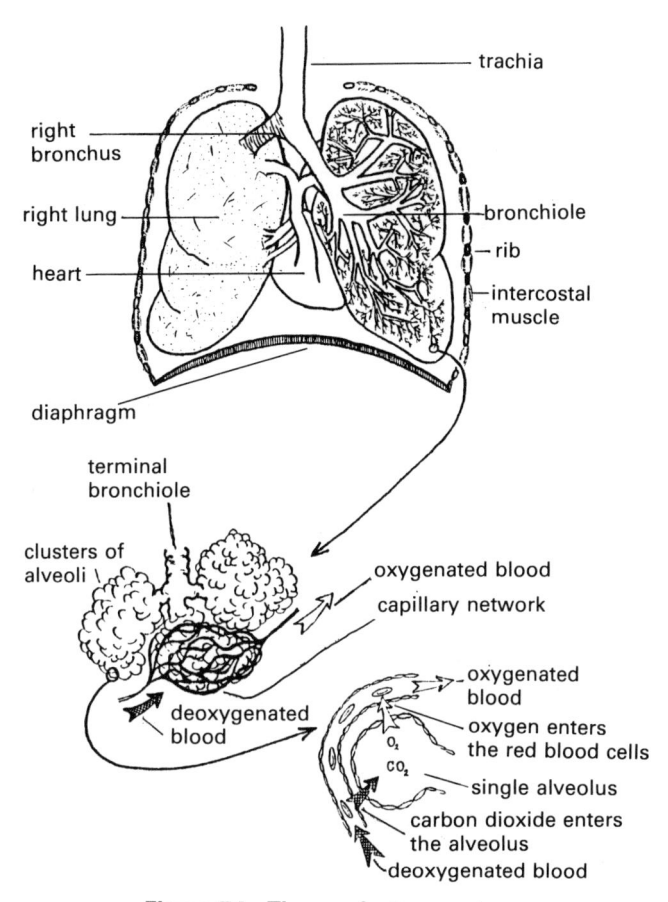

Figure 74 The respiratory system

This whole process is often referred to as *external respiration*. The transfer of oxygen to the muscles of the body from the red blood cells is then known as *internal respiration*.

THE NERVOUS SYSTEM

The nervous system is that part of the body that is responsible for controlling all our senses and movements. It consists of:

(a) the brain,
(b) the spinal cord, } these form the central nervous system
(c) other nerves.

The brain

The brain controls all the body activities. It is extremely delicate and contained within the cranium of the skull and suspended in cerebrospinal fluid for protection. However, there is some room for movement of the brain within the cranium (particularly when the body has become partially dehydrated), and it may be damaged by blows or pressure to the head.

The spinal cord

The spinal cord is made up of nerve fibres and extends from the brain through the spinal canal almost to the base of the spine, protected by the bones of the vertebrae. It is along the spinal cord that information and instructions are carried to and from the brain to all the peripheral nerves of the body.

Other nerves

Other nerves include:

(a) spinal nerves which are connected directly to the spinal cord;
(b) peripheral nerves which spread to all parts of the body, including the muscles, skin and sense organs.

The peripheral nerves have specialised functions:

Sensory nerves carry information or sensory impulses to the central nervous system.
Motor nerves carry instructions or motor impulses from the central nervous system to the muscles.

The instructions from the central nervous system may be the result of a deliberate thought or decision, in which case they are said to be *voluntary*. Through practice and repetition the pathways along which these impulses travel are strengthened and improved, eventually making certain movements and skills much easier to perform until they virtually become automatic. It is therefore important that physical skills, especially in sport, are practised precisely as, eventually, they become almost automatic. Once this has occurred faults in technique can be very difficult to correct.

Many instructions are not voluntary. They occur very rapidly, often to

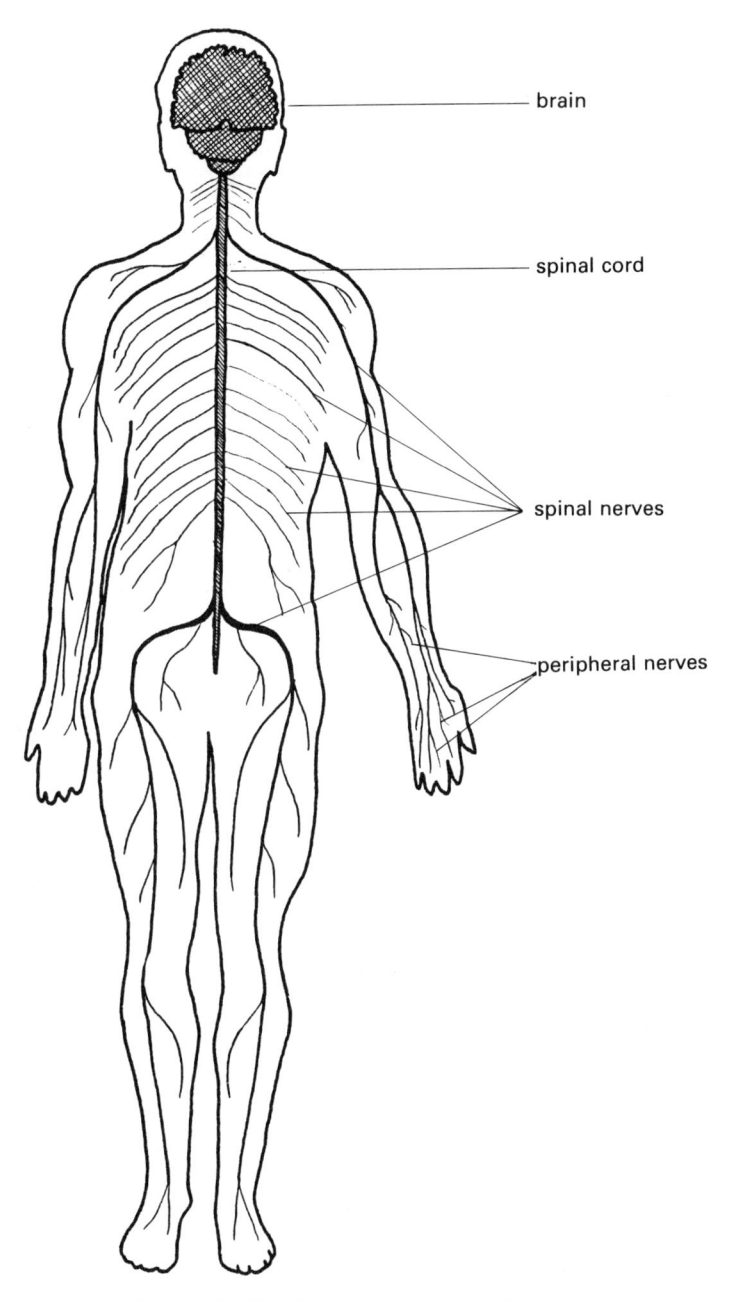

Figure 75 The human nervous system

protect the body from injury, without conscious thought. These actions are known as *reflex actions*. In sport reflex actions are responsible for many of the subtle adjustments that the body makes in order to avoid injury. Once the body is injured, however, the nerves and the sense organs responsible for giving information about the positions of the muscles, tendons and joints (called proprioceptors) take longer to repair and consequently athletes frequently tend to aggravate old injuries (eg by "turning over" on an injured ankle) if they return to playing sport too quickly. There is evidence to suggest that the use of a "rocker board" or a "wobble board", once the other tissues have mended, may help prevent such recurrences as it allows the nerves and proprioceptors to re-establish the limits of safe movement for the joint.

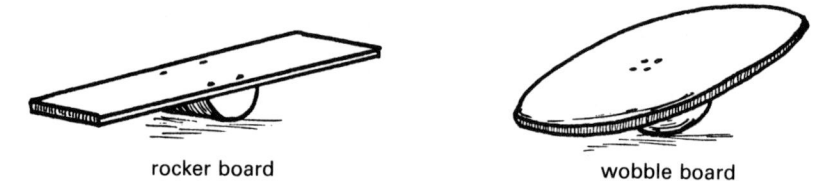

rocker board   wobble board
Figure 76   Rocker board and wobble board

Other actions of the body that are controlled by the central nervous system are completely automatic (eg the actions of the digestive system) and are controlled by the *autonomic* nervous system. It is of little concern to the athlete, other than the need to be aware that its functions may affect exercise (eg after a heavy meal) and that meals and training times may have to be adjusted accordingly.

INJURIES ASSOCIATED WITH RECREATIONAL ACTIVITIES

Although sport is generally regarded as being a "healthy" activity, having all the benefits of regular exercise attributed to it, there is also widespread acceptance of the idea of "sports injuries" associated with particular activities.

Injuries, often very serious ones, do occur when people are participating in recreational activities, particularly in sports competitions, strenuous training sessions and "adventure" activities (eg mountaineering, rock climbing, pot holing and skiing). However, it is not the actual participation in these activities that results in injury but the additional incidents or stresses to which an athlete is exposed during the course of their participation.

Rock climbing does not cause serious injury — falling 10 metres on to rocks most certainly does. Similarly, playing football does not cause serious injury but having both legs kicked away from underneath a player by a reckless or dangerous tackle might. The injuries received following such incidents may be identical to those received in a car crash. The fact that they were received during participation in a sporting or recreational activity need not make them different in any way.

These incidents or stresses which can lead to damage may be referred to as the mechanism causing a particular injury. The causal chain involved is illustrated in the figure below:

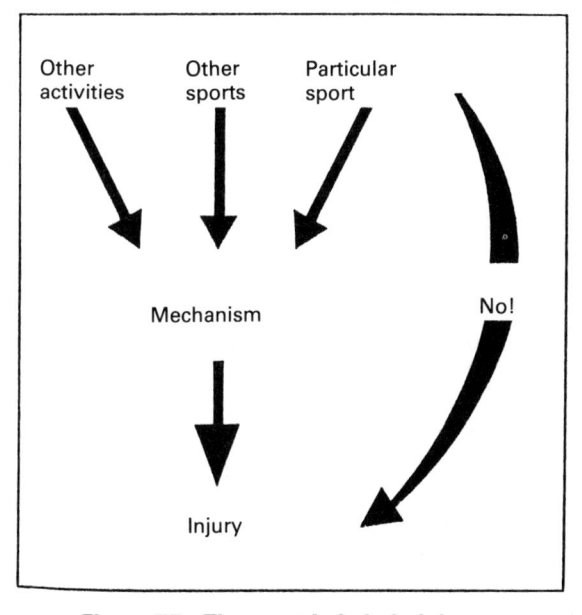

Figure 77 The causal chain in injury
Reproduced from Williams JGP, A Colour Atlas of Injury in Sport, 1980 by kind permission of Wolfe Medical Publications Ltd.

209

CLASSIFICATION OF SPORTS INJURIES

Sports injuries may be classified as being:

(a) intrinsic,
(b) extrinsic.

Intrinsic injuries

Intrinsic injuries derive directly from some act or action of the athlete which causes stress to be developed *within* his or her own body resulting in injury. In this sense they may be considered as being "self-inflicted".

Extrinsic injuries

Extrinsic injuries are those which occur as a direct result of forces and stresses applied from *outside* the body of the injured athlete.

The cause of these extrinsic injuries may be another athlete, an implement or vehicle of some kind or factors associated with the environment.

Such injuries can be very severe as the forces exerted may be considerable.

An alternative way of classifying sports injuries is to consider the way in which they were received (ie suddenly or as a result of repeated stresses over a period of time). Thus injuries may also be classified as being caused as a result of:

(a) sudden stress or a traumatic incident;
(b) repeated stresses or overuse.

Traumatic incident

This is where the injury resulted from sudden stress to the body (eg as a result of a direct blow or violence).

Overuse

Overuse injuries occur as a result of repeated stresses to the body over a period of time, possibly even weeks or months, and are often caused as a result of not allowing sufficient time between training sessions or matches for the body to fully recover or as a result of using faulty or inappropriate equipment or techniques.

It is possible to use both these methods of classification of sports injuries in conjunction with one another as set out in the following figure.

CLASSIFICATION	SUDDEN STRESS (traumatic incident)	SUSTAINED REPEATED STRESS (overuse)
INTRINSIC	Pulled hamstring Ruptured Achilles tendon	"Shin splints" Metatarsalgia
EXTRINSIC	Fractured tibia/fibula (from a violent tackle in football) Fractured skull (from striking head on the ice whilst ice skating)	Achilles tendonitus (from running in badly designed training shoes) Blistered hands (from oars when rowing or from rings/bar in gymnastics)

Figure 78 **Classification of sports injuries — examples**

FACTORS AFFECTING INJURY

The extent to which any individual participant is at risk of injury may depend to a greater extent upon factors related to the participant than they do to those connected with the activity itself.

The factors affecting injury may be listed as:

(a) physical fitness
(b) psychological fitness
(c) physique
(d) technique
(e) environment
(f) age
(g) sex
(h) drugs
(i) equipment.

Physical fitness

This is the most important factor in avoiding injury in sports or recreational activities. In addition to training for the specific needs of the activity, flexibility training can also reduce the likelihood of injury, particularly from pulls and strains. Participants also need sufficient physical endurance for the activity in which they are participating.

Fatigue can break down the reflexes and reactions, and with tiredness the risk of injury increases.

A thorough warm-up, including stretching exercises, will also help to reduce the risk of injury in competition or strenuous training but the most important thing to remember is that where strenuous or competitive sport is concerned the rule is:

GET FIT TO PLAY SPORT *NOT* PLAY SPORT TO GET FIT!

Psychological fitness

This affects the risk of injury to an individual player in a number of ways:

(a) The style of play adopted, whether it is energetic and aggressive, placing a high reliance upon power and commitment, and the extent to which the athlete is aroused or "psyched-up" and in control of his or her actions.

(b) Confidence, a lack of which may result in a player pulling out of a tackle or being unable to perform techniques effectively. This is of particular importance in activities such as rock climbing where, if a climber loses confidence, the grip may be lost.

(c) The extent of the need or desire to win, which may either cause a player to continue to play or compete whilst injured, thus causing much more serious damage, or to cheat and break the rules of the game, thus injuring other players.

(d) The extent to which a player has learned to come to terms with his or her physical limitations. This is particularly important as players get older — middle-aged players may strive too hard to reach the standards that they once achieved and thus suffer from pulled muscles and ruptured ligaments. Older players have often learned to come to terms with this and consequently are able to continue to participate on a regular basis with minimal risk.

Physique

The physique of the athlete should be appropriate to the activity being undertaken, otherwise abnormal stesses may be placed upon the body causing injury or, alternatively, the individual may be vulnerable to injuries caused by other players.

A slim, light frame may be ideal for long distance running but offers the athlete little protection in a sport where there may be a considerable degree of body contact (eg Rugby football). On the other hand a well-built heavy frame may be a considerable asset in such a contact sport, yet suffer badly from stresses to the joints and cardio-vascular system in activities where sustained effort over a period of time is required (eg half marathon running).

Technique/skill

Some techniques, even performed skilfully, are dangerous in themselves, either to the performer or to other players. In many instances the use of these techniques is prohibited by the rules of the sport itself (the short arm tackle or deliberate collapsing of the scrum in Rugby, and head diving into the mat in order to throw an opponent in judo, are all prohibited techniques because they could cause severe spinal injuries). Good supervision is of considerable value in ensuring that dangerous play is prevented. Generally it is true to say, however, that the more skilfully the technique is performed the less risk there is of injury. Poor technique can cause abnormal stresses to the body resulting in overuse injuries or cause the performer to be at greater risk of an accident (eg bad running technique can cause knee and ankle injuries, particularly in the case of fun runners attempting half marathons, and novice ice skaters tend to be prone to falling heavily on to the ice). Limitations in technique can also lead to a reliance upon physical effort and power, with the extra risks involved, in order to compete effectively.

Another aspect of skilled performance which affects the degree of risk of injury is judgement or the assessment of risk and danger. Poor judgement can lead to much greater risks being taken, particularly in adventure sports like mountaineering, rock climbing and caving. Safety equipment can sometimes lead to a false sense of security. It has been remarked that less people might be injured falling from climbing walls if the crash mats were replaced by metal spikes!

Environment

Factors such as heat, cold, humidity and lighting can all affect performance and the degree of stress that the body is exposed to; judgement and coordination may also be affected. However, serious injuries can arise due to factors such as inappropriate surfaces (or wet patches on indoor floors) and projections into, or equipment at the side of, the playing or training area.

In outdoor activities the list of environmental hazards is much greater. Altitude, adverse weather conditions, rock falls, tides and currents all add to the factors which could bring about an accident resulting in serious injury or death.

Age

Although injuries are common at all ages in sport, participants are more prone to particular types of injury at different ages.

Children, whose bones are still developing and who generally lack strength, are particularly vulnerable to direct violence and overuse injuries. This tendency continues into adolescence when, despite increased muscle development, muscle strains and tears occur.

There are also considerable variations between the size, weight and strength of adolescents at different stages of puberty and this can put the smaller ones at risk in contact sports and games.

After adolescence and during early adulthood, athletes are at the peak of their abilities. Training is much more strenuous, sustained and serious. This can lead to a combination of overuse injuries and strains (particularly if strenuous or inappropriate weight training is engaged in). Impacts in contact sports tend to be more severe at this time as well.

In middle age participants tend to have more work and family commitments and less time available to achieve or maintain a high level of fitness. Bones become more brittle, ligament and tendon injuries can occur and injuries take much longer to heal.

Sex

There are certain skeletal differences between men and women, primarily between the relative width and strength of the pelvic and shoulder girdles. Women also tend to have lighter skeletons.

These differences tend to make women more susceptible to certain types of injury. The lighter narrower shoulder girdle of women is less suited to power production and the greater width of the pelvic girdle means that there is a greater slant to the thigh bones (femurs) which can increase the likelihood of knee injuries.

The lighter frame can also make them more susceptible to stress fractures.

In some sports this may mean that the range of techniques used and the way in which they are applied may have to be adapted. This approach has been very successfully adopted by the British Judo Association's Women's Judo Team, which has produced a constant stream of World and European champions in recent years. Apart from separating men and women in sports where strength and power are essential features of the sport, there are no other reasons why both sexes should not compete against one another where equal participation is fair and acceptable.

Drugs

Any substance which adversely affects fitness and health will increase the risk of injury. In this context both alcohol and nicotine must be included. Alcohol affects timing and judgement almost immediately, as well as having long term effects, whilst the adverse effects of smoking on the heart, lungs and circulatory system are so well documented that it is difficult to understand why any serious athlete could even consider the habit.

It is, however, with those drugs that are taken in an attempt to improve sports peformance that there is most concern. Not only do they have dangerous side effects, but if successful athletes are thought or known to be using them then this increases the pressure upon lesser or younger athletes to take them. The 1988 Olympics in Seoul highlighted the range of different drugs that are currently known to be being taken by athletes. The use of anabolic steroids in power production events such as weight lifting and sprinting is known to lead to severe side effects. Apart from ligament injuries, there is also a serious risk of kidney or liver cancer. In 1987 a 27 year-old bodybuilder died as a result of taking anabolic steroids.

The use of pain killers, too, has caused considerable debate. Pain is the body's way of warning us that something is wrong; by taking drugs to mask this warning in order to continue to participate athletes are risking doing irreparable damage to themselves.

The use of diuretics to lower bodyweight for sports such as judo, boxing and other events where athletes are separated by weight categories also carries the risks associated with dehydration and consequent lowering of physical performance.

The dangers associated with the taking of stimulants have been known for many years. Their use allows the body to be pushed well beyond its normal limits but at the risk of stressing it to the point of collapse. The most well known instances of this were the deaths of the cyclists Knud Jensen in the 1960 Rome Olympics and Bobby Simpson on the mountain stage of the 1967 Tour de France. Both were found to have traces of amphetamines (a stimulant) in their bodies at the time of their deaths.

Equipment

All equipment used when participating in sports and recreational activities should be well maintained and suitable for the purpose for which it is being used. This also applies to clothing and footwear in particular, which should be the correct size, well designed and appropriate to the sport and the surface upon which it is being played. A large proportion of stress injuries suffered by runners are caused by training in poorly designed or ill-fitting training shoes.

Apparatus, particularly that used for gymnastics and trampolining, must be well maintained and set out correctly. If apparatus collapses whilst being used then the athelete is likely to suffer severe extrinsic injury. The same considerations apply when vehicles are being used (eg in motor racing).

INJURIES ASSOCIATED WITH SPECIFIC RECREATIONAL ACTIVITIES

Different recreational activities tend to have particular injuries commonly associated with them. Certain of these injuries may also be more specifically associated with a particular role or position within a given sport. Perhaps the best example of this is cricket where those injuries commonly associated with bowlers are quite different from those suffered by batsmen and fielders. Goalkeepers also tend to suffer from different injuries to those experienced by their outfield colleagues.

Examples of recreational activities, together with some of the injuries commonly associated with them, are illustrated on the following pages.

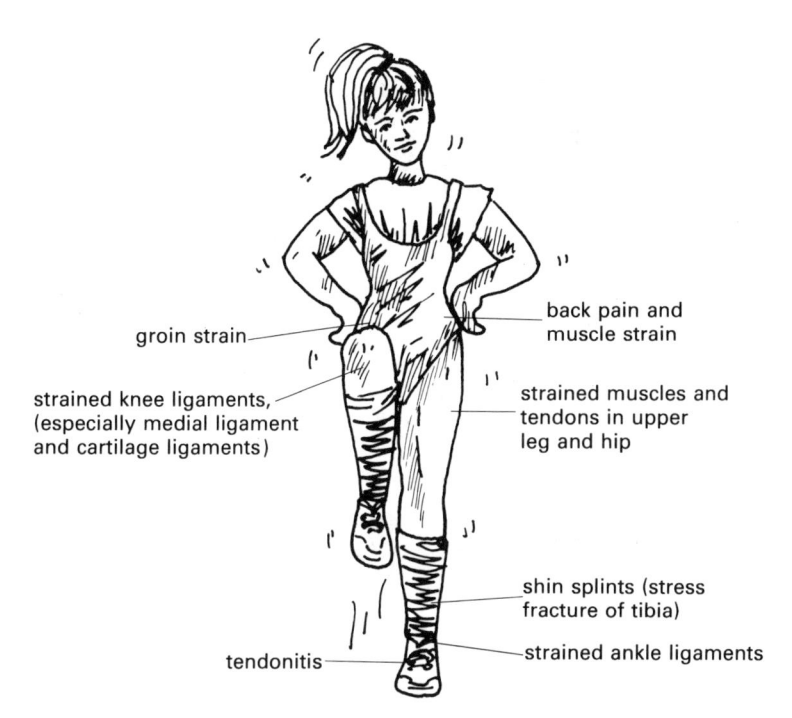

Figure 79 Sports injuries associated with aerobics and dance

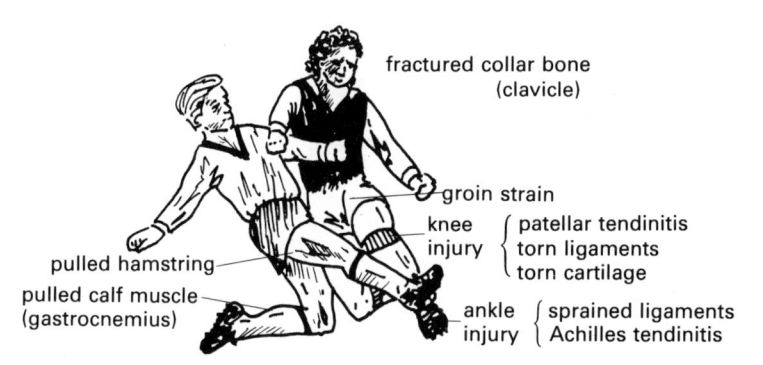

- groin strain
- strained knee ligaments, (especially medial ligament and cartilage ligaments)
- back pain and muscle strain
- strained muscles and tendons in upper leg and hip
- shin splints (stress fracture of tibia)
- tendonitis
- strained ankle ligaments

Figure 80 Sports injuries associated with Association football

- fractured collar bone (clavicle)
- groin strain
- knee injury { patellar tendinitis, torn ligaments, torn cartilage
- pulled hamstring
- pulled calf muscle (gastrocnemius)
- ankle injury { sprained ligaments, Achilles tendinitis

217

Figure 81 Sports injuries associated with basketball

Blows from the ball are the most common cause of injury to batsmen and fielders:

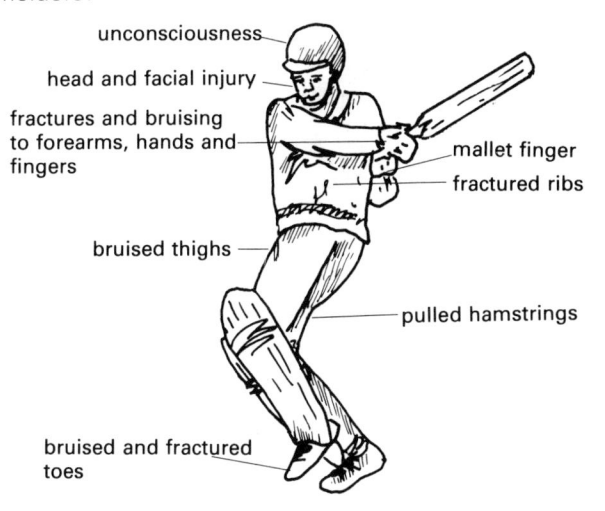

- unconsciousness
- head and facial injury
- fractures and bruising to forearms, hands and fingers
- mallet finger
- fractured ribs
- bruised thighs
- pulled hamstrings
- bruised and fractured toes

Figure 82   Sports injuries associated with batting in cricket

Most of the injuries associated with batting at cricket are also experienced by fielders. Some of these injuries can be very serious — the facial injuries suffered by Mike Gatting, then England captain, in the West Indies could easily have proved fatal and, indeed, deaths have occurred to players and spectators as a result of being struck by the ball.

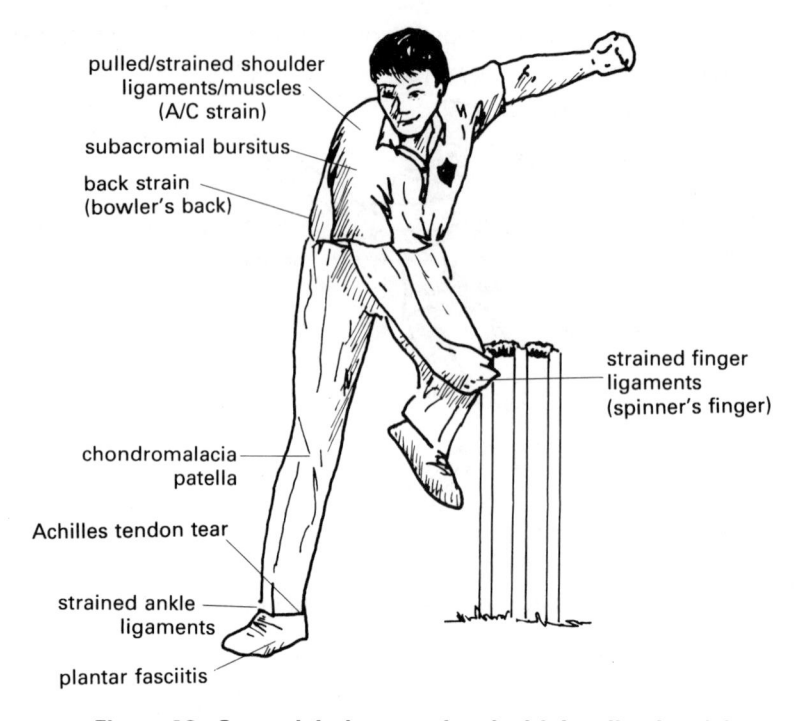

Figure 83 Sports injuries associated with bowling in cricket

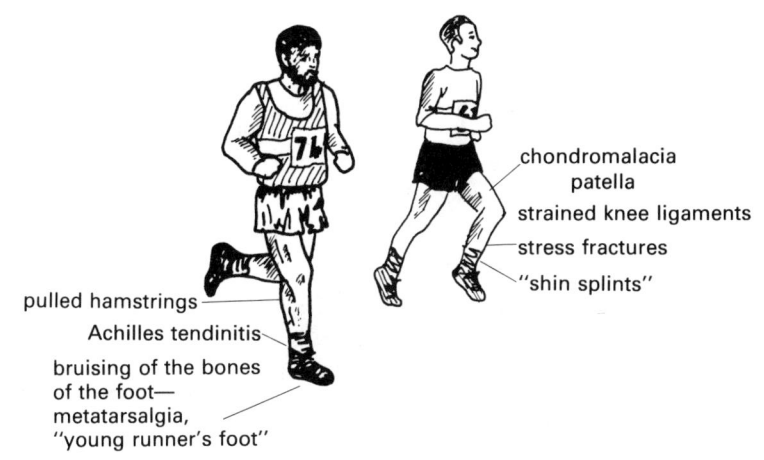

Figure 84 Sports injuries associated with cross country, jogging, distance, hill and road running

- chondromalacia patella
- strained knee ligaments
- stress fractures
- "shin splints"
- pulled hamstrings
- Achilles tendinitis
- bruising of the bones of the foot—metatarsalgia, "young runner's foot"

Almost all the injuries associated with distance running are those which are regarded as stress or overuse injuries.

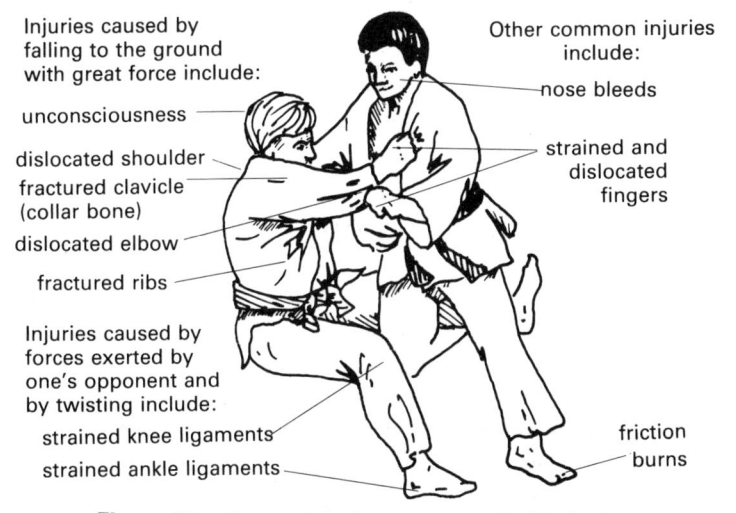

Injuries caused by falling to the ground with great force include:

- unconsciousness
- dislocated shoulder
- fractured clavicle (collar bone)
- dislocated elbow
- fractured ribs

Injuries caused by forces exerted by one's opponent and by twisting include:

- strained knee ligaments
- strained ankle ligaments

Other common injuries include:

- nose bleeds
- strained and dislocated fingers
- friction burns

Figure 85 Sports injuries associated with judo

Although serious spinal injuries have occurred in judo and there have also been deaths associated with players having been strangled unconscious, such incidents are extremly rare and could not be regarded as typical.

221

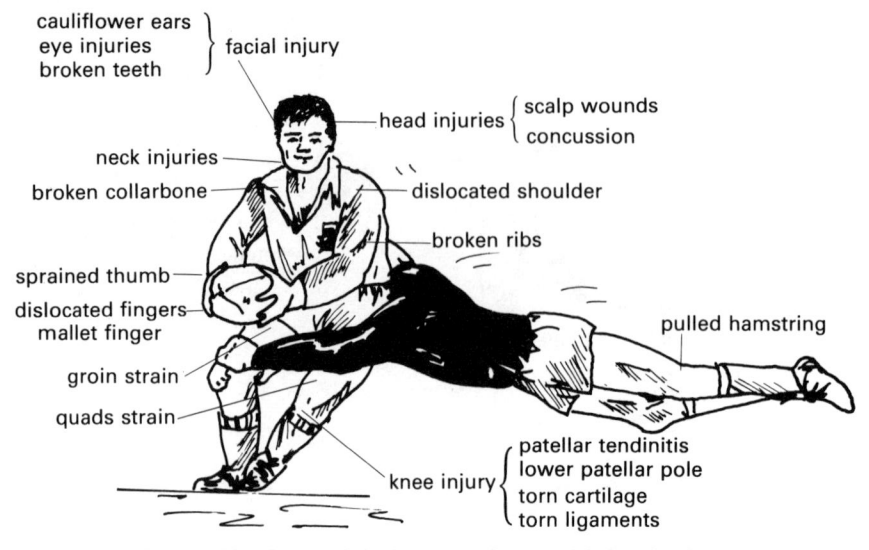

Figure 86 Sports injuries associated with Rugby football

Labels: cauliflower ears, eye injuries, broken teeth, facial injury, head injuries {scalp wounds, concussion}, neck injuries, broken collarbone, dislocated shoulder, broken ribs, sprained thumb, dislocated fingers, mallet finger, pulled hamstring, groin strain, quads strain, knee injury {patellar tendinitis, lower patellar pole, torn cartilage, torn ligaments}

As a result of the considerable degree of body contact in Rugby football, bruising, joint injuries, dislocations and fractures are quite common. Serious neck injuries can also occur as a result of mistimed tackles, "short arm" tackles around the head and when scrums collapse. It is especially important that players learn to tackle correctly and play within the rules of the game.

FIRST AID FOR SPORTS INJURIES

It must be stressed at the outset that this section is included only to give a simple background to the immediate action to be taken when confronted with the most commonly encountered sports injuries. It is designed to be of assistance to those following the City and Guilds Parts I and II Certificates. It is not a substitute for attending a recognised first aid course and gaining a formal qualification in first aid which is very strongly recommended.

Principal aims of a first aider

There are three principal aims of a first aider. These are:

(a) to preserve life;

(b) to prevent the casualty's condition worsening;
(c) to promote recovery.

In most sports and recreational activities, with the notable exception of outdoor adventure pursuits such as mountaineering and potholing, qualified medical help is likely to be close at hand and situations which are genuinely life threatening are very uncommon. Those life threatening situations which require immediate action that may be encountered include:

(a) near drowning,
(b) heart attack,
(c) severe trauma (eg broken neck).

In all these instances immediate resuscitation of the casualty may be necessary. This may involve *artificial ventilation* (mouth to mouth/nose) and *external chest compression*.

It is most unlikely that no other person will be present. If no one else has taken charge, then you must. Send one of the bystanders for assistance or to summon an ambulance immediately, then check to see if the casualty is breathing:

(a) does the chest rise and fall?
(b) can you hear breathing?
(c) can you feel breath coming out of the mouth?

If not, start artificial ventilation

(a) open the airway by tilting the head back and quickly check that it is clear by making sure that there are no obstructions (eg vomit) or that the tongue has dropped back;
(b) pinch the casualty's nose, make a good seal by placing your mouth firmly over his or hers and blow out into the victim's mouth;
(c) watch to see that the casualty's chest rises;
(d) take your mouth away and allow the casualty to exhale;
(e) give two good breaths and then check the pulse in the neck — if there is a pulse present then it is only necessary to continue to give mouth to mouth ventilation at the rate of one breath every five seconds;
(f) continue until the casualty starts to breathe again on his or her own, or until qualified help arrives.

(Note: beware of the casualty vomiting — especially in cases of near drowning.)

223

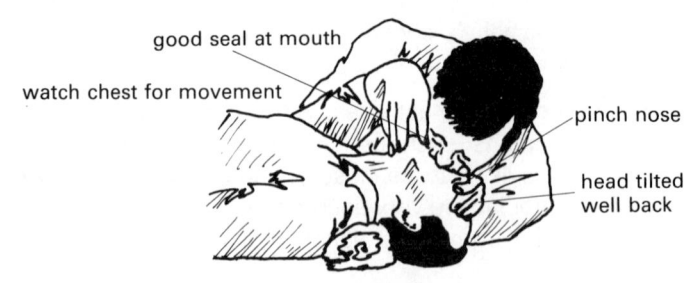

Figure 87 Artificial ventilation

If, when you check (e), there is no pulse then you will also need to do chest compression:

(a) the casualty must be on a firm surface;
(b) place the heel of one hand on the centre of the lower half of the breast bone with the heel of the other hand on top of it — keep your fingers off the casualty's chest;
(c) keep the arms straight and firm and rock forwards pressing down very firmly 15 times at the rate of 80 compressions per minute;
(d) give two more full breaths of mouth to mouth ventilation and then repeat 15 compressions, two breaths, until either the pulse returns or qualified help arrives;
(e) check for a pulse after the first minute and then every three minutes.

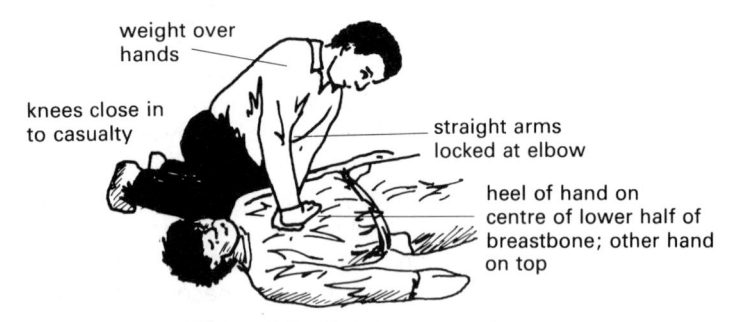

Figure 88 Chest compression

Note: external chest compression, to be effective, needs to be done *very* firmly. Successful compression frequently results in the casualty sustaining broken ribs — check carefully that there is *no* pulse before administering the technique.

Provided that neck or back (spinal) injuries are not suspected, then unconscious patients who are breathing may be placed in the recovery position (Figure 89).

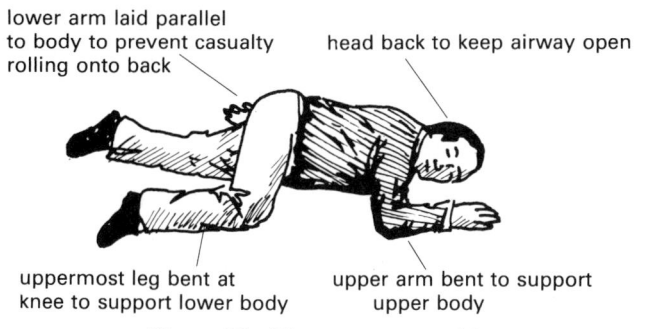

Figure 89 The recovery position

Labels on figure:
- lower arm laid parallel to body to prevent casualty rolling onto back
- head back to keep airway open
- uppermost leg bent at knee to support lower body
- upper arm bent to support upper body

If a broken neck or back is suspected then the casualty **must not be moved** unless absolutely essential — any movement could cause death or paralysis. If in doubt *play safe* and assume the worst! It is always good policy, provided that the victim is breathing, not to move any casualty, and to prevent anyone else from touching him or her, until you have had a chance to assess the situation. Injured athletes have been known to try to stand on broken legs or attempt to carry on participating in competitions with broken or dislocated limbs (including broken necks!). No match or game is that important, and children are just as likely as adults to try to continue under such circumstances.

Furthermore, because they are so much lighter, children are at much greater risk of being picked up and carried by well meaning adults, no matter what condition they may be in.

More typically, casualties with serious leg injuries will remain on the floor. Unless it is outdoors, or on an ice rink, and there is a danger of exposure if they remain where they are, then they need not be moved. Keep them warm, give them *nothing* to drink (or eat) and wait for the ambulance crew. They are very good at dealing with this sort of situation.

Casualties who have injuries to the arm, shoulder and collar bone very often support themselves in a way that feels comfortable. It is not a good idea to dive in and interfere, strapping everything up with yards of bandages. Support things where they are, if this causes no discomfort, and convey the casualty to hospital if possible, or call for an ambulance if other means of transport are not available.

Bleeding, especially severe bleeding, has to be stopped. Direct pressure should help reduce the flow of blood whilst the casualty is conveyed to hospital, but remember everything wrapped around the injury has to be unwrapped before a doctor or nurse can look at it. Often a large, preferably sterile, dressing or pad is sufficient.

With bleeding the "look, press, lower, raise" method of dealing with incidents is very effective:

Look — for where the injury is
— whether there is any foreign body in the wound.

Press — for 5–10 minutes, until the bleeding has stopped; where possible use a sterile pad.

Lower — the casualty to the floor or to a seat
(the casualty may faint and this position makes it easier to raise the injured part).

Raise — the injured part that is bleeding above the heart
(this helps stem the flow of blood).

The casualty should also be asked to seek medical advice concerning the need for tetanus cover.

First aiders should also ensure that they protect themselves as far as is possible from contact with casualty's blood otherwise they may run the risk of contracting serious diseases and infections such as AIDS or hepatitis.

Eye injuries

All eye injuries are potentially serious. The most frequent situations where such injuries may occur are encountered in squash (where the ball hits the eye at speed), and contact sports such as Rugby and judo (where there is the risk of fingers accidently poking the eyes).

Cover the eye with a sterile pad or dressing and convey the casualty to hospital.

Thumb injuries

Because of the complicated structure of the joint, which permits a very wide range of movement, thumb injuries should also be taken seriously. If they do appear at all serious medical advice should be sought.

Promoting recovery

In terms of promoting recovery, injuries such as pulls, strains and bruises are likely to mend much quicker and be less painful if they are dealt with using the RICE method:

REST — stop using the injured part immediately.

ICE — use an ice pack (a bag of frozen peas is an excellent substitute) to reduce bleeding and swelling, for about ten minutes.

COMPRESSION — over the ice pack, either manually or by means of a bandage, again in order to reduce bleeding and swelling — but do not apply it too tightly.

ELEVATION — to help drain excess fluid away from the damaged area.

Such action should promote recovery but if the injury appears at all serious medical advice should be sought promptly.

Minor cuts and grazes can be dealt with in the following way:

(a) wash your hands;
(b) lightly rinse the cut or graze;
(c) clean the surrounding area whilst protecting the wound with a sterile swab;
(d) gently dry the wound;
(e) dress with a plaster or dressing;
(f) if in any doubt seek medical advice.

It must be stressed that there is no substitute for attending a recognised first aid course. Further information on local courses may be obtained from the local branch or division of the following organisations:

St John Ambulance,

St Andrew's Ambulance Association,
The British Red Cross Society.

COACHING AND OFFICIATING QUALIFICATIONS

These are of particular importance in leisure and recreation as they can give an indication of the experience and competence of an individual with respect to a particular sporting activity. This is especially the case when the activity concerned has a relatively high degree of risk attached to it (eg gymnastics, trampolining and weight training) or if it is proposed to organise a major competition.

Therefore the acquisition of one or two carefully chosen coaching qualifications, together with a current first aid certificate and an appropriate life-saving award (eg RLSS bronze medallion) may be of considerable value to anyone hoping to start work in sport and leisure centres.

It is important to note that there is a distinction between a coaching qualification and an officiating qualification.

Coaching qualifications

Coaching and teaching qualifications are concerned with:

- (a) teaching the skills of a sport;
- (b) bringing about increased levels of performance.

Generally speaking, there are different levels of coaching qualifications appropriate to the different levels of skills being taught. These range from basic to advanced levels and are usually awarded on the basis of satisfactory attendance on an approved course together with some form of practical and written assessment.

The different levels of coaching qualifications that may be available are illustrated by the following examples:

(a) *Trampolining* BTF trampoline assistant
　　　　　　　　　BTF coach grade 1
　　　　　　　　　BTF coach grade 2 (advanced)
(b) *Judo*　　　　 BJA preliminary club coach
　　　　　　　　　BJA club coach
　　　　　　　　　BJA senior club coach.

Officiating qualifications

Officiating qualifications are concerned with:

(a) making decisions upon scoring and rule infringements;
(b) implementing the rules of the sport.

These qualifications concern referees, line judges, scorers and timekeepers. Examples include:

BJA competition controller
BJA recorder and timekeeper
BTF judge
FA referee class 3
LTA umpire.

Obtaining information on sports qualifications

Information on the rules and regulations of particular sports may be obtained from a number of sources:

(a) by contacting the governing body of the sport concerned direct — addresses may be obtained from either the Sports Council or the CCPR should they be difficult to obtain;
(b) by contacting a local club direct — many local authorities produce handbooks containing this information. These are usually available from libraries, council and information offices;
(c) by attending a coaching or officiating course — details of these are often available at local sports centres;
(d) by looking up the information in books on the sport which may be found in a local library or bought or ordered from a local bookshop, although it should be remembered that rules and regulations are frequently altered and that the information in books may quickly become out of date.

481-1 PRODUCT KNOWLEDGE

Exercise 1

Draw out and complete the following tables:

VITAMINS		
VITAMIN	USED FOR	SOURCE
C	Protecting the body against infections. Maintaining healthy teeth and gums	Fresh fruit, vegetables

MINERALS		
MINERAL	USED FOR	SOURCE
IRON	Needed for forming haemoglobin in the blood cells	Liver eggs, green vegetables

Exercise 2

Many people who train in fitness centres do so because they wish to alter the weight or shape of their body, as well as improve their fitness.

(a) What NUTRITIONAL advice would you give someone who wished to
   (i) lose weight (become less fat)
   (ii) gain weight (increase muscle mass)?

(b) What advice would you give someone with regard to the TYPE of training that should be undertaken to
   (i) lose weight
   (ii) gain weight?

Exercise 3

Draw a sketch of an athlete or athletes participating in a leisure, sporting or recreational activity and indicate by means of labels the most common injuries associated with that activity.

Do not select as your chosen activity one of those already illustrated in the text. A further example is illustrated below:

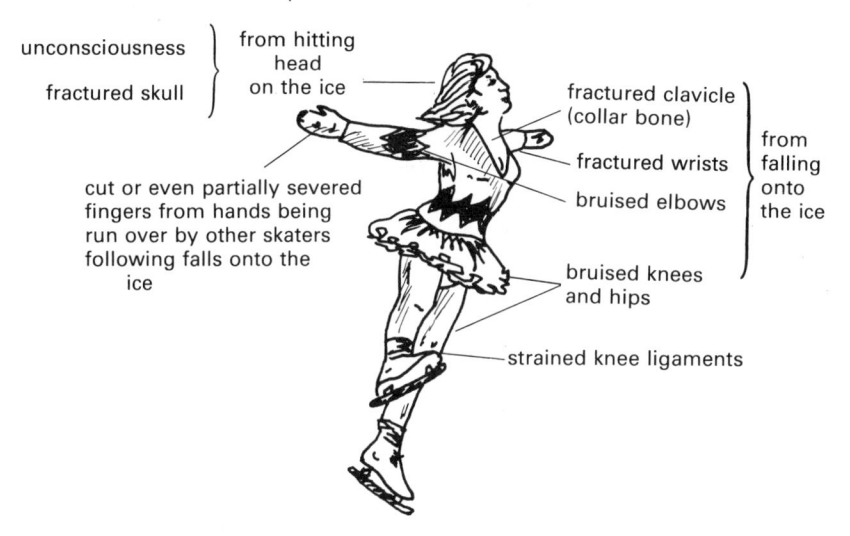

Figure 90 Sports injuries associated with ice skating

Exercise 4

(a) Make a table of typical sports-related injuries associated with each of the following sports, together with the mechanism associated with that injury and the immediate action to be taken.

SPORT	Associated INJURY	Typical MECHANISM	Immediate ACTION
Rock climbing	Broken neck	Falling from rock to the ground	DO NOT MOVE* Send for ambulance
Association football			
Rugby football			
Squash			
Keep fit			
Jogging			
Cricket			
Swimming			
Diving			
Badminton			
Basketball			
Netball			
Aerobics			
Hockey			
Ice Skating			

*Provided that the casualty is still breathing — otherwise the minimum movement required to facilitate artificial resuscitation will be necessary.

(b) List three recreational activities where spinal injuries may occur:

(i)
(ii)
(iii)

Exercise 5

(a) Make a list of TEN governing bodies of sport, also giving the initials by which they are usually known,
eg swimming — the Amateur Swimming Association; ASA. The list should include TWO team sports, TWO racket sports and TWO water sports.

(b) For THREE of these identify and list:
  (i) the main coaching qualifications;
  (ii) the range of officiating qualifications.

Do not select your chosen sports from the examples already given in the text.

481–1
PRODUCT KNOWLEDGE

Part I Written paper

Past examination questions related to diet and health

1. List FIVE components of a balanced diet, giving for EACH an example of a suitable source. (5 marks)
(December 1987)
2. (a) Explain why it is unwise to eat a heavy meal immediately before taking vigorous exercise. (2 marks)
(Extract June 1987)
   (b) Briefly explain why cramp may occur if a swimmer has recently eaten a heavy meal. (3 marks)
(Extract December 1986)
3. (a) List THREE disorders that may trouble an overweight person. (3 marks)
   (b) Overweight people should not undertake violent exercise without medical consultation.
   List TWO other medical conditions where advice should be sought. (2 marks)
(December 1990)
4. List FIVE conditions whose sufferers should seek medical advice before taking exercise. (5 marks)
(December 1987)

Past examination questions related to anatomy and physiology

1. (a) List THREE functions of the human skeleton. (3 marks)
   (b) What type of joint is
       (i) the hip joint
       (ii) the knee joint? (2 marks)
(April 1990)
2. (a) List THREE examples of the skeleton providing protection for vital organs, naming the organs concerned. (3 marks)
(Extract December 1990)
   (b) Explain how muscles and the skeleton can create movement. (2 marks)
(Extract June 1990)

3. (a) List the FOUR words labelled 1–4 which are missing in the diagram of blood circulation given below. (2 marks)
   (b) Name the FOUR chambers of the heart. (2 marks)
   (c) What is the name of the major artery carrying blood away from the heart? (1 mark)
   (April 1990)

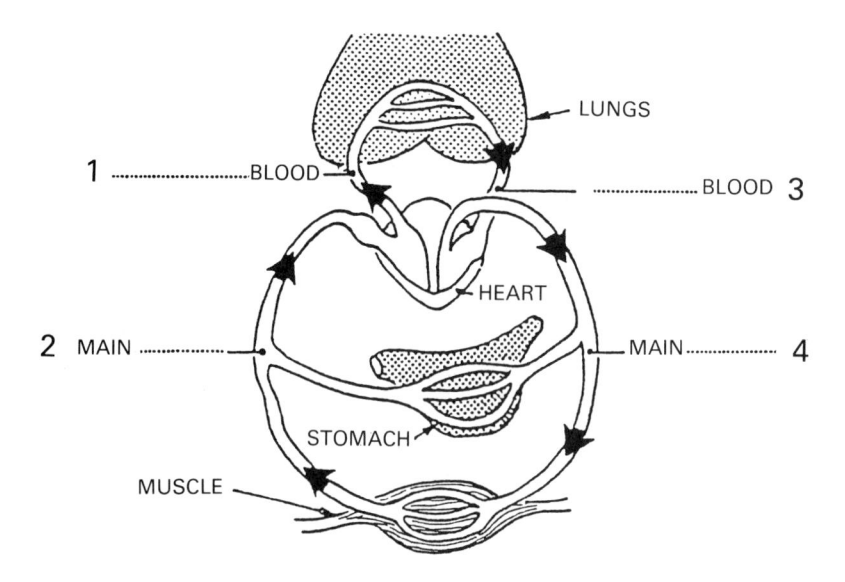

```
                            LUNGS
1 ............BLOOD                    ............BLOOD 3

                        HEART
2 MAIN ............              MAIN............ 4

             STOMACH
  MUSCLE
```

(a) What is the long term effect of regular exercise on the pulse? (1 mark)
(b) List TWO immediate effects of exercise on the heart. (2 marks)
(c) Name the gases carried principally by

   (i) arteries
   (ii) veins. (2 marks)
   (April 1990)

4. (a) List THREE types of blood vessel in the human body. (3 marks)
   (Extract December 1990)
   (b) Blood in the body is named after the two major types of blood vessel which transport it. State the name of the blood

   (i) leaving the heart
   (ii) returning to the heart. (2 marks)
   (Extract December 1986)

5. (a) Explain how the gases are introduced into and removed from the body. (2 marks)
   (b) What is the short term effect of heavy exercise on the lungs? (2 marks)
   (c) What is the long term effect of exercise on the lungs? (1 mark)

   (June 1990 amended)

Past examination questions related to first aid

1. List the THREE principal aims of a first aider. (3 marks)
   (December 1985)
2. You are on duty when you are called to a young trampolinist who has clearly sprained an ankle.
   (i) Briefly describe the treatment that you would give. (2 marks)
   (ii) List the details that you would record in the accident book afterwards. (2 marks)
   (May–June 1985)
3. A customer has gashed his head on a coat hook in the changing room. List the necessary steps in rendering assistance. (2 marks)
   (December 1984)

Past examination questions related to coaching and officiating

1. (a) Explain the difference between coaching and officiating qualifications. (2 marks)
   (b) List THREE purposes of qualifications to coach. (3 marks)
   (June 1990)
2. (a) List two different officials from EACH of THREE of the following sports:

   soccer, netball, hockey, cricket, squash. (2 marks)
   (Extract April 1990 amended)
   (b) List THREE of the officials required in THREE of the following

   (i) athletics
   (ii) basketball
   (iii) tennis
   (iv) volleyball
   (v) swimming. (3 marks)
   (Extract December 1990)

481-2

PRODUCT KNOWLEDGE

Part II Paper 1 Technical aspects, health and safety

Past examination questions related to exercise, fitness and the main body systems

1. State FIVE ways in which regular exercise could promote good health. (5 marks)
   (April 1990)
2. List FIVE elements of physical fitness. (5 marks)
   (April 1991)
3. State TWO SHORT TERM effects of exercise on EACH of the following systems

   (a) respiratory
   (b) circulatory. (5 marks)
   (April 1990)
4. State TWO LONG TERM effects of exercise on each of the following systems

   (a) respiratory
   (b) circulatory. (5 marks)
   (June 1990)
5. Briefly explain the following terms:
   (a) anaerobic
   (b) aerobic. (5 marks)
   (June 1991)
6. List TWO functions of EACH of the following body systems

   (a) circulatory
   (b) nervous
   (c) respiratory
   (d) muscular
   (e) skeletal. (10 marks)
   (December 1986)

Past examination questions related to sports injuries and first aid

1. Explain, giving ONE example in each case, the main difference between extrinsic and intrinsic injuries. (5 marks)
   (April 1991)
2. Name FIVE factors that affect injury to the body. (5 marks)
   (June 1990)
3. State a common injury associated wtih EACH of the following recreational activities

   (a) soccer
   (b) jogging
   (c) hockey
   (d) squash
   (e) swimming. (5 marks)
   (April 1991)
4. Name TWO sporting activities where spinal injuries may occur and give an example of where and how such injuries may be caused in each activity. (5 marks)
   (Centre-set paper, December 1985)
5. (a) State a common injury associated with EACH of the following sports

    (i) indoor soccer
    (ii) netball OR basketball
    (iii) cricket. (3 marks)

   (b) Describe briefly the immediate treatment required for EACH of the injuries given in (a). (7 marks)
   (June 1986, amended)
6. Describe FIVE stages that should be taken by the first aider in dealing with a person injured whilst playing a sport. (5 marks)
   (June 1990)

REFERENCES AND FURTHER READING

Exercise, Fitness and the Main Body Systems

Beashel, P and Taylor, J Sport Examined. Macmillan Education, 1986
Kapit, W and Elson, LM The Anatomy Colouring Book. Harper and Row, 1977
McArdle, WD, Katch, FI, Katch, VL, Exercise Physiology – Energy, Nutrition, and Human Performance. Lea and Febiger, 1981
Perrott, JW Anatomy for students and teachers of Physical Education. Arnold, 1959
Physiology and Performance. National Coaching Foundation, 1986
The Body in Action. National Coaching Foundation, 1984

Sports Injuries and First Aid

Beashel, P and Taylor, J Sport Examined. Macmillan Education, 1986
First Aid Manual, St John Ambulance *et al.* 1982
Gray, M Football Injuries. Arnold, 1980
Injuries and Sport. Scottish Sports Council
Muckle, DS Sports Injuries, Oriel/RKP
Read, M Sports Injuries. Breslich and Foss, 1984
Safety First For Coaches. National Coaching Foundation, 1986
Safety in Outdoor Pursuits, DES Safety Series No 1. HMSO, 1979
Safety in Physical Education, DES Safety Series No 4. HMSO, 1978
Williams, JGP Injury in Sport. Bayer, 1980
Williams, JGP Injury in Sport — A Colour Atlas of. Wolfe Medical, 1980

Index

Accidents, recording details.................. 103–4
Areas of Outstanding Natural Beauty.......... 51
Arts Council 56–8

Bibliographies,
   marketing... 31
   product knowledge 239
   provision and control 85–6
   resource management 177–8
Bisham Abbey N.S.C. 37
British Tourist Authority 61–2

Central Council of Physical Recreation
   The 43–4
Chemicals... 104–8
   burns.. 108
   cleaning.. 104–5
   poisoning 108
   soft landscapes 106
   swimming pool water 105–6
   toilets 105
Chessington World of Adventure............... 10
Children's play areas........................... 158–63
   equipment.. 161–2
   safety 159–60
   siting 163–3
   supervision.. 161
   toilet facilities 162
Circulatory system 202–4
Coaching and officiating...................... 228–9
Codes of practice 101
Colne Valley Park 10, 54–5
Commercial organisations 73–4
Community groups 74, 75
Control and provision, *see* provision and
   control
Country parks 53
Countryside Commission 44–5
Countryside Council for Wales.............. 60–1
Crystal Palace N.S.C. 37

Data recording, storage and retrieval 90–2
Dealing with people 89–90

Emergency services 102–3
English Heritage 71–2
English Nature (Nature, Conservancy
   Council for England)...................... 59–60
English Tourist Board 62–4
Enterprise Neptune 70
Environmental Protection Act 1990 ....44, 59
Examination questions,
   marketing... 26–7
   product knowledge 234–8
   provision and control 80–4
   resource management.................. 168–76
Exercises,
   marketing... 26–7
   product knowledge 230–3
   provision and control 77–9
   resource management................... 164–7

Filtration systems in swimming
   pools... 122
Food and diet 179–3
Foot infections 129–30
Footpaths, long-distance 51–3
Forest Parks 58
Forestry Commision 58–9

Governing bodies of sport..................... 66–8
Government departments 34–5

Health and safety...................................... 97
   lifting heavy weights 101–2
Health and Safety at Work, etc, Act,
   1974 98–101
Holme Pierrepont National Water
   S.C. 38
Hygiene
   parks and open spaces, in 96–7
   river banks and outdoor water
     sports areas.. 97
   swimming pools, in 96, 121
   sports complexes, in 96

Injuries 208–28
  age 214
  artificial ventilation 223–4
  basketball 218
  chest compression 224
  classification 210–11
  cricket 219–20
  dance and aerobics 217
  drugs 215–6
  environment 213–4
  equipment 216
  eye 226
  first aid 222–8
  football 217
  ice skating 231
  judo 221
  lifting heavy weights 101–2
  physical fitness 211–12
  physique 212–13
  psychological fitness 212
  recording accidents 103–4
  recovery 227
  recovery position 225
  Rugby football 222
  running 221
  sex 214–5
  technique 213
  thumb 226–7

Joint Provision Centres 72

Lake District Appeal 70
Leisure pools 117–20
Lilleshall N.S.C. 38
Local authorities 72–3

Maintenance 110–15
  facilities design 111
  materials 110–11
  pattern and type 111–12
  planning schedule 112–13
  supervision 113–15

Marketing 1–27
  benefits 4
  bibliography 31
  Chessington World of Adventure 10
  Colne Valley Park 10, 54–5
  cultural influences 11
  customers 2–3
  disabled people 20
  economic factors 13
  ethnic minority groups 21–2
  examination questions 28–30

exercises 26–7
fashion 12
leisure 6
location 9–10
marketing process 1
mix 5
mothers with children 21
National Parks 10
non-sporting activities 7–8
philosophy of use 13
play 6
political factors 13
pricing 4
products 4
programming 13–16
promotion 4–5
publicity 23–4
recreation 6
resources 3
services 4
social factors 10–11
specific groups 19–23
sports 6–7, 8
targeting promotion 5
Thorpe Park 10
Markings, court and pitch 155–8
Members' clubs 75
Muscular system 195–201

National Nature Conservancy Councils . 59–60
National organisations 33–76
National Parks 10, 45–51
  Council for 51
National Rivers Authority 64–6
National Sports Centres 36–40
National Trust 69–71
Nervous system 205–8
Non-activity areas 108–10
Non-sporting activities 7–8
Non-verbal communications 88–9

Offices, Shops and Railway Premises
  Act 1963 102

Pest control 106
Plant in swimming pools 122
Plas Y Brewin N.C. 40
Playing surfaces 145–55
  appropriate surfaces 154
  artificial surfaces 146–8
  friction 151
  markings, court and pitch 155–8
  natural surfaces 146

241

performance parameters 148–53
rebound resilience 149–50
resistance to set 152
rolling resistance 151
spin 151–2
sprung floors 153
stiffness 151
substrate effects 150–1
wear and weathering 152
Pollution in swimming pools 123
Product knowledge 179–229
bibliography 239
circulatory system 202–4
coaching and officiating 228–9
examination questions 234–8
exercise 186
exercises 230–3
fitness 187
food and diet 179–83
illnesses and infections 185
injuries 216–22
meals 185
muscular system 195–8
nervous system 205–8
overweight 184
physical condition 184–6
respiratory system 204–5
skeletal system 190–5
training 187–90
Provision and control 33–86
Areas of Outstanding Natural
Beauty 51
Arts Council 56–8
bibliography 85–6
British Tourist Authority 61–2
Central Council of Physical
Recreation 43–4
Colne Valley Park 54–5
commercial organisations 73–4
community groups 74–5
Council for National Parks 51
Country Parks 53
Countryside Commission 44–5
English Heritage 71–2
English Nature 59–60
English Tourist Board 62–4
examination questions 80–4
exercises 77–9
Forest Parks 58
Forestry Commission 58–9
governing bodies of sport 66–8
Government departments 34–5
joint provision centres 72
local authorities 72–3

national organisations 33–71
National Parks 45–50
National Playing Fields Association 68–9
National Rivers Authority 64–6
National Sports Centres 36–40
National Trust 69–71
Nature Conservancy Council, for
England 59–60
Regional Parks 53
Regional Sports Councils 40–3
sponsorship 74
Sports Council 35–6
Tourist Boards 61–4
Water Act 1989 64
Publicity 23–5

Reception duties 87–90
Regional Parks 53
Regional Sports Councils 40–3
Resource management 87–178
bibliography 177–8
chemicals 104–8
childrens' play areas 158–63
codes of practice 101
data recording, storage and
retrieval 90–2
dealing with people 89–90
emergency services 102–3
examination questions 168–76
exercises 164–7
health and safety 97–101
hygiene 96–7
maintenance 110–15
non-activity areas 108–10
non-verbal communcation 88–9
Offices, Shops, and railway
Premises Act, 1963 102
pest control 106
playing surfaces 145–55
reception duties 87–8
shift work 92–5
soft landscapes .... ,137–45
sports halls 115–6
swimming pools 105, 107, 117–37

Soft landscapes 137–45
costing 139–40
design 138–9
establishment 144–5
layout 140
materials 140
planning 138–9
soil cultivation 141
Sponsorship 74
Sports Council 35–6

Sports halls 115–6
Supervision of maintenance 113–4
Swimming pools 105, 107, 117–37
   changing room areas 135–6
   commercial interest in 136-7
   energy saving 136
   eye irritation 123–4
   foot infections 129–30
   hygiene 96, 121
   leisure pools 117–20
   plant and filtration 122
   pollution 123
   rectangular tank 117, 118
   safety 131–3
   water 105–6, 124–7

Thorpe Park 10
Tourist Boards 61–4

Unemployed adults 22–3

Water Act 1989 64
Water in swimming pools 105–6, 124–7
   circulation 126–7
   filtration 122, 124–5
   heating 126
   sterilisation 124
   tests 128–9

Youth groups 75

243